CONTENTS

Section

INDEX TO QUESTIONS AND ANSWERS

Managerial Level

Paper P4

Organisational Management and Information Systems

Exam Kit

CIMA

British Library Cataloguing-in-Publication Data

A catalogue record for this book is available from the British Library.

Published by Kaplan Publishing UK
Unit 2
The Business Centre
Molly Millars Lane
Wokingham
Berkshire
RG41 4QZ

ISBN 978 1 84710 698 8

© Kaplan Financial Limited, December 2008

Printed and bound in Great Britain

Acknowledgements

We are grateful to the Chartered Institute of Management Accountants, the Association of Chartered Certified Accountants and the Institute of Chartered Accountants in England and Wales for permission to reproduce past examination questions. The answers have been prepared by Kaplan Publishing.

INTRODUCTION

We have worked closely with experienced CIMA tutors and lecturers to ensure that our Kits are exam-focused and user-friendly.

This Exam Kit includes an extensive selection of questions that entirely cover the syllabus – this ensures that your knowledge is tested across all syllabus areas. Wherever possible questions have been grouped by syllabus topics.

All questions are of exam standard and format – this enables you to master the exam techniques. Section 1 contains Section A-type questions you will come across in your exam, Section 2 contains Section B-type questions and Section 3 contains Section C-type questions.

May and November 2008 exams are at the back of the book – try these under timed conditions and this will give you an exact idea of the way you will be tested in your exam.

SYLLABUS AND LEARNING OUTCOMES

Learning aims

This syllabus aims to test the student's ability to:

- describe the various functional areas of an organisation and how they relate to one another;
- apply theories, tools and techniques appropriate to a functional area in support of the organisation's strategy;
- prepare reports and plans for functional areas;
- evaluate the performance of functional areas.

Learning outcomes and syllabus content

A – INFORMATION SYSTEMS – 20%

Learning outcomes

On completion of their studies students should be able to:

- explain the features and operations of commonly used information technology hardware and software;
- explain how commonly used technologies are used in the work place;
- identify opportunities for the use of information technology (IT) in organisations, particularly in the implementation and running of the information system (IS);
- evaluate, from a managerial perspective, new hardware and software and assess how new systems could benefit the organisation;
- recommend strategies to minimise the disruption caused by introducing IS technologies;
- explain how to supervise major IS projects and ensure their smooth implementation;
- evaluate how IS fits into broader management operations.

Syllabus content

- Introduction to hardware and software in common use in organisations.
- Hardware and applications architectures (i.e. centralised, distributed, client server) and the IT required to run them (PCs, servers, networks and peripherals).
- General Systems Theory and its application to IT (i.e. system definition, system components, system behaviour, system classification, entropy, requisite variety, coupling and de-coupling).
- Recording and documenting tools used during the analysis and design of systems (i.e. entity-relationship model, logical data structure, entity life history, dataflow diagram, and decision table).

- Databases and database management systems. (*Note:* Knowledge of database structures will not be required.)
- The problems associated with the management of in-house and vendor solutions and how they can be avoided or solved.
- IT-enabled transformation (i.e. the use of information systems to assist in change management).
- System changeover methods (i.e. direct, parallel, pilot and phased).
- IS implementation (i.e. methods of implementation, avoiding problems of non-usage and resistance).
- The benefits of IT systems.
- IS evaluation, including the relationship of sub-systems to each other and testing.
- IS outsourcing.
- Maintenance of systems (i.e. corrective, adaptive, preventative).

B – CHANGE MANAGEMENT – 10%

Learning outcomes

On completion of their studies students should be able to:

- explain the process of organisational development;
- discuss how and why resistance to change develops within organisations;
- evaluate various means of introducing change;
- evaluate change processes within the organisation.

Syllabus content

- External and internal change triggers (e.g. environmental factors, mergers and acquisitions, re-organisation and rationalisation).
- The stages in the change process.
- Approaches to change management (e.g. Beer and Nohria, Kanter, Lewin and Peters, Senge et al).
- The importance of managing critical periods of change through the life cycle of the firm.

C – OPERATIONS MANAGEMENT – 20%

Learning outcomes

On completion of their studies students should be able to:

- evaluate the management of operations;
- analyse problems associated with quality in organisations;
- evaluate contemporary thinking in quality management;
- explain the linkages between functional areas as an important aspect of quality management;
- apply tools and concepts of quality management appropriately in an organisation;
- construct a plan for the implementation of a quality programme;
- recommend ways to negotiate and manage relationships with suppliers;
- evaluate a supply network;
- explain the concept of quality and how the quality of products and services can be assessed, measured and improved.

Syllabus content

- An overview of operations strategy and its importance to the firm.

- Design of products/services and processes and how this relates to operations and supply.

- Methods for managing inventory, including continuous inventory systems (e.g. Economic Order Quantity, EOQ), periodic inventory systems and the ABC system. (*Note:* ABC is not an acronym. A refers to high value, B to medium and C to low value inventory.)

- Strategies for balancing capacity and demand including level capacity, chase and demand management strategies.

- Methods of performance measurement and improvement, particularly the contrast between benchmarking and Business Process Re-engineering (BPR).

- Practices of continuous improvement (e.g. quality circles, Kaizen, 5S, Six Sigma).

- The use of benchmarking in quality measurement and improvement.

- Different methods of quality measurement (i.e. operational, financial and customer measures).

- The characteristics of lean production: flexible workforce practices, high commitment human resource policies and commitment to continuous improvement. Criticisms and limitations of lean production.

- Systems used in operations management: Manufacturing Resource Planning (MRP), Optimised Production Technologies (OPT), Just-in-Time (JIT) and Enterprise Resource Planning (ERP).

- Approaches to quality management, including Total Quality Management (TQM), various British Standard (BS) and European Union (EU) systems as well as statistical methods of quality control.

- External quality standards (e.g. the various ISO standards appropriate to products and organisations).

- Use of the intranet in information management (e.g. meeting customer support needs).

- Contemporary developments in quality management.

- The role of the supply chain and supply networks in gaining competitive advantage, including the use of sourcing strategies (e.g. single, multiple, delegated and parallel).

- Supply chain management as a strategic process (e.g. Reck and Long's strategic positioning tool, Cousins' strategic supply wheel).

- Developing and maintaining relationships with suppliers.

D – MARKETING – 20%

Learning outcomes

On completion of their studies students should be able to:

- explain the marketing concept;

- evaluate the marketing processes of an organisation;

- apply tools within each area of the marketing mix;

- describe the business contexts within which marketing principles can be applied (consumer marketing, business-to-business marketing, services marketing, direct marketing, interactive marketing);

- evaluate the role of technology in modern marketing;

- produce a strategic marketing plan for the organisation.

Syllabus content

- Introduction to the marketing concept as a business philosophy.

- An overview of the marketing environment, including societal, economic, technological, physical and legal factors affecting marketing.

- Understanding consumer behaviour, such as factors affecting buying decisions, types of buying behaviour and stages in the buying process.

- Market research, including data-gathering techniques and methods of analysis.

- Marketing Decision Support Systems (MDSS) and their relationship to market research.

- How business to business (B2B) marketing differs from business to consumer (B2C) marketing.

- Segmentation and targeting of markets, and positioning of products within markets.

- The differences and similarities in the marketing of products and services.

- Devising and implementing a pricing strategy.

- Marketing communications (i.e. mass, direct, interactive).

- Distribution channels and methods for marketing campaigns.

- The role of marketing in the strategic plan of the organisation.

- Use of the internet (e.g. in terms of data collection, marketing activity and providing enhanced value to customers and suppliers) and potential drawbacks (e.g. security issues).

- Market forecasting methods for estimating current (e.g. Total Market Potential, Area Market Potential and Industry Sales and Market Shares) and future (e.g. Survey of Buyers' Intentions, Composite of Sales Force Opinions, Expert Opinion, Past-Sales Analysis and Market-Test Method) demand for products and services.

- Internal marketing as the process of training and motivating employees so as to support the firm's external marketing activities.

- Social responsibility in a marketing context.

E – MANAGING HUMAN CAPITAL – 30%

Learning outcomes

On completion of their studies students should be able to:

- explain the role of the human resource management function and its relationship to other parts of the organisation;

- produce and explain a human resource plan and supporting practices;

- evaluate the recruitment, selection, induction, appraisal, training and career planning activities of an organisation;

- evaluate the role of incentives in staff development as well as individual and organisational performance;

- identify features of a human resource plan that vary depending on organisation type and employment model;

- explain the importance of ethical behaviour in business generally and for the Chartered Management Accountant in particular.

Syllabus content

- The relationship of the employee to other elements of the business plan.

- Determinants and content of a human resource (HR) plan (e.g. organisational growth rate, skills, training, development, strategy, technologies and natural wastage).

- Problems in implementing a HR plan and ways to manage this.

- The process of recruitment and selection of staff using different recruitment channels (i.e. interviews, assessment centres, intelligence tests, aptitude tests, psychometric tests).

- Issues relating to fair and legal employment practices (e.g. recruitment, dismissal, redundancy, and ways of managing these).

- Issues in the design of reward systems (e.g. the role of incentives, the utility of performance-related pay, arrangements for knowledge workers, flexible work arrangements).

- The importance of negotiation during the offer and acceptance of a job.

- The process of induction and its importance.

- Theories of Human Resource Management (e.g. Taylor, Schein, McGregor, Maslow, Herzberg, Handy, Lawrence and Lorsch).

- High performance work arrangements.

- The distinction between development and training and the tools available to develop and train staff.

- The importance of appraisals, their conduct and their relationship to the reward system.

- HR in different organisational forms (e.g. project-based firms, virtual or networked firms).

- Personal business ethics and the CIMA Ethical Guidelines.

REVISION GUIDANCE

Planning your revision

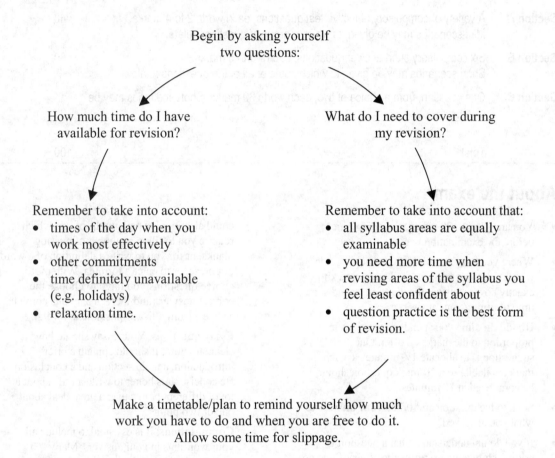

Begin by asking yourself
two questions:

How much time do I have
available for revision?

What do I need to cover during
my revision?

Remember to take into account:
- times of the day when you work most effectively
- other commitments
- time definitely unavailable (e.g. holidays)
- relaxation time.

Remember to take into account that:
- all syllabus areas are equally examinable
- you need more time when revising areas of the syllabus you feel least confident about
- question practice is the best form of revision.

Make a timetable/plan to remind yourself how much
work you have to do and when you are free to do it.
Allow some time for slippage.

Revision techniques

- Go through your notes and textbook **highlighting the important points**

- You might want to produce your own set of **summarised notes**

- **List key words** for each topic to remind you of the essential concepts

- **Practise exam-standard questions**, under timed conditions

- **Rework questions** that you got completely wrong the first time, but only when you think you know the subject better

- If you get stuck on topics, **find someone to explain** them to you (your tutor or a colleague, for example)

- **Read recent articles** on the CIMA website and in *Financial Management*

- **Read** good newspapers and professional journals

THE EXAM

Format of the exam

There will be a written exam paper of three hours, with the following sections: *Number of marks*

Section A	A variety of compulsory objective test questions, each worth 2 to 4 marks. Mini-scenarios may be given, to which a group of questions relate.	40
Section B	Six compulsory short answer questions, each worth 5 marks. Short scenarios may be given to which some or all of the questions relate.	30
Section C	One question, from a choice of two, each worth 30 marks. Short scenarios may be given.	30
	Total:	100

About the exam

- You are allowed 20 minutes' reading time before the examination begins.

- Where you have a **choice of question**, decide which questions you will do. Unless you know exactly how to answer the question, spend some time **planning** your answer.

- **Divide the time** you spend on questions in proportion to the marks on offer. One suggestion is to allocate 1½ minutes to each mark available, so a 10-mark question should be completed in 15 minutes.

- Stick to the question and **tailor your answer** to what you are asked.

- If you do not understand what a question is asking, **state your assumptions**. Even if you do not answer in precisely the way the examiner hoped, you should be given some credit, if your assumptions are reasonable.

- If you **get completely stuck** with a question, leave space in your answer book and **return to it later.**

- Spend the last **five minutes** reading through your answers and **making any additions or corrections**.

- You should do everything you can to make things easy for the marker. The marker will find it easier to identify the points you have made if your **answers are legible**.

- **Objective test questions** include true/false questions, matching pairs of text and graphic, sequencing and ranking, labelling diagrams and single and multiple numeric entry, but

could also involve paragraphs of text which require you to fill in a number of missing blanks, or for you to write a definition of a word or phrase, or to enter a formula. With multiple-choice questions you have to choose the correct answer (and there is only *one* correct answer) from a list of possible answers.

- **Essay questions**: Your essay should have a clear structure. It should contain a brief introduction, a main section and a conclusion. Be concise. It is better to write a little about a lot of different points than a great deal about one or two points.

- **Computations**: It is essential to include all your workings in your answers. Many computational questions require the use of a standard format: company income statement account, balance sheet and cash flow statement for example. Be sure you know these formats thoroughly before the examination and use the layouts that you see in the answers given in this book and in model answers.

- **Scenario-based questions:** read the scenario carefully, identify the area in which there is a problem, outline the main principles/theories you are going to use to answer the question, and then apply the principles/theories to the scenario.

- **Reports, memos and other documents**: some questions ask you to present your answer in the form of a report or a memo or other document. So use the correct format – there could be easy marks to gain here.

Section 1

SECTION A-TYPE QUESTIONS

All the section A-type multiple-choice questions carry 2 marks unless otherwise stated.

INFORMATION SYSTEMS

1   **Bar code readers, scanners and keyboards are examples of:**

   A   hardware input devices

   B   software input devices

   C   systems processing devices

   D   hardware processing devices

2   **Local area networking is used for:**

   A   communication between computers within a limited geographical area

   B   structuring an organisation within a division or business unit

   C   exchange of information through a trade association or region

   D   managing a complex operational issue by global interface with trade associations and professional bodies

3   **Entropy is a term used to describe:**

   A   the tendency of a system to break down into randomness

   B   the tendency of a system to develop over time leading to randomness

   C   a means of testing candidates in an interview to overcome randomness

   D   a means of developing open learning using computers

4   **Many large organisations have established a computer intranet for the purpose of:**

   A   providing quick, effective and improved communication amongst staff using chat rooms

   B   providing quick, effective and improved communication to staff

   C   providing quick, effective and improved communication to customers

   D   providing quick, effective and improved ordering procedures in real time

5   **The main advantages of a database management system include:**

   A   the development of separate data sources

   B   unlimited access and open communication

   C   end user flexibility and a devolution of responsibility

   D   data integrity and elimination of duplication

6   **An expert system describes:**

A   a database built upon past knowledge and experience

B   a powerful off the shelf software solution

C   an on-line library of operating advice and handy hints

D   an electronic version of working papers assembled by the Research and Development
        department

7   **What name is given to system maintenance for an IT system that is concerned with re-writing
        software for the system to meet new user requirements that emerge after the system has been
        implemented?**

A   Adaptive maintenance

B   Constructive maintenance

C   Corrective maintenance

D   Perfective maintenance

8   **When an old computer system and a new computer system are both operated throughout an
        organisation for a period of time, and the outputs from the two systems are compared with
        each other, the system changeover method is known as:**

A   direct changeover

B   parallel running

C   pilot testing

D   phased changeover

9   **A system designer has produced the following diagram as part of the documentation for a new
        system under development.**

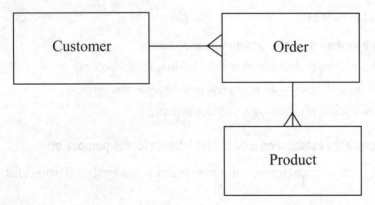

This is an example of:

A   a data flow diagram

B   an entity relationship model

C   structured programming

D   an entity life history diagram

10   A firm of travel agents has several branches. Each branch has terminals (PCs) linked to a central computer at head office. The central computer has links to the computer systems of all the main airlines and holiday firms. When a customer wishes to book a holiday of a flight with the agent, the branch submits a request for booking to the firm's central computer, which then sends on the request to the appropriate airline or holiday firm. Confirmation of bookings are returned by the same route.

The relationship between a terminal in a branch office and the computer at the firm's head office is known as:

A   a star configuration

B   a WAN

C   client/server

D   distributed data processing

11   A company uses a computer system for its middle management that can be used to assist with working out possible solutions to management problems. The system includes modelling and forecasting facilities, such as linear regression analysis and statistical analysis.

This type of system is:

A   a management information system (MIS)

B   an expert system

C   an executive information system (EIS)

D   a decision support system (DSS)

12   What is the name given to software that controls the communications between different software applications and files within a database system?

A   Server

B   Database

C   Database management system

D   Database administrator

13   A customer file holding data about customers was used by the sales force to plan direct mailing sales campaigns. However, the information on the file was not kept up-to-date, and the sales force has now stopped using it. This is an example of:

A   decoupling in a system

B   entropy in a system

C   a closed system

D   sub-optimisation in a system

14   In systems theory a sensor is:

A   the person who acts on 'results'

B   sensitive personal data used as input

C   the process of being sensitive to (mindful of) the wider environment

D   any device that measures and records the output of a system

15   'Corrective' refers to a type of systems maintenance performed to:

    A   remedy software defects

    B   allow executive level unstructured decision-making

    C   adjust applications to user preferences

    D   prevent future operation delays

16   'Centralised' and 'distributed' are examples of:

    A   hard systems approaches to change

    B   star networks

    C   value chain approaches

    D   systems configurations

17   When an organisation securely shares part of its private network with customers or other outside parties it is said to operate:

    A   an internet

    B   an intranet

    C   an extranet

    D   a joint venture

18   A network server:

    A   routes messages over a network

    B   manages files in a network

    C   acts as a workstation in a network

    D   is the main computer in a network

19   The following decision table shows the logic for a program to determine the credit to be offered to customers:

Conditions					
Sales value $500 or less?	Y	N	N	N	N
Sales value less than $5,000?	–	Y	Y	N	N
New customer?	–	Y	N	Y	N
Action					
No credit	X				
30 days' credit		X			
60 days' credit			X	X	
90 days' credit					X

If a regular customer purchases items costing $4,900, what length of credit will be granted?

    A   None

    B   30 days

    C   60 days

    D   90 days

20   An oil company uses a mainframe computer for a major system, and the management believe that it is essential that the continuity of processing must be assured at all times. Which of the following risk control measures is the most appropriate for ensuring that this happens?

A   A secure password protection system

B   A standby mainframe

C   Surplus capacity in the memory of the operational mainframe

D   Fire safety measures

21   Within the context of information systems, the term 'peripheral' refers to:

A   a hardware device that is added to expand functionality

B   an insignificant computer output

C   an outsourced staffing arrangement

D   an unnecessary systems operation

22   A computer system consists of several locally based computers linked in a communications network via a central computer. The local computers can share routine processing tasks. This type of system is best described as:

A   a multi-user system

B   a database system

C   an online real time system

D   a distributed data processing system

23   A network in which a number of smaller computers are linked directly to a larger central computer is called:

A   a ring network

B   a tree network

C   a hierarchical network

D   a star network

24   Entity life histories, data flow diagrams and decision tables are all examples of:

A   requisite variety and system entropy

B   evaluation techniques when appointing a preferred supplier

C   recording techniques used during the analysis and design of a system

D   software considerations in project design

25   A main aim of electronic data interchange (EDI) is:

A   to improve communication exchanges within an organisation

B   to replace conventional documentation with structured electronically transmitted data

C   to allow employees to work at home

D   to create a shared data resource within an organisation

26   Explain the purpose of tools such as data flow diagrams, entity life histories, entity-relationship models and decision tables.   **(4 marks)**

27   Explain why a phased system changeover for a computer development might help employees cope better with technological change.   **(4 marks)**

28   Describe the main benefits of in-house developed information systems.   **(4 marks)**

29   Explain the functions that a file server might perform within a computer system.   **(4 marks)**

30   De-coupling is a term used in general system theory. A DBMS is an example of de-coupling within a computer system.

      (a)   Explain briefly what is meant by de-coupling.

      (b)   Explain why a DBMS is an example of de-coupling.   **(4 marks)**

31   Explain the nature of system software, and describe the three main types of system software.

                                                                                   (4 marks)

32   The operating system:

      A   forms part of a system's software

      B   forms part of a system's hardware

      C   is another term for a system's hardware

      D   is a standalone end-user (operator) system solution

33   Describe the main advantages of an organisation developing and using an 'extranet'.

                                                                                   (4 marks)

34   Explain the relationship between open systems and adaptive maintenance.   **(4 marks)**

35   Parallel running and pilot schemes are methods of systems changeover. Explain the reasons why an organisation might instead choose a direct approach to a system changeover.

                                                                                   (4 marks)

36   Describe the types of test that should be conducted before a new information system goes 'live'.   **(4 marks)**

37   When identifying the requirements of a new system explain what 'functional' and 'physical' aspects should be taken into account.   **(4 marks)**

38   Describe the four elements used in a data flow diagram.   **(4 marks)**

39   Explain the relationship between 'data independence' and a database approach to flexible data management.   **(4 marks)**

40   Data redundancy arises as a result of:

      A   viruses and computer misuse

      B   downsizing the organisation

      C   a lack of password controls

      D   duplication of data held

41 **A network topology refers to:**

A   the physical arrangement of a computer network

B   the type of hardware used

C   the hierarchy of access

D   the range of software operated

42 **Data integrity refers to its:**

A   accuracy

B   security of storage

C   adaptability for multiple use

D   ethical use of personal details

43 **Entity relationship modelling is a technique used within:**

A   an assessment centre test used in staff selection

B   market research and product testing

C   database analysis and design

D   business process re-engineering

44 **The main advantages of a database include:**

A   the development of separate data sources

B   unlimited access and open communication

C   end user flexibility and devolution of responsibility

D   data integrity and elimination of duplication

45 **Input devices are communication links:**

A   between the user and the computer

B   between hardware and software

C   between processing devices

D   within data processing

CHANGE MANAGEMENT

46 **Activities associated with organisational development:**

A   require universal agreement that change must take place

B   require 'interventions' into the social processes of an organisation

C   naturally occur through a shared sense of purpose and a strong organisational culture

D   result from the effect of Greiner's life cycle model

47   The technique of force field analysis depicts:

A   change as occurring through a series of restraining and driving forces

B   growth of organisations through evolution and revolution

C   an organisation's environment as a series of opportunistic and threatening factors

D   aggressive management styles used to drive change

48   According to Kurt Lewin, the final stage of his three-stage model of change is called:

A   unfreezing

B   refreezing

C   unbundling

D   support and facilitation

49   Which of the following would be an internal trigger for change in an organisation?

A   A major acquisition

B   A major development in IT technology

C   New legislation for protection of the environment

D   Trade union demands for a shorter working week for all employees

50   Kurt Lewin's force field theory of change in organisation identifies driving forces and restraining forces that influence change. When there is strong resistance to change, Lewin recommended that the most effective way for management to achieve the desired change would be to:

A   increase the strength of the driving forces

B   reduce the strength of the driving forces

C   increase the strength of the restraining forces

D   reduce the strength of the restraining forces

51   Senge argued that learning organisations adapt best because they have mastered five disciplines or 'component technologies'. Which of the following is one of these component technologies?

A   Effective control systems

B   Participation by everyone in decision-making

C   Building a shared vision

D   Overcoming resistance to change

52   Kanter argued that change-adept organisations, which are organisations that manage change successfully, share three key attributes. These are:

A   imagination to innovate, openness to collaborate, professionalism to perform

B   openness to collaborate, professionalism to perform, resilience to survive

C   professionalism to perform, imagination to innovate, resilience to survive

D   resilience to survive, openness to collaborate, imagination to innovate

53   Beer and Nohria identified two approaches to transformational change within an organisation, the Theory E and Theory O approaches. Theory E is a 'hard' approach based on maximising economic value and Theory O is a 'soft' approach based on organisational capability.

According to Beer and Nohria, when the management of an organisation wish to implement transformational change, the most effective approach is to use:

A   the Theory O approach only

B   the Theory E approach first, followed by the Theory O approach

C   the Theory O approach first, followed by the Theory E approach

D   the Theory E and Theory O approaches simultaneously

54   Which of the following is an example of incremental change within an organisation?

A   Downsizing

B   Introducing a new IT system

C   Restructuring

D   Changing the corporate culture

55   The management of a hospital are trying to persuade its doctors and qualified medical staff that due to a chronic shortage of trained medical staff throughout the country, the problems that the hospital faces in dealing with patients will be eased if unqualified staff are given training to carry out certain types of medical treatment on patients.

According to Lewin's three-step model of change, which stage in the process is gaining acceptance by qualified staff of the need to allow unqualified staff to treat patients?

A   Unfreezing

B   Movement

C   Refreezing

D   None of these

56   At what stage in Kurt Lewin's model of organisational change does the process of unfreezing take place?

A   The termination stage

B   The diagnostic stage

C   The intervention stage

D   The evaluation stage

57   Planned organisational change is most commonly triggered by the need to respond to new threats or opportunities presented by:

A   the organisation's culture

B   developments in the external environment

C   the internal environment

D   action by the organisation's management

58   Which *one* of the following factors is most likely to lead to successful organisational change?

A   Imposed by external consultants

B   Maintaining existing policies and procedures

C   Autocratic leadership

D   Initiated and supported by top management

59   An approach that focuses on the adaptation of organisations to change is commonly associated with the use of management consultants as agents of change, who apply diagnostic and problem-solving skills to an organisation's problems. This type of change management is known as:

A   Total Quality Management

B   Business Process Re-engineering

C   continuous improvement

D   organisational development

60   Establishing a staff help line when attempting to cope with resistance to change is an example of:

A   facilitation

B   manipulation

C   coercion

D   co-optation

61   In defining a learning organisation, Senge distinguished between adaptive and generative learning organisations. Explain the difference between these types of learning and their relevance to organisational change.   **(4 marks)**

62   Kurt Lewin's ideas on change are based on the view that change is:

A   capable of being planned

B   emergent

C   inevitable and uncontrollable

D   transformational

63   The intervention of a consultant or change agent is a common feature of:

A   co-operation and negotiation strategies for change

B   an inclusive culture

C   high levels of management visibility

D   a programme of Organisational Development (OD)

OPERATIONS MANAGEMENT

64 **The 5-S model refers to:**

A internal analysis involving structure, sub-structure, systems, sub-systems and strategy

B internal analysis involving style, shared values, skills, staffing and 'soft' information

C operations management practices of structurise, systematise, sanitise, standardise and self-discipline

D the Japanese six-sigma model adapted to Western practice

65 **Approval of documentation, procedures manuals and work instructions is associated with:**

A registration under the standards required for quality certification

B total quality management (TQM)

C lean production methods

D job evaluation

66 **Kaizen is a quality improvement technique that involves:**

A continuous improvement by small incremental steps

B a complete revision of all organisational processes and structures

C immediate, often radical 'right first time' changes to practice

D a problem-solving fishbone technique to identify cause and effect

67 **Describe the relationship between operations management and (using Mintzberg's terminology) the organisational technostructure.** **(4 marks)**

68 **Identify the reasons why an organisation might attempt to actively manage its relationship with its suppliers.** **(4 marks)**

69 **Identify examples of external failure costs, and explain their significance for an organisation with a reputation for quality.** **(4 marks)**

70 **Quality management thinker J.M. Juran once suggested that 85% of an organisation's quality problems are:**

A a result of ineffective control by supervisors and managers

B a result of ineffective systems

C a result of ineffective workers

D a result of ineffective incentive bonus schemes

71 **The five S (5S) practice is a technique aimed at achieving:**

A effective investment of resources in training and recruitment

B standardised procedures to improve the physical and thinking organisational environments

C excellence in strategy, style, skills, staff and structure

D diversity of activity and independence of thought in order to achieve closeness to the customer

72   Optimised production technologies (OPT) is an operations management system which aims to:

A   improve distribution networks

B   improve supply sourcing alternatives

C   integrate operations and quality assurance

D   reduce production bottlenecks

73   W.E. Deming promoted concepts of quality management, and his work is most closely associated with:

A   the quality planning road map

B   continuous improvement

C   the concept of zero defects

D   statistical quality control

74   The TQMEX model is a framework that integrates processes associated with:

A   total quality management experience through accreditation

B   supply chain management

C   both operations and quality management

D   organisational development

75   Hammer and Champy identified the main themes of Business Process Re-engineering as:

A   process re-orientation, creative use of IT, ambition and rule-breaking

B   effective process documentation, control and incentive bonus schemes

C   documentation, a clear business ethos and an investment in training

D   process review and enlightened HR practices

76   Which of the following statements about MRP I is correct?

A   MRP I is a computer system that uses a database to integrate the systems for all functions within the organisation, such as operations management, engineering, sales and marketing and accounting

B   MRP I ensures that inventory levels are maintained at sufficiently high levels to avoid the risk of 'stock-outs'

C   MRP I is a computerised system for scheduling production based on economic batch quantities

D   MRP I converts a master production schedule into production schedules for sub-assembles and parts and purchasing schedules for parts and raw materials

77   Which of the following statements about TQM is correct?

A   TQM relies on motivating employees to improve quality rather than on quality standards and statistical control methods

B   The level of defects must remain below a minimum acceptable level

C   All individuals within the organisation must be involved in quality improvements

D   The aim should be to eliminate all costs relating to quality

78   For an organisation following a strategic approach to supply, describe the organisational factors ('spokes in a wheel') that need to be integrated, co-ordinated and developed.

(4 marks)

79   The Toyota Production System, from which the concept of lean manufacturing was derived, identified seven types of waste in manufacturing. These included:

A   making defective products; motion; over-production

B   motion; overspending; inventory and work-in-progress

C   over-production; waste in processing; system defects

D   waiting; human error; transportation

80   A characteristic of lean manufacturing or a lean process is:

A   production initiated by 'supply push' rather than 'demand pull'

B   large batch production

C   small work cells

D   workers with specific skills

81   Which of the following is a concept in Just-in-Time production?

A   The aim at all times should be to achieve maximum capacity utilisation of production resources

B   It is better to have one large and complex machine than several small and simpler machines

C   Set-up times should be increased

D   The layout of a shop floor and the design of work flow can reduce production times

82   Which type of sourcing strategy for purchases uses a single but different source of supply at each of its plants or factories?

A   Single sourcing

B   Multiple sourcing

C   Parallel sourcing

D   Network sourcing

83   Which strategy for balancing capacity and demand has the objective of trying to balance available capacity with sales demand?

A   Level capacity planning

B   Chase demand planning

C   Demand management planning

D   Yield management planning

84 **Which of the following approaches to operations management is inconsistent with the concept of continuous improvement?**

    A   BPR

    B   6 Sigma

    C   Quality circles

    D   5S

85 **International standard ISO 14001** *Environmental Management Systems* **encourages processes for controlling and improving an organisation's:**

    A   performance on 'green' issues

    B   performance on quality issues as they relate to the competitive environment

    C   performance on scanning an industry environment

    D   performance on its internal investment in people

86 **Compare and contrast Kaizen and Business Process Re-engineering (BPR).**   **(4 marks)**

87 **Explain how computer software can assist in achieving quality in a manufacturing organisation.**
                                                                                        (4 marks)

88 **Distinguish quality control from quality circles.**   **(4 marks)**

89 **Describe the underlying concept of the Six Sigma approach to quality management.**

                                                                                        (4 marks)

90 **Explain briefly the difference between MRP II and ERP.**   **(4 marks)**

91 **Core features of world-class manufacturing involve:**

    A   competitor benchmarking and an investment in training and development

    B   an investment in IT and technical skills

    C   global sourcing networks and an awareness of competitor strategies

    D   a strong customer focus and flexibility to meet customer requirements

92 **An ABC system refers to:**

    A   a Japanese style problem solving device that is particularly helpful in inventory management

    B   an inventory management method that concentrates effort on the most important items

    C   accuracy, brevity and clarity in the quality of system reporting

    D   a mainframe solution to managing inventory

93 Corrective work, the cost of scrap and materials lost are:

A   examples of internal failure costs

B   examples of external failure costs

C   examples of appraisal costs

D   examples of preventative costs

94 Economies of scope refers to:

A   the economic viability of making alterations to systems

B   an organisation becoming economically viable through a process of 'rightsizing'

C   mass production assembly lines achieving economies through volume of output

D   economically producing small batches of a variety of products with the same machines

95 According to Porter's value chain, the final primary activity is referred to as:

A   marketing and sales

B   outbound logistics

C   procurement

D   service

96 Supply chain partnerships grow out of:

A   quality accreditation

B   recognising the supply chain and linkages in a value system

C   an expansion of trade

D   adopting a marketing philosophy

97 Which practice or activity is defined as 'the process of identifying, understanding and adapting outstanding practices and processes from organisations anywhere in the world to help your organisation improve its performance'?

A   Total Quality Management

B   Continuous improvement

C   Business Process Re-engineering

D   Benchmarking

98 State the main principles of Total Quality Management.   **(4 marks)**

99 Explain the meaning of a 'quality chain' within an organisation and suggest how service level agreements can be used to strengthen the quality chain.   **(4 marks)**

100 ISO 9001 : 2000 *Quality Management Systems: Requirements* requires that, to meet the required quality management standards, an organisation should document key processes and activities.

Explain why documentation is necessary and what processes or activities should be documented.   **(4 marks)**

MARKETING

101   Effective product promotion is centred on:

A   production processes

B   customers and communication

C   bonuses for sales staff and product quality

D   effective systems of monitoring and control

102   Conventional marketing wisdom suggests that, for successful segmentation of markets, segments must be:

A   relatively unsophisticated in their needs

B   economic, efficient and effective

C   measurable, accessible and substantial

D   currently lacking in providers

103   Distribution channels, transport, warehouse and sales outlet locations are all examples of:

A   'place', one component of the marketing mix

B   'promotion', one component of the marketing mix

C   'physical evidence', one component of the marketing mix

D   the management of operations for a service organisation

104   Distinguish between push and pull marketing policies and their impact on the promotion of goods.   **(4 marks)**

105   A company is deciding to sell its designer jewellery products over the internet for the first time, using its web site to display its product range and accept orders and payments. This represents a change in which of the following elements of the marketing mix?

A   Product

B   Price

C   Place

D   Promotion

106   Which *one* of the following statements explains 'concentrated marketing'?

A   The entity produces one product for a number of different market segments

B   The entity introduces several versions of the product aimed at several market segments

C   The entity produces one product for a mass market

D   The entity produces one product for a single segment of the market

107   Briefly explain two techniques that might be useful in forecasting future market demand for an organisation's products or services.   **(4 marks)**

108   Differentiated marketing is a marketing strategy based on:

A   offering a range of different products to one segment of the market

B   offering one product only to one segment of the market

C   offering the same range of products to all segments of the market

D   offering a number of different products, each to a different segment of the market

109   Market research into the size of the market that might exist for a new product or service is market research into the:

A   market potential

B   market penetration

C   sales potential

D   sales demand110

110   An organisation's credit policy represents a variable within:

A   the price marketing mix

B   the product marketing mix

C   product placement

D   the matrix of potential sales and growth

111   The primary aim of the marketing strategy for a commercial organisation should be to:

A   sell its products or services to customers

B   meet the overall business objectives by satisfying customer needs

C   promote a marketing culture amongst all its employees

D   maximise sales efficiency

112   Which of the following is an example of interactive marketing?

A   Television advertising

B   Direct mail

C   Telemarketing

D   Advertising on a web site

113   An exercise to assess the attitudes of customers or potential customers towards a particular consumer product is classified as:

A   market research

B   marketing research

C   a survey of buyers' intentions

D   test marketing

114   A marketing decision support system (MDSS) might be used to:

A   provide a list of customers to target with a direct mail shot

B   provide a forecast of future sales from an analysis of past sales

C   provide sales reports comparing actual with budgeted sales

D   hold a record of the buying history of each customer

115   Differential pricing means:

A   charging different prices for the same product in different parts of the market

B   charging prices that are different from those of competitors' products in the same market

C   charging different prices for the same product at different times of the day

D   offering price discounts for purchasing in large quantities

116   Which of the following is marketing or selling with a 'pull' effect?

A   Placing products in display baskets or 'gondolas' in a supermarket, to encourage impulse buying

B   Offering a low price to a distributor to persuade him to stock the product

C   Direct selling by members of the sales team

D   Television advertising for a product

117   Which of the following market research data-gathering techniques is most likely to be effective in estimating how many people buy a consumer product, in what quantities and how often?

A   Sample surveys

B   Observation

C   Analysis of past sales

D   Group interviewing

118   Which of the following is the most suitable definition of internal marketing?

A   Marketing the organisation's products to its own employees

B   Training employees who deal with customers to provide customer satisfaction in the work they do

C   Marketing activities carried on from the organisation's own premises, such as direct mail activities and telemarketing

D   Training employees in the features of the products and services sold by the organisation

119   'Market shakeout' involves the weakest producers exiting a particular market and occurs in a period between:

A   growth through creativity and growth through direction

B   introduction and market growth

C   market growth and market maturity

D   market maturity and decline

120 Analysing a market into sub-groups of potential customers with common needs and behaviours in order to target them through marketing techniques is called:

    A   market research

    B   market development

    C   segmentation

    D   product adaptation

121 Separate people or groups such as initiators, influencers, buyers and users are all involved in a buying decision in the context of:

    A   fast-moving consumer goods marketing

    B   business-to-business marketing

    C   business-to-consumer marketing

    D   services marketing

122 When planning the activities of a sales force, management must decide to which selling activities the sales staff should give priority. A distinction can be made between the following sales force activities:

    (a)   'hunting' versus 'farming'

    (b)   'selling' versus 'servicing'.

Explain the differences between these types of activities. **(4 marks)**

123 Explain why a firm might choose not to engage in market segmentation after conducting appropriate research. **(4 marks)**

124 In what ways does B2B marketing differ from B2C marketing? **(4 marks)**

125 Describe the stages in a product life cycle, and explain how the concept of the product life cycle might be relevant to marketing. **(4 marks)**

126 Public relations activity can be used within marketing as part of:

    A   marketing decision support activities

    B   a promotional mix

    C   customer feedback processes

    D   segmentation practices

127 Charging a very low price on one item in order to generate customer loyalty and increased sales of other items is called:

    A   market penetration

    B   loss leader pricing

    C   product penetration

    D   skim pricing

128 Explain the concept of physical evidence when applied to the marketing mix. **(4 marks)**

129 Identify the potential benefits of a marketing database and the source data from which it might be constructed. **(4 marks)**

MANAGING HUMAN CAPITAL

130 Charles Handy's vision of a 'shamrock' organisation suggests a workforce that comprises three different type of worker, namely:

A strategic, operational and support

B qualified, trainee and unskilled

C 'white collar', 'blue collar' and e-worker

D core, contractual and flexible labour

131 Job family structures are examples of:

A motivational tools

B similar levels of responsibility reflected across several distinct functions or disciplines

C Japanese employment practice

D pay structures for jobs within distinct functions or disciplines

132 Abraham Maslow's theory of motivation is often represented as:

A a hierarchy of needs

B individual behaviour labelled X or Y

C a scientific relationship between work and reward

D a series of negative and a series of positive factors

133 The set of activities designed to familiarise a new employee with an organisation is called:

A job analysis

B induction

C selection

D manipulation and co-optation

134 Recruitment involves:

A advertising a vacancy and interviewing

B conducting interviews and tests

C advertising a vacancy and initial screening of candidates

D ensuring that contract negotiation complies with organisational policy

135 **Three hundred and sixty degree (360°) feedback is normally associated with:**

A   exit interviews

B   quality circle activity

C   appraisal processes

D   reflection as part of a cycle of learning

136 **When someone commences a new job, the process of familiarisation is known as:**

A   probationary period

B   recruitment

C   appraisal

D   induction

137 **An effective appraisal system involves:**

A   assessing the personality of the appraisee

B   a process initiated by the manager who needs an update from the appraisee

C   advising on the faults of the appraisee

D   a participative, problem-solving process between the manager and appraisee

138 **The motivating potential score, developed by Hackman and Oldham, is calculated to assess:**

A   the knowledge of an individual

B   the satisfaction with work

C   the content of the job

D   the quality of work performed

139 **Job rotation involves:**

A   a redesign of a person's post based upon job analysis

B   the movement of an individual to another post in order to gain experience

C   the expansion and enrichment of a person's job content

D   the relocation of a post holder in order to benefit from the experience of a number of potential mentors

140 **A grievance procedure is established by an organisation in order that:**

A   there is a standing process to deal with the arbitration of disputes

B   the organisation can fairly discipline members of the workforce for wrongdoing

C   the workforce might formally raise issues where ill treatment has occurred

D   collective bargaining between the employer's side and the workforce might proceed smoothly

141 An 'assessment centre' approach is used:

A   as part of an appraisal process

B   as part of a process of training and development

C   as part of a selection process

D   as part of an exit interview process

142 Selection tests that fail to produce similar results over time when taken by the same candidate are:

A   contradictory

B   unreliable

C   too general

D   unstable

143 According to F.W. Taylor, which one of the following is a characteristic of scientific management?

A   Work specialisation

B   Group working

C   Socio-technical system

D   The informal organisation

144 Why is succession planning desirable in a large organisation?

A   To ensure that promotion opportunities exist

B   To ensure business continuity

C   To ensure competence in key functions

D   To prevent natural wastage of staff

145 When it wishes to appoint full-time office staff, a company might use the services of an employment agency for:

A   recruitment and selection only

B   recruitment and screening only

C   screening and selection only

D   screening only

146 In which of the following situations is it most likely that an unfair dismissal has occurred?

A   An employee leaves his job claiming that the employer was in breach of contract by demoting him

B   The employer terminates a fixed term contract with a sub-contractor without notice

C   The employer dismisses a lorry driver who has been banned from driving by the court

D   The employer dismisses an employee because of redundancy

147 **What is the major difficulty in establishing a basic pay structure for knowledge work?**

A   Job evaluation

B   Benchmarking

C   Scarcity of individuals with knowledge skills

D   Performance evaluation

148 **Intelligence, aptitudes and disposition are often factors identified in:**

A   a job description

B   appraisal targets

C   a person specification

D   360 degree documentation

149 **What is the main practical reason for asking an applicant for a reference from a former employer, as part of the selection process for a vacant job?**

A   To gain another person's opinion about the suitability of the candidate for the job

B   To find out whether the candidate has any personal faults or weaknesses

C   To assess what the candidate's future performance in the job might be

D   To establish whether the candidate has been telling the truth about his previous employment history

150 **The purpose of job evaluation is to:**

A   assess the personal qualities required to do the job

B   assess what the responsibilities of the job should be

C   assess the performance of the job holder

D   assess a fair rate of pay for the job

151 **Which of the following factors can be both a hygiene factor and a motivator for employees?**

A   Pay

B   The quality of management

C   Working conditions

D   The level of responsibility the individual is given

152 **Lawrence and Lorsch argued that specialisation within an organisation and greater decentralisation are most needed in organisations:**

A   with a stable and predictable environment

B   where there is a low level of change in its environment and technology

C   where there is a high level of predictable change in its environment and technology

D   where there is a high level of unpredictable change in its environment and technology

153   What are the three ingredients in Handy's motivation calculus?

    A   Needs, motivation, satisfaction

    B   Needs, effectiveness, results

    C   Participation, pay, recognition

    D   Motivation, effort, rewards

154   One of the major consequences of changing an organisation towards a virtual structure will be:

    A   less trust of employees

    B   fewer meetings

    C   a reduction in outsourcing

    D   less motivation to perform

155   The following assumptions underlie a well-known theory of motivation.

    (1)   The expenditure of physical and mental effort at work is as natural as play or rest.

    (2)   If a job is satisfying, then the result will be commitment to the organisation.

These assumptions apply to:

    A   Maslow's hierarchy of needs

    B   McGregor's Theory X

    C   McGregor's Theory Y

    D   Ouchi's Theory Z

156   According to Likert, which of the following is not a feature of effective management?

    A   The motivation to work must be supplemented by a system of rewards

    B   Employees should be seen as individuals with needs, whose self-worth should be developed

    C   An organisation should be developed as a closely-knit structure of effective work groups, all committed to achieving the organisation's objectives

    D   Supportive relationships must exist within each work group, characterised by mutual respect not actual support

157   According to Herzberg, one of the motivator factors in employment is:

    A   advancement

    B   status

    C   interpersonal relations

    D   the employer's policies and administration

158   Performance-related pay involves:

A   rewarding employees with a proportion of total profits

B   rewarding employees with a proportion of total profits in excess of a target minimum level

C   rewarding employees on the basis of the amount of work they have done

D   rewarding employees for achieving agreed personal targets

159   Rensis Likert argued that the most effective style of management:

A   is benevolent authoritarian

B   is participative

C   is consultative

D   depends on the circumstances and the situation

160   Recent developments towards greater employee involvement, flexible working and flatter organisational structures have placed greater emphasis on which one of the following styles of management?

A   Exploitative authoritative

B   Autocratic

C   Participative

D   Benevolent authoritative

161   Any claim that unethical behaviour is in an organisation's best interests is an attempt to:

A   follow the principle of procedural justice

B   do the right thing for society

C   rationalise the unethical conduct

D   look after the interests of oneself

162   Activities aimed at attracting a number of suitable candidates interested in joining an organisation are called:

A   human relationship marketing

B   recruitment

C   selection

D   human capital harvesting

163   According to M.A. Devanna, which one of the following describes the components of the HR cycle?

A   Job design, selection, involvement, appraisal, rewards

B   Selection, performance appraisal, rewards, development

C   Performance, job design, appraisal, involvement, development

D   Appraisal, development, job design, involvement, rewards

164   According to F.W. Taylor, which one of the following is a characteristic of scientific management?

    A   Work specialisation

    B   Group working

    C   Socio-technical system

    D   The informal organisation

165   Which of the following HR activities should be the most difficult to outsource to an external organisation?

    A   Staff development

    B   Re-location

    C   Training

    D   Recruitment

166   In staff recruitment, an appraisal method based on identifying the skills required for a job and assessing which applicant has those required skills is known as:

    A   psychometric testing

    B   work sample tests

    C   a competence-based approach

    D   an assessment centre

167   An assessment centre:

    A   helps selection by assessing job candidates by using a comprehensive and interrelated series of techniques

    B   is the training headquarters where job interviews take place

    C   is a desk-based process of reviewing job application forms for suitability

    D   is a place where job applicants are subjected to psychological testing

168   Training workers in methods of statistical process control and work analysis:

    A   overcomes a crisis of control in an organisation's life cycle

    B   is part of a succession planning approach to Human Resources

    C   is part of a quality management approach

    D   is part of a scientific management approach

169   The expectations that the individual and the organisation have of one another are referred to as:

    A   a hygiene factor

    B   a psychological contract

    C   dual theory motivation

    D   a person specification

170 **According to Douglas McGregor:**

A   'Theory X' people dislike work, need direction and avoid responsibility

B   'Theory Y' people dislike work, need direction and avoid responsibility

C   self-actualising people dislike work, need direction and avoid responsibility

D   hygiene factors determine whether people like work, need direction or take responsibility

171 **The processes of job analysis and individual performance appraisal are related in the sense that:**

A   they are different terms for the same process

B   performance appraisal is based on job analysis

C   both form part of the selection process

D   job analysis is based on performance appraisal

172 **It is the role of 'outplacement consultants' to:**

A   provide help to redundant employees including training and finding jobs

B   provide help to employees wishing to gain experience in other roles

C   arrange for placing products in an untested market place

D   arrange for placing under-used assets at the disposal of start-up businesses

173 **F.W. Taylor's thinking on motivation in the workplace involved a belief that:**

A   social groups and individuals as part of a culture should be key considerations

B   reward for effort and workplace efficiency should be key considerations

C   managers had two different sets of assumptions about their subordinates

D   'motivators' and 'hygiene factors' should be key considerations

174 **In terms of employment CIMA's Ethical Guidelines require members to:**

A   act responsibly in the way that all other professionals do

B   act responsibly but in a way that satisfies organisational demands and pressures

C   act responsibly but in a way that satisfies the individual's own ethical code

D   act responsibly, honour any legal contract of employment and conform to employment legislation

175 **Identify the main stages involved in developing human resource plans and programmes following the production of a corporate plan.**   (4 marks)

176 **Explain the difference between:**

(a)   job enlargement

(b)   job rotation

(c)   job enrichment   (4 marks)

177   Identify eight important documents and pieces of information to which an interviewer should
       have access when conducting a job selection interview.   **(4 marks)**

178   Describe the difference between 'hard' and 'soft' human resources management.

                                                                                        (4 marks)

179   Explain how reliability (the same result for a repeated event) might be improved in selection
       interviews.   **(4 marks)**

180   Frederick Herzberg's study of work and people is of significance to managers because it
       identifies:

       A   a framework for HRM involving appraisal, training and motivation

       B   the need to assess the personality of job applicants

       C   factors associated with job satisfaction called motivators

       D   satisfaction from a participative, problem-solving environment

181   Adding new tasks to a person's job, so increasing their responsibility, is called:

       A   process re-engineering

       B   job enrichment

       C   HR development

       D   career scoping

182   Remuneration is an example of:

       A   self-actualisation reward

       B   an intrinsic reward

       C   an extrinsic reward

       D   an individual's work/life balance

183   Rodger's seven-point plan refers to:

       A   quality targets for world-class operations

       B   implementation guidelines for introducing new hardware

       C   the likely headings to be found as part of a person specification

       D   lean production processes

184   In the expectancy theory of motivation 'valence' refers to:

       A   a belief that an outcome will satisfy organisational tasks

       B   a person's own preference for achieving a particular outcome

       C   a belief that the outcome will be shared by others equally

       D   an understanding of the probability of an event happening

185   In HR planning how might an organisation match the projected 'supply' of human resources to
       future demand.   **(4 marks)**

186 Identify the advantages and disadvantages of a policy of succession planning for a large organisation. **(4 marks)**

187 Identify both the advantages and disadvantages of a decentralised Human Resource provision for an organisation that has many business units and sites. **(4 marks)**

Section 2

SECTION B-TYPE QUESTIONS

188   SPEC

SPEC manufactures spectacles and sunglasses, which it sells through retail organisations and specialist opticians. It is planning to introduce a major new computer system for marketing. The new system will be developed in-house. In the past, the company has neglected both IT and marketing activities, and the managing director has been calling for major changes in the way that marketing staff think and operate. He has accused the marketing management of being too sales-oriented and not sufficiently marketing-oriented. He sees the new computer system as an opportunity to introduce big changes. opponents

At a recent project development meeting, the IT director and senior systems analyst presented ideas for the design of the new system. These were presented largely in the form of diagrams and tables: data flow diagrams, entity-relationship models, entity life histories and decision tables. Several points were raised at the meeting.

(1)   The managing director is very concerned about the problems of implementing what he regards as major changes into the organisation, particularly marketing activities. He believes that the change must be managed carefully.

(2)   The marketing director is looking forward to having the new system, which will provide a marketing decision support system and a customer database. He believes that the database will be useful for direct marketing.

(3)   The managing director added that he has been advised to check whether the new system will raise any legal issues that the company will have to consider.

Required:

(a)   Explain the potential benefits of a new IT system to the organisation.   **(5 marks)**

(b)   Explain the purpose in systems development of:

   (i)   data flow diagrams

   (ii)   entity-relationship models

   (iii)   entity life histories

   (iv)   decision tables.   **(5 marks)**

(c)   Suggest an approach to the management of change within the organisation, based on the views of Beer and Nohria.   **(5 marks)**

(d)   Explain the difference between mass marketing, direct marketing and interactive marketing, giving examples of each.   **(5 marks)**

(e)   Explain how market research can be used to support a marketing decision support system.   **(5 marks)**

(f)   Describe three legal issues that might affect the marketing of spectacles and sunglasses.   **(5 marks)**

(Total: 30 marks)

189   NEW SYSTEM

A company is planning a major new IT system for order processing, inventory control and order despatch operations. Senior management would prefer to develop a bespoke system, although an off-the-shelf software package is available that could be used instead. The IT manager recognises the need for the new system to be introduced quickly, and has suggested that the systems development, if done in-house, would make use of prototyping.

One of the main reasons for introducing the new system is that customers for the company's products demand reliable delivery dates for the items they order, and several rival companies have been gaining market share because they have been able to develop better order delivery systems. All the customers of the company are businesses. The company's new system will be used for taking customer orders and informing customers about the availability of the items, and will provide the customer with a 'guaranteed' delivery date.

Another feature of the new system is that it will speed up order processing, and it is expected that about 100 staff will be made redundant. The staff who are kept on will need training in the use of the new system.

Required:

(a)   Explain the main disadvantages of buying off-the-shelf software rather than developing a bespoke information system.   **(5 marks)**

(b)   Explain how prototyping would speed up system implementation and improve the quality of the final system.   **(5 marks)**

(c)   The new computer system is intended to improve operating processes within the company. Explain the importance of operations strategy for the company.   **(5 marks)**

(d)   Suggest how the new IT system might be seen as an element of the marketing mix by the company's marketing management.   **(5 marks)**

(e)   Suggest how staff should be trained in operating the new system.   **(5 marks)**

(f)   Suggest the procedures the company should follow if it has to make some staff redundant.   **(5 marks)**

(Total: 30 marks)

190   HUBBLES (PILOT PAPER)

Hubbles, a national high-street clothing retailer has recently appointed a new Chief Executive. The company is well established and relatively financially secure. It has a reputation for stability and traditional, quality clothing at an affordable price. Lately, however, it has suffered from intense competition leading to a loss of market share and an erosion of customer loyalty.

Hubbles has all the major business functions provided by 'in house' departments, including finance, human resources, purchasing, strategy and marketing. The Strategy and Marketing Department has identified a need for a comprehensive review of the company's effectiveness. In response, the new Chief Executive has commissioned a review by management consultants.

Their initial findings include the following:

- Hubbles has never moved from being sales-oriented to being marketing-oriented and this is why it has lost touch with its customers;

- Hubbles now needs to get closer to its customers and operate a more effective marketing mix;

- Additional investment in its purchasing department can add significantly to improving Hubbles' competitive position.

The Chief Executive feels that a presentation of interim findings to senior managers would be helpful at this point. You are a member of the management consultancy team and have been asked to draft a slide presentation of some of the key points. The Chief Executive has identified six such points.

Required:

Prepare a slide outline, and brief accompanying notes of two to three sentences, for each of the Chief Executive's key points identified below. (Your responses should be contained on no more than six pages in total.)

(a) Describe the difference between a company that concentrates on 'selling' its products and one that has adopted a marketing approach.   **(5 marks)**

(b) Explain how Hubbles might develop itself into an organisation that is driven by customer needs.   **(5 marks)**

(c) Explain what is meant by the 'marketing mix'.   **(5 marks)**

(d) Identify examples of ways in which the management of Hubbles could make use of the marketing mix to help regain its competitive position.   **(5 marks)**

(e) Describe the main areas in which Hubbles' Human Resources Department might reasonably contribute to assist the Purchasing Department.   **(5 marks)**

(f) Explain how an efficient Purchasing Department might contribute to effective organisational performance.   **(5 marks)**

(Total: 30 marks)

191   STAND PRODUCTS

Stand Products is a manufacturing organisation that has been established for many years, producing electrical and electronic products. It is currently facing tough market conditions. The management of the company believe that the market as a whole is currently expanding quite rapidly, but the annual sales revenue of Stand Products is growing much more slowly and the company is losing market share.

At a recent meeting of the senior management to discuss the difficulties facing the company, there was general agreement that the company had suffered badly from a general lack of innovation and new thinking, and that change was urgently needed.

The marketing director believes that the need for change was being driven by a variety of factors outside the company, which he calls 'triggers for change'. The managing director disagrees: his view is that too much authority has been delegated to the profit centre managers within the company and that head office was now losing control of its operations and marketing strategies. He thinks the time has come, given the continuing growth of the company's business, to make organisational changes and bring back more power and influence to head office.

The managing director has also stated the view that even if changes are introduced, the company will have to make some staff redundant in order to cut costs.

The operations director stated his view that many of the difficulties of the company were caused by difficulties that the company was having with suppliers, and with poor performance in some of the company's manufacturing centres. Referring to the concept of the supply wheel, he would like to carry out a strategic review of the entire supply chain and consider outsourcing many of the company's current manufacturing operations. He has also argued that if manufacturing continues to be carried on in-house rather than outsourced, he will carry out a major review of performance objectives and performance measurements in manufacturing operations. He thinks that there is currently too much emphasis on cost control and not enough on other elements of performance.

Required:

(a)   Kanter, in *The Change Masters: Corporate Entrepreneurs at Work*, argued for the need for organisations to be creative and encourage change, and criticised the widespread management indifference in the US to innovations suggested by employees.

Describe the ways in which she suggested that creativity should be encouraged within organisations.   **(5 marks)**

(b)   Describe the nature of external triggers for change that affect organisations.

(5 marks)

(c)   The views of the managing director are compatible with Greiner's growth model. Describe the five stages in Greiner's growth model, and suggest which stage the company might have reached, if the managing director's views are correct.

(5 marks)

(d)   When an employer needs to make some employees redundant, it may use measures that reduce the need for compulsory redundancies.

Define 'compulsory redundancies' and suggest measures that might be taken to reduce or avoid the amount of compulsory redundancies.   **(5 marks)**

(e)   Describe the concept of the supply wheel and the elements within it, and the implications for the company.   **(5 marks)**

(f)   Explain what types of performance objectives and performance measurement criteria the operations director could introduce to help improve the management of the company's operations.   **(5 marks)**

(Total: 30 marks)

192   HILO CONSULTANCY

Hilo Consultancy specialises in providing IT solutions to business clients. The company has been growing successfully, and is a project-based organisation. A project team is created whenever a client commissions new work, and is disbanded when the work is completed. The company assembles the teams from a pool of its own full-time staff, and also employs temporary staff as required to meet the particular skills requirements for each project. Much of the company's work is involved with developing complex databases for clients, such as marketing databases.

The company's organisation structure and reward systems are based on high-performance arrangements, although there have been some problems recently with members of staff who are dissatisfied with their salaries and career prospects.

The HR manager attributes much of the success of the company to the excellent leadership qualities of the managing director, who has great skills in dealing with the highly-skilled and intelligent work force. The HR manager has described the work force as a mixture of 'self-actualising man' and 'complex man'.

The managing director recognises that as the company grows and develops, changes will be needed. He is particularly interested in the need to reinforce the company's policies for high-quality working, and he is an advocate of quality management. Some clients have already asked whether Hilo Consultancy has any certification of its quality standards. The managing director believes that in several years' time, a significant number of potential clients might insist on certification of quality management standards from its suppliers, and he intends that Hilo Consultancy should apply for certification under the ISO 9000 series.

Required:

(a) Describe the nature and purpose of a customer database for marketing, and explain how might a database be used. **(5 marks)**

(b) Explain the meaning of 'high performance work arrangements'. **(5 marks)**

(c) Describe the main features of a project-based organisation and explain the particular problems for HR management in this type of organisation. **(5 marks)**

(d) The views of the HR manager about the leadership skills of the managing director relate to the views of Schein on motivation. Describe the four types of employee behaviour identified by Schein, and explain their relevance to management.

(5 marks)

(e) The ISO 9000 series of quality management standards is based on certain quality principles. Explain the purpose of the ISO 9000 quality standards and describe the quality principles on which they are based. **(5 marks)**

(f) Explain the framework for an exercise to establish quality management systems in conformity with ISO 9001: *2000 guidelines*. **(5 marks)**

(Total: 30 marks)

193 PMK MANUFACTURING

PMK Manufacturing, a division of a global manufacturing company, has been experiencing difficulties with its operations in manufacturing and purchasing and supply. A new managing director for the division has been appointed, with the task of improving the division's performance.

He has found several features of the management and organisation that he does not like. The previous managing director had concentrated on improving efficiency through work organisation and work standards. The new managing director considers this approach to be rather old-fashioned, and too much like scientific management; worse still, it has not been successful.

He has also found that the management information systems are poor. Reports are often produced late, and do not provide the feedback that operations managers need to control work quality and work flow adequately. Feedback reporting systems will need to be improved.

In his previous job in another division of the company, the managing director had worked with his management team and employees to develop a continuous improvement programme, which had been very successful. However, he is not convinced that a continuous improvement programme would be appropriate for the PMK division, in view of the culture change required, and he suspects that an overhaul of operational and purchasing systems based on a business process re-engineering approach might be more appropriate. He considers that a reorganisation of production on a Just-In-Time basis might be appropriate, and that there will have to be a major improvement in purchasing and supply.

He supports the views of Reck and Long, that purchasing should be used as a strategic weapon to promote competitiveness, but the division has so far failed to engage in any long-term relationships with its suppliers.

(a) F.W. Taylor is regarded as the founder of scientific management. Describe the objectives of management as suggested by Taylor. Why might the managing director consider the approach to be old-fashioned? **(5 marks)**

(b) Feedback systems provide negative and positive feedback for control purposes. Explain the difference between positive and negative feedback in a management information system, and give an example of a management system in which feedback is used. **(5 marks)**

(c)   Describe the features of continuous improvement or Kaizen.   **(5 marks)**

(d)   Describe the nature of Business Process Re-engineering (BPR) and explain the principles on which it is based.   **(5 marks)**

(e)   Describe the operational requirements for a system of JIT production.   **(5 marks)**

(f)   Explain the approach of Reck and Long to supply strategy, and describe their four stages in the development of purchasing to becoming a competitive weapon in a company's strategic planning and battle for markets.   **(5 marks)**

(Total: 30 marks)

194   SOFT DIVISION

The Soft Division of TTFN International has had a poor reputation for human relations management, and a new management team has been installed to introduce change and improvements. The new team has found that the previous management used a very authoritarian style of leadership, and had discouraged innovative ideas and suggestions for improvements from their employees.

Although the new team expect to use a different style of leadership, they have discovered several other problems that demand their attention. A major cause of concern is the lack of adequate HR planning by the division. The division is undergoing a period of great change, with new technology and increasing environmental regulations affecting both product design and production systems. New skills will be needed from employees and some of the existing skills of the work force will no longer be required after the next one or two years.

A second problem is that for some jobs in the division, the wrong type of person has been employed and recruitment methods ought to be introduced. The new management favour the use of testing of job applicants, such as psychometric testing. In addition, they believe that there ought to be a formal system of job appraisal. The senior management of TTFN International have indicated that the Soft Division would be permitted to introduce a performance-related pay scheme, if this would improve the efficiency and performance of the division.

A third issue is that employees need to be alerted to the growing significance of social and environmental issues, particularly in view of the increasing environmental regulations, and the new management intend to pursue a corporate social responsibility policy.

Required:

(a)   In the 1980s, Kanter criticised the lack of innovation in many US companies, and accused senior management of discouraging new ideas and change. Describe six ways in which senior management might discourage innovation.   **(5 marks)**

(b)   Describe the methods that might be used by the HR department to forecast the organisation's demand for employees over the next five years.   **(5 marks)**

(c)   A company might identify from its HR plan that it will need fewer of a particular group of employees in about two years' time, and some employees might have to be made redundant.

Suggest measures that the company might take now, based on the HR plan, to reduce the amount of redundancies in the future.   **(5 marks)**

(d)   Explain the nature of psychometric testing, and the advantages and disadvantages of using this form of testing for recruitment purposes.   **(5 marks)**

(e)   (i)   Explain the purpose of an appraisal system.

(ii)   Explain the problems that a organisation might have to deal with in operating a performance-related pay scheme for its employees.   **(5 marks)**

(f)   Explain the concept of corporate social responsibility (CSR) and suggest how CSR might be relevant for the marketing of an organisation's products or services.

(5 marks)

(Total: 30 marks)

195 CHAPTERLAND (NOV 06 EXAM)

The country of Chapterland has a principle that healthcare should be free to its citizens at the point of access. Healthcare is funded from national taxation and organised through a series of large health units, one of which is known as 'Q2'. Q2 operates a huge, single site hospital and offers a variety of community services (such as health visiting) that are taken to the local population. Q2 has a management structure consisting of eight clinical and administrative directors who report to Q2's Chief Executive Officer (CEO). The Q2 CEO is directly accountable to the national government through regular returns of information and year-end reporting.

Published 'quality league tables' of hospital performance against government targets suggest that Q2 has one of the worst records in the country. (Targets are for cleanliness of hospital wards, treatment waiting times and staff employed per patient cases dealt with.) In addition, Q2 has in recent years been operating to a budget in excess of its funding, which is against government regulations. The current year budget again exceeds projected funding.

Last year, Q2's previous CEO decided that certain changes were necessary including:

- better cost control
- improved performance measurement; and
- benchmarking.

He revealed this thinking for the first time in a global email he sent to Q2's staff. Later, when conducting the annual performance appraisal of the Director of Human Resources (HR), he tasked her with implementing 'each and every form of benchmarking' within the next four months so that 'true' performance deficiencies could be addressed. However, the Director of HR left for a new job elsewhere within that period. The CEO then undertook to manage the changes himself but was surprised to find directors unenthusiastic and even unco-operative. Under pressure from the government the CEO resigned 'for personal reasons' and no progress was made with his initiatives.

A new CEO has just been appointed. Her immediate concern is to reduce expenditure and improve performance. On her first day as CEO she spoke of a need to re-establish a culture of 'care through quality' within Q2. She wishes to discuss a number of ideas and issues with her clinical and administrative directors at a special 'away day' meeting to be arranged soon. You work in the CEO's central policy team and she has informed you that some ideas for initiatives include outsourcing, improved supply management and new performance management measures.

Required:

You have been asked to provide the new CEO with briefing notes on a number of issues that will help prepare her for the 'away day' meeting. These notes should:

(a)   explain why the changes attempted by the previous CEO were unsuccessful **(5 marks)**

(b)   explain the role Human Resources could perform in supporting any new initiatives for change **(5 marks)**

(c)   analyse the potential of outsourcing as a means of overcoming some of the problems facing Q2 (the CEO has identified two services initially – IT/IS and cleaning)

(5 marks)

(d)   discuss which forms of benchmarking Q2 should use in order to contribute to better performance management   **(5 marks)**

(e)   discuss how a culture of 'care through quality' might be established within Q2
                                                                                (5 marks)

(f)   describe the performance measures that will be needed in order to satisfy future management and strategic reporting requirements of Q2.   **(5 marks)**

(Total: 30 marks)

196   GOURMET COMPANY

Gourmet Company is a private European company. Its founder and main shareholder began in business by manufacturing food processing equipment. This remains an important part of the company's operations, but it has diversified into the manufacture of Gee-May branded food products and also into operating a chain of Gee-May food stores and a chain of Gee-May restaurants. Gourmet Company is now a large and successful international company, with over ten different divisions operating as investment centres.

Each division is structured and organised in a different way from the other divisions, according to the circumstances in which the division operates. Central management do not impose a particular management or organisation structure on its divisions, even though some divisions need to work together in close co-operation.

However, divisional managers are continually being urged by head office to improve their operational performance. There have been several innovations recently in efforts to improve systems and operations.

(i)   The division that manufactures food processing equipment has recently introduced an MRP I system to improve production and inventory planning and control.

(ii)   The food stores division is trying to introduce a Just-In-Time philosophy into the operation of its food stores, with the aim of improving customer service.

(iii) The food stores division has also introduced a new user-friendly computer system, that enables customers in its shops and stores to check out and pay for their own purchases, without having to queue for service at a cash desk.

(iv)   The company is continually producing new products to maintain competitive advantage, and the marketing departments in the various divisions collaborate with operational management in product screening and in developing new products of a very high quality, in keeping with the Gee-May brand name.

Required:

(a)   The organisation structure of Gourmet Company is consistent with the contingency theory of organisation. Explain the basic proposition in contingency theory, and explain how the requirements for differentiation and integration affect the efficiency of an organisation structure. (Your answer should refer if possible to the work of Lawrence and Lorsch.)   **(5 marks)**

(b)   (i)   Explain the difference between continuous inventory management, periodic inventory systems and ABC inventory management.

       (ii)   Explain, giving your reason, which type of inventory management system is appropriate for an MRP I system of production scheduling.   **(5 marks)**

(c)   Explain how the JIT philosophy might be applied to the provision of services to customers.   **(5 marks)**

(d)   Explain the meaning of a 'user-friendly' computer system, and suggest what the user-friendly features of the check-out system in the food stores might be.   **(5 marks)**

(e)   Explain the nature of concept screening in the product design process.   **(5 marks)**

(f)   Explain the purpose of branding consumer products.   **(5 marks)**

(Total: 30 marks)

197   V COSMETICS (MAY 05 EXAM)

V is an innovative company run according to the principles of its entrepreneurial owner. V operates a package distribution service, a train service, and sells holidays, bridal outfits, clothing, mobile telephones, and soft drinks. V is well known for challenging the norm and 'giving customers quality products and services at affordable prices and doing it all with a sense of fun'. V spends little on advertising but has great brand awareness thanks to the 'visibility' of its inspirational owner.

V has just announced the launch of 'V-cosmetics' to exploit a gap in the market. The cosmetic range will be competitively priced against high street brands and have the distinctive V logo.

You work for a market analyst who is about to appear on a radio discussion of V's business interests. You have been asked to provide a clear, short briefing for the market analyst on the thinking behind V-cosmetics. Your research of the V-cosmetics range identifies innovative marketing proposals. V-cosmetics will not be on sale in shops, instead it will use two approaches to promotion and selling, namely:

- The use of 'cosmetic associates'. Individuals may apply to become an associate and, if accepted, will be required to buy a basic inventory of every V-cosmetic product. The associate will then use these products as samples and 'testers'. After initial training associates organise parties in the homes of friends and their friends where they take orders for products at a listed price. Associates receive commission based on sales.

- The internet and mobile telephone technology will also be heavily used to offer Vcosmetic products to the public.

Required:

Prepare brief notes containing bullet points and no more than two to three sentences for each of the key points identified below. (Your notes should be contained on no more than six pages in total.)

(a)   Explain how the proposed approach can be understood within the context of the marketing mix.   **(5 marks)**

(b)   Explain the human resource implications of using 'cosmetic associates'.   **(5 marks)**

(c)   Explain the concept of direct marketing.   **(5 marks)**

(d)   Explain the advantages of the internet as a marketing channel.   **(5 marks)**

(e)   Describe how V might use internet and mobile phone technology as part of its marketing approach.   **(5 marks)**

(f)   Identify the main ethical issues associated with the proposal to market V cosmetics.

(5 marks)

(Total: 30 marks)

198   XX (MAY 07 EXAM)

XX is a manufacturing firm with a past reputation for offering a diverse range of innovative products to a traditional market. Three years ago the previous Chief Executive invested in e-commerce as a way of making longer term cost reductions and establishing an advantage over XX's competitors (all of whom trade by more traditional means). A second initiative involved building a carefully designed headquarters (HQ) to cater for a growing central staff needed to control operating activities more tightly. These initiatives were financed by a number of measures including:

- the suspension of all other plans for the purchase of computer hardware and software

- abandoning both training and research and development (R&D) in the short term

- reducing both marketing and finance budgets

- suspending all new recruitment even for posts falling vacant.

The Chief Executive explained that:

- e-commerce would replace all other forms of trading and both old and new customers would be beating at our door

- the new HQ would be a visible symbol that 'XX means innovation'.

Although the new HQ won a prestigious design award, other matters did not go so well and after successive years of financial losses a new Chief Executive was appointed. The new Chief Executive soon recruited a small management team with particular expertise in company analysis and recovery. Its report into XX's problems indicated:

- a weakening position relative to competitors due to inappropriate strategies

- poor management at all levels and a neglect of XX's core business and products

- weak financial control and management accounting information

- inappropriate marketing practices and a failure to manage the company's product portfolio leading to unprofitable lines and few new products.

The new Chief Executive indicated several priorities to turnaround the company including:

- halting further investment in e-commerce

- reconsidering budgetary priorities including reducing central costs

- delayering, decentralisation and re-skilling of the workforce

- funding the re-establishment of XX's position in the marketplace

- using software solutions to improve XX's manufacturing operation.

The Chief Executive wishes to present these ideas at the next Board meeting and has asked you to prepare brief notes to support the presentation.

Required:

Prepare brief notes for the new Chief Executive for each of the sub-questions she has identified below.

(a)   Explain how XX can address any **two** of the issues identified by the management team.

(5 marks)

(b)   Explain why delayering is more appropriate than downsizing in helping to turnaround XX.

(5 marks)

(c)   Explain the disadvantages of using the internet as XX's sole marketing tool.

(5 marks)

(d)   Describe the factors that need to be considered by XX when deciding whether to invest in a product. **(5 marks)**

(e)   Identify the types of software application that would produce most advantage to a manufacturing firm trying to improve its production operations. **(5 marks)**

(f)   Describe the potential benefits of XX resuming its investment in training. **(5 marks)**

(Total: 30 marks)

199   MOTIVATION ASSUMPTIONS

R Company employs about 50 sales people, each of whom covers his or her own territory. They are between 25 and 63 years old, have served for varying lengths of time, and include both married and single people. They have a basic salary and can earn a similar amount again in commission. The company now feels that this method of payment has become inequitable because of variable conditions in each region. Some of the sales people have also commented that the company's reliance on the state pension arrangements compares unfavourably with alternative employers.

It has now been decided to abandon the commission system and to compensate the sales people by:

• consolidating part of their commission into a higher salary

• establishing a non-contributory pension scheme

• providing more prestigious cars for them

• increasing their holiday entitlement by 25%.

Required:

(a)   Describe briefly the assumptions underlying the following theories of human motivation:

(i)   Maslow's need-based theory **(5 marks)**

(ii)   Herzberg's motivation-hygiene theory **(5 marks)**

(iii) McGregor's Theory X and Theory Y. **(5 marks)**

(b)   Explain what effect the following changes may have on the sales people at R Company and on other staff:

(i)   consolidating part of their commission into a higher salary **(5 marks)**

(ii)   establishing a non-contributory pension scheme **(5 marks)**

(iii) changing the car and holiday entitlements. **(5 marks)**

(Total: 30 marks)

200   S & C (MAY 06 EXAM)

S & C is a medium-sized firm that is experiencing rapid growth as evidenced by increased sales revenue. It has been able to develop a range of new consultancy and specialist business advisory services that it offers to its growing customer base. To cope with these developments, several organisation-wide initiatives have been launched over the past two years.

The existing financial systems are struggling to cope with these developments, but replacement software is due to be installed within the next six months. The new system was justified partly because it could reduce costs, although precise details have not been given. The application software does not fit existing business processes exactly. However, it has the clear advantage of giving S & C access to an industry best practice system and is identical to that used by all its main competitors and some of its clients.

A three-person project steering group has recommended that a phased approach to introduction should be used and has undertaken most of the project planning. A programme of events for implementing the system has been agreed but is not yet fully operational. This group has not met for a while because the designated project manager has been absent from work through illness.

You are Head of S & C's Central Support Unit. You also serve on the project steering group.

A partners' meeting is due to take place soon. The firm's senior partner has asked you to prepare a PowerPoint presentation to other partners on implementation issues. You understand that the partners are conscious that system implementation represents a form of further organisational change. They are asking questions about the approach that will be taken to the introduction of the new system, likely changes to practices, critical areas for success, system testing, support after implementation, system effectiveness, etc.

Required:

Produce **outline notes** that will support your eventual PowerPoint presentation. These notes should:

(a)   discuss the options to overcome the fact that the software does not fit existing business processes exactly **(5 marks)**

(b)   explain why a phased approach to introducing the system is, in this case, more suitable than a direct 'big bang' approach **(5 marks)**

(c)   discuss the ways in which particular individuals and groups within S & C are important for implementation to succeed **(5 marks)**

(d)   explain how users should be involved in the implementation phase of the project

(5 marks)

(e)   describe the training that should be given to targeted groups within S & C **(5 marks)**

(f)   explain the aims of a post-implementation review. **(5 marks)**

(Total: 30 marks)

201   TF7 (NOV 07 EXAM)

TF7 is a progressive manufacturing company, which is open to new approaches and willing to learn from good ideas wherever they are practised. One of the first within its industry to invest heavily in new technology, TF7 runs its database over office-wide networks and links employees' computers by wireless local area network (LAN) connections.

TF7 has, in the past, only dealt with wholesalers but, thanks to email links from a new internet home page, it now receives a substantial number of enquiries from ultimate consumers of its products. TF7 feels that this will represent the majority of its business in the future.

In response to employees spending more time communicating with potential customers by email, TF7 is considering expanding its technology, including the connection of its database to a web server. This would enable potential customers to search for product specifications, availability and delivery and price information for themselves. It would also allow customers to place orders and view shopping cart items through a browser facility. Before making such an investment, TF7 has commissioned management consultants to conduct an organisational review.

The consultants have produced a draft report in which they outline a number of interim findings, including the following:

- TF7 should gain significant benefits over its rivals through its existing database operations.

- TF7 should consider developing further the interconnection of applications so long as contingency plans are made for the potential of systems failure.

- Although there has been considerable expenditure on hardware, TF7 now needs to invest in software applications.

- TF7's management information systems and executive information systems are undeveloped to the detriment of the company both operationally and strategically.

- Culturally, TF7 needs to adjust fully from business to business trading (B2B) to business to consumer trading (B2C).

- Currently training is conducted by TF7's own staff. The staff training programme needs to be reviewed to take account of new skill requirements demanded by new working practices. In-house training should continue but a mixture of TF7 trainers (and managers) and specialist providers should deliver a programme designed by TF7's Human Resources Department. The effectiveness of staff training events needs to be more carefully assessed.

- The experiment of using quality circles, which has recently been piloted, is unique within the industry and is worth developing further.

You work in TF7's technical department and report directly to the Chief Executive, who has asked for a series of brief notes so that he is prepared when discussing the draft report with the management consultants.

Instructions

Your notes can take any form so long as they comply with the limit of six pages and might include diagrams, tables, sentences or bullet points, etc.

Required:

Provide appropriate briefing notes for the Chief Executive for each of the following issues.

(a) Describe the benefits TF7 should be enjoying as part of its current database operations. **(5 marks)**

(b) Explain the value of good management information systems and executive information systems. **(5 marks)**

(c) Explain what issues TF7 needs to be aware of when adjusting from business to business trading (B2B) to business to consumer trading (B2C). **(5 marks)**

(d) Explain how TF7 can assess the effectiveness of staff training events. **(5 marks)**

(e) Identify the advantages that TF7 might achieve by using specialist providers as well as its own staff in delivering a training programme. **(5 marks)**

(f) Describe the ways in which TF7 might encourage the development of the use of quality circles. **(5 marks)**

(Total: 30 marks)

202 ROUND THE TABLE (NOV 05 EXAM)

You are a researcher employed by a topical business discussion television show 'Round The Table'. Next week's discussion is about managing supply to achieve quality and customer satisfaction. Invited guests will be a leading academic, public and private sector senior managers and the chief executive of a car producer. You have been asked to prepare an outline briefing that will give some background information to the show's presenter.

Your research shows that the automobile industry is highly competitive and globally suffers from 'overcapacity'. In certain countries however, there is unfulfilled demand for specialist makes and models, implying some under capacity 'hot spots'. You understand that, for any organisation, whether producing goods or services, effective capacity management is vital. It ensures that customers' needs are more fully met and that there are fewer unfulfilled delivery date promises. There are several ways of dealing with variations in demand and matching production capacity including:

- concentrating on inventory levels (a 'level capacity' strategy)

- concentrating on demand (a 'demand' strategy)

- adjusting levels of activity (a 'chase' strategy).

As part of your investigation you note that distinctive issues exist for service organisations (such as those found in the public sector) compared with manufacturing organisations (such as car producers).

Required:

As the show's researcher you are required to produce guidance notes to support the show's presenter which:

(a)   discuss why a level capacity strategy might be difficult for a firm wishing to adopt a just-in-time (JIT) philosophy   **(5 marks)**

(b)   discuss the impact of demand strategies on an organisation's marketing practices
                                                                                        (5 marks)

(c)   discuss the relationship between chase strategies and the flexible organisation
                                                                                        (5 marks)

(d)   identify the ways that service organisations differ from manufacturing organisations when considering capacity management   **(5 marks)**

(e)   describe the types of software applications a manufacturing firm might introduce to improve its inbound logistics   **(5 marks)**

(f)   describe the types of computerised assistance that could be used by those involved in selling cars and wanting to improve demand.   **(5 marks)**

Notes: (a) to (d) should have particular regard to quality, capacity and other organisational issues.

(Total: 30 marks)

Section 3

SECTION C-TYPE QUESTIONS

Note: With effect from the May 2007 diet, section C of this paper have comprised one 30-mark question from a choice of two. Previously, the questions in this section were worth 20 marks each.

INFORMATION SYSTEMS

203   PROJECT MANAGEMENT

Developing and implementing large-scale administrative computer systems requires a formalised and disciplined approach to project management and control.

Required:

(a)   Outline an approach to project management suitable for controlling the development of such a system.   **(15 marks)**

(b)   How can computers be used to help in the administrative support and technical development of a project?   **(5 marks)**

(c)   Discuss the advantages and disadvantages of writing the software associated with a new project in-house rather than using a third party supplier.   **(10 marks)**

(Total: 30 marks)

204   E-MAIL

E-mail is becoming one of the most common forms of communication, both for sending messages within organisations and across the Internet.

Required:

(a)   Discuss the impact of communication by e-mail on work practices.   **(12 marks)**

(b)   Discuss situations where e-mail would NOT be an appropriate communication medium.   **(10 marks)**

(c)   Explain why many organisations forbid the use of email for personal purposes.

(8 marks)

(Total: 30 marks)

205 SMALL CHAIN

A small chain of four department stores is located in and around a major metropolitan area. It is about to implement, in all stores, a point of sale system with linkages to a central computer. The stores all currently use conventional cash registers. You have been asked to assist in the conversion to the new system.

You are required to produce:

(a) an evaluation of the various approaches to the system changeover **(10 marks)**

(b) a checklist, in sequence, of the activities likely to be carried out during implementation **(6 marks)**

(c) suggestions as to how the new system might be evaluated after three months of operational running **(8 marks)**

(d) a list of the personnel problems that might be created by the introduction of this system. **(6 marks)**

(Total: 30 marks)

206 IN-HOUSE SOLUTION

MTK is a large construction company that operates internationally in highly-competitive markets. The board of directors of the company have decided that a major new computer system is required for planning and controlling projects. It has also decided that in order to give the company a competitive advantage over its rivals, the system must be designed and developed in-house.

The directors recognise, however, that there are significant problems with developing a major new computer system in-house, and that measures should be taken to ensure that any such problems are either avoided or resolved.

Required:

Explain the risks or problems that are commonly encountered with a major new in-house system development, and suggest how they might be managed. **(30 marks)**

207 DATABASE

TUN currently has different computer application systems for production scheduling, inventory control, accounting, purchasing, product design and engineering, marketing and human relations. A decision has been taken to develop a new database for the company's operations.

An IT consultant advising management has commented that a database with a database management system (DBMS) achieves de-coupling of applications from data, and that a DBMS can bring substantial benefits to the company.

Required:

(a) Explain the difference between a database and a DBMS, and why there is de-coupling of data from applications. **(4 marks)**

(b) Describe the advantages of a database and DBMS over having a different computer system for each major application. **(16 marks)**

(c) Explain how a database and DBMS might be used in conjunction with an executive information system (EIS). **(10 marks)**

(Total: 30 marks)

CHANGE MANAGEMENT

208 ZED BANK (PILOT PAPER)

Required:

(a) Using prescriptive, planned change theory, as outlined by Lewin and others, describe how any major new organisational initiative can be successfully implemented.

(10 marks)

(b) Zed Bank operates in a fiercely competitive market and has decided to implement a number of important initiatives, including:

- enhancing its current services to customers by providing them with on-line internet and telephone banking services; and

- reducing costs by closing many of its rural and smaller branches (outlets).

In an attempt to pacify the employee representatives (the Banking Trade Union) and to reduce expected protests by the communities affected by branch closure, a senior Bank spokesperson has announced that the changes will be 'incremental' in nature.

In particular, she has stressed that:

- the change will be implemented over a lengthy time period

- there will be no compulsory redundancies

- banking staff ready to take on new roles and opportunities in the online operations will be retrained and offered generous relocation expenses.

For customers, the Bank has promised that automatic cash dispensing machines will be available in all the localities where branches (outlets) close. Customers will also be provided with the software needed for Internet banking and other assistance necessary to give them quick and easy access to banking services.

The leader of the Banking Trade Union is 'appalled' at the initiatives announced. He has argued that the so-called 'incremental' change is in fact the start of a 'transformational' change that will have serious repercussions, not only for the Union's members but also for many of the Bank's customers.

Required:

(i) Distinguish incremental change from transformational change. Explain why the Bank spokesperson and the trade union leader disagree over their description of the change. **(10 marks)**

(ii) Explain whether Zed Bank might benefit from allowing employees to participate in the management of the change process. **(10 marks)**

(Total: 30 marks)

209 ORGANISATIONAL DEVELOPMENT

The B Company, a long-established food company with about 200 employees, is experiencing a number of problems including the need to implement new hygiene regulations, changes in consumer tastes, rising cost of materials, increasing competition and a demand for higher pay from its employees. But, rather than rising to the challenges as was the case in the past, the current staff seem unable to respond effectively. Morale is generally at a low level, departments are not co-operating and there have even been instances of conflict between quality control and operations. There also seems to be a lack of confidence in the management in general and a feeling that the company has lost direction.

A consultant called in to assist the B Company has recommended the use of techniques drawn from the field of organisational development as one means of tackling B's problems.

Required:

(a) Describe the overall approach of organisational development. **(8 marks)**

(b) Explain how you would use methods and techniques of organisational development to deal with the problems in the B Company. **(14 marks)**

(c) Explain how you would go about selecting a suitable consultant to facilitate the organisational development process. **(8 marks)**

(Total: 30 marks)

210 EVERLAND BANKS (MAY 06 EXAM)

Banking services within the country of Everland are provided exclusively by a few well-established banks, all offering broadly similar 'traditional' banking services. Overall, the industry performance is viewed from within as satisfactory and historically all banks have maintained stable profits and employment levels. Marketeers would describe the industry as being classically 'product oriented'. The profile of senior Everland bank officials and managers is of well-qualified professionals, possessing long banking industry experience and considerable financial skills. Within the combined workforce other business skills (in, for instance, HR or marketing) are noticeably lacking.

In the external environment, the government will soon pass new legislation that will effectively break the oligopoly-type position of banks and open the market up to other providers. Senior bank officials, however, are unconcerned, feeling that banks are in 'reasonable shape' to face any new challenge.

You work for the Everland Banking Advisory Group (EBAG), an independent body, and have been asked to analyse the banking industry in the country of Utopia to identify lessons that might be learnt. Your investigation reveals that, since the sector opened up to more competition, a much wider range of financial institutions offer banking services. Despite this, banks in Utopia have all prospered over the past few years. This is thanks to wide-ranging changes in how they operate, the products and services they offer and their organisational structures. You identify some significant trends within the banking industry of Utopia, including:

- the use of marketing techniques
- a clearer focus on customers (who have become increasingly more demanding)
- a new generation of bank employees, many with commercial backgrounds
- banks now exhibiting a strong sense of ethical and social responsibilities towards customers.

Required:

(a) Discuss the dangers to Everland banks if they do not change. **(8 marks)**

(b) Discuss the types of change that Everland banks could be making in order to survive and prosper. **(12 marks)**

(Total: 20 marks)

211 K COMPANY

K Company is experiencing rapid change. Increasing competition necessitates continual updating of its product offerings, its technology and its methods of working. Like other companies today, K Company has to be responsive to frequently changing customer requirements, the challenges posed by fast-moving competitors and the many other threats from a changing world.

One of the ways in which K Company might seek to cope with the challenges of the rapidly-changing environment is to become a 'learning organisation'.

Required:

(a)   Advise K Company what would be involved in building a learning organisation.

(10 marks)

(b)   The changing environment has implications for K Company's selection process and, given the limitations of interviews and selection tests that constitute the traditional methods of selection, the company has decided to make use of an assessment centre to improve its chances of obtaining people who fit the needs of the company.

Describe the key features of an assessment centre and explain why it is considered to be more effective than traditional methods of selection.   **(10 marks)**

(c)   K Company's chief executive has suggested that a new corporate vision statement might focus the attention of every member of staff and management and create a much tighter sense of cohesion.

Describe the problems that can be created by the adoption of corporate vision statements.   **(10 marks)**

(Total: 30 marks)

212   R & L (MAY 05 EXAM)

R & L is a large manufacturing firm that is well known as a 'good employer'. Over the past few years, R & L has experienced difficult times with reducing sales and mounting losses. In desperation it employed management consultants to analyse its situation. The consultants have concluded that the downturn in sales is permanent and that R & L needs to reduce its workforce by 50% over the next year in order to survive. Reluctantly, R & L's board of directors has accepted these findings, including the need to reduce the number of staff. The directors have also agreed to act as honestly and as fairly as possible, but realise that any changes they propose will be unpopular and may meet with resistance.

Required:

(a)   Discuss what initiatives R & L can take to achieve the job reductions needed given the company's reputation for being a good employer. (Your answer should include reference to appropriate support for any individuals affected.)   **(10 marks)**

(b)   Discuss the potential strategies available in order to overcome resistance to change, and identify those strategies that would be most suitable for R & L.   **(10 marks)**

(Total: 20 marks)

213   T COMPANY

T Company was, until recently, a national telephone company that enjoyed monopoly status, but a decision to deregulate by the government means that it is now exposed to aggressive competition from new entrants. T Company's competitive position has also been undermined by developments in wireless technology. As customers increasingly choose to use mobile phones, T Company's vast investment in fixed line technology is becoming increasingly uneconomic. This change in technology and the associated shift in consumer tastes have left T Company with no option but to invest in mobile technology itself.

T Company also suffers from its history as a monopoly provider; its bureaucratic culture and structure means that it tends to be slower to respond to market changes than the new entrants. The high proportion of telephone engineers who belong to the telecoms trade union does not help this situation. When earlier this year, T Company announced job cuts, the trade union members voted for industrial action that lasted for several weeks and cost the Company millions in lost revenue.

The development of broadband digital technology, however, allows high speed access to the Internet. This has meant a new lease of life for fixed line operators like T Company because existing fixed line systems can be adapted for broadband use. This opportunity has been seized by T Company's senior management. The Company has been successful in attracting 50,000 subscribers to the new broadband service in its first year of operation. The Company has also introduced a service that allows people on the move to access the Internet at selected public venues using a wireless enabled laptop.

This installation of broadband does, however, require training in new skills and the engineers required to undertake this training have threatened strike action in support of a large pay increase to compensate them for using the new skills required for the job.

Required:

(a) Identify the internal and external triggers for change in the strategy and operations of T Company. Discuss the difficulties that the Company is likely to experience in introducing the change programme. **(8 marks)**

(b) Evaluate the success of T Company in managing the change process to date. By application of any model of change management, explain how T Company might go about managing change in the future. **(12 marks)**

(c) Assuming that the need to transform T Company was identified and championed by senior management, describe some of the political mechanisms that they might have used to deal with any reluctance of middle managers to resist change. **(10 marks)**

(Total: 30 marks)

214 CHAPTERLAND (NOV 07 EXAM)

The country of Chapterland has 12 regions, each with a democratically elected regional government responsible for education, law and order. (Other public services are provided directly by the Chapterland government.) SW1 is the country's biggest region. Following last year's election, SW1 has a new regional government which wishes to simplify the several pay structures that exist in the education and law and order services as well as increase employee flexibility and productivity.

A detailed investigation by SW1's new regional government indicates that:

- employee groups performing similar activities in different public services are paid on different pay scales and all have different annual leave, maternity leave and sickness entitlements

- pay scales and conditions of service have developed over time as a result of national negotiations between representatives of regional employers (including SW1) and respective national trade unions

- all university lecturers have the same fixed holidays, meaning no teaching takes place for five weeks of the year. In addition, weekend working is prohibited under current terms and conditions of service

- police officers receive generous allowances to assist in paying for their accommodation costs

- traffic wardens (who act as police enforcement officers for motoring regulations and deal with traffic-related issues) receive allowances for laundering their uniforms and replacing their footwear

- 'pay for performance' schemes do not operate

- the unions have traditionally conducted negotiations collectively at a national level.

It is the regional government's intention that in future:

- a new unified pay scheme will be introduced and will incorporate a performance management system. Basic pay will be reduced but high bonus payments for hitting performance targets will be possible

- promotion policy will be based on achievement of individual targets instead of length of service and loyalty

- more flexible working will be expected from all groups.

SW1's regional government instructed a negotiating team to meet with regional union representatives collectively in order to persuade them to abandon nationally negotiated contracts, and give up certain benefits. In return, SW1 is prepared to offer 'one-off' payments to compensate staff. Although regional bargaining such as this has never been tried in Chapterland, the national government has indicated that it supports SW1's ideas.

The negotiating team has met many times with the regional union groups over the past ten months but progress has been slow. It is clear that, although agreement is close for all other groups, the university lecturers' union is reluctant to recommend to its members changes to the current nationally negotiated pay and conditions. This is halting any overall agreement.

SW1's regional government is frustrated by this slow progress and has instructed the negotiating team to meet with regional union groups separately to agree the size of the one-off payments for their respective groups. The regional university lecturers' union is to be made a 'final' offer and, if rejected, SW1 will write to all lecturers personally offering them a new contract of employment with different conditions of service. As an incentive, those lecturers accepting a new contract within 30 days will receive a small payment immediately. Those not signing a new contract will be considered to have resigned from their jobs. The local regional newspaper finds out about these plans and the headlines in the evening newspaper reads 'SW1 government's unethical plans'.

Required:

(a) Evaluate the way in which resistance to change is being managed by SW1's regional government. **(10 marks)**

(b) Discuss the ethical issues associated with the regional government's attempts to alter pay and conditions. **(10 marks)**

(c) Discuss the possible difficulties for SW1 in operating a reward scheme based upon achievement of performance targets. *Note:* Your answer should include both design and operational issues. **(10 marks)**

(Total: 30 marks)

OPERATIONS MANAGEMENT

215   YO (MAY 07 EXAM)

YO employs buyers, designers, machinists, tailors and sales people to produce and sell its coats, jackets, trousers, dresses and skirts. YO has a long-standing relationship with MX which sells directly to the public from a chain of out of town stores. Over 80% of YO's sales are to MX whose approach has been to sell clothing in great volumes at lower prices than the high street stores. It expects its suppliers (including YO) to take account of new fashion designs and manufacture its clothes at competitive prices.

MX is rethinking its strategy and wishes to move more 'upmarket' by introducing a better quality clothing range, which it believes its customers will be prepared to pay a little more for. Already YO has noticed that MX has started to be more demanding by sending back any batches it feels are in the slightest way unsuitable.

MX wants to work with fewer suppliers but develop a better relationship with each of them. MX wants to renegotiate its contract with YO (which expires soon in any case). MX is prepared to talk with YO about the need to improve the quality of its products and has indicated that, if it receives the right assurances, it would be prepared to pay a slightly higher unit price per item. It also proposes to work more closely with YO's designers to maximise production of the type of clothing that it feels its customers want.

If these talks are unsuccessful, MX will use one of its other suppliers when the existing contract expires. YO is aware that MX has experimented by using a few trusted overseas suppliers who have managed to achieve both relatively low prices and superior quality through the adoption of total quality management (TQM) techniques.

Anxious to maintain its relationship with MX, YO recognises that it must change from its present focus on price to one that includes quality considerations.

Required:

(a) Evaluate the way in which MX is proposing to manage its suppliers as part of a value system. **(10 marks)**

(b) Discuss the requirements for achieving total quality within YO. **(10 marks)**

(c) Describe how YO must change in order to meet MX's new requirements. In your answer you should only consider how YO's human resource practices and the attitude and behaviour of its employees must change. **(10 marks)**

(Total: 30 marks)

216 PRODUCTION SCHEDULING

VB Production has a large production plant where it makes three products, A, B and C. Items are produced in batches, and the production planning and control department uses the economic batch quantity model to decide the batch sizes for each product.

Recently, there have been some production scheduling difficulties, and for short periods there has been a stock-out of one of the products. At a meeting of the production management team, it has been suggested that it might be appropriate to introduce a levelled scheduling system for the three products.

Estimates of sales demand in the next four weeks have been provided for the meeting:

Product	A	B	C
	Units	Units	Units
Week 1 demand	5,000	8,000	5,000
Week 2 demand	6,000	11,000	5,000
Week 3 demand	3,500	12,000	8,000
Week 4 demand	4,500	7,000	6,000

Another suggestion that has been put to the meeting is that the company should switch to Just in Time production methods.

Required:

(a) Explain how a levelled scheduling system would differ from batch production based on economic batch quantities, and suggest the problems that would have to be addressed if the company were to move to a levelled scheduling production system.

(15 marks)

(b) Explain how a levelled scheduling system differs from a Just-In-Time production system, and suggest the problems that would have to be addressed if the company were to move to a JIT production system. **(15 marks)**

(Total: 30 marks)

217 PIPE DREAM

Pipe Dream manufactures a wide range of pipes and tubes. The company has recently appointed a new chief executive who has announced his intention to convert Pipe Dream into a world class company. After several months in the job, he has succeeded in converting his management team to his point of view. He has argued that although the company's operations appear to be fairly efficient, there are many areas in which improvements need to be made.

A major planning meeting has been called, to discuss the steps that might be needed to introduce Total Quality Management (TQM) concepts into the company.

Required:

Prepare a discussion paper for the meeting in which you:

(a)   describe the main features of TQM   **(12 marks)**

(b)   recommend an approach for introducing TQM into the company, and the problems
        you would expect to encounter   **(12 marks)**

(c)   justify the use of TQM for a company whose products do not need to be manufactured
        to the very highest level of precision.   **(6 marks)**

(Total: 30 marks)

218 URBAN DANCE

Urban Dance is a small company operating a number of dance schools. The owner of the company, who also acts as managing director, spent many years working in schools for the arts, such as dance schools, music schools and art schools, in both the public and private sector of the economy, and he is well-known and well-respected in the profession.

Urban Dance was established eight years ago, and the company has performed reasonably well during that time. Students come from many parts of the country, and many are referred from state-owned schools and private schools. The ages of students range from 14 to 18, and students are given a normal academic education as well as specialising in dance.

The owner/managing director would like to open more schools, but he believes that before he can do this, he needs to improve various aspects of the current schools and make them better-managed. He is interested in the idea of benchmarking.

Required:

(a)   Suggest methods of benchmarking that might be used to assess the performance of the
        schools explaining how benchmarking might be used to help the company improve
        performance.   **(12 marks)**

(b)   Recommend the initial steps that management should take to establish a benchmarking
        programme.   **(8 marks)**

(c)   Identify some potential problems and shortcomings associated with benchmarking.

(10 marks)

(Total: 30 marks)

219   VIRTUAL

At a recent conference of purchasing and supply managers, a guest speaker discussed the view that within a few years, many international companies might be able to operate almost as virtual companies. He argued that outsourcing, supply chain management and global sourcing were all that was necessary to create a company that could sell its products successfully in markets around the world.

Required:

Suggest how a virtual company might use outsourcing, supply chain management and global sourcing to make consumer durable products and deliver them to markets around the world.

(30 marks)

MARKETING

220   MARKETING FUNCTION: CONCEPTS

Marketing mix has been defined as 'the set of controllable variables and their levels that the firm use to influence the target market'. There are a great number of marketing mix variables, the most popular classification being the four Ps.

(a)   Outline the characteristics of each of the four Ps.   **(12 marks)**

(b)   Discuss how you would expect a manager to apply many, but not necessarily all, of the principles of the four Ps to the marketing of a well-established tourist attraction, for example a theme park, whose popularity is beginning to fall slightly.   **(18 marks)**

(Total: 30 marks)

221   GREEN COMPANY

Green Company produces gardening equipment which it sells mainly through garden centres and retail outlets in domestic markets, although there are a few sales to distributors in other countries. Its products are well-established, and its Greengrowers brand name for gardening equipment is well-known. The market is very competitive, and the company is continually designing and developing new products and new models. However, the sales management have expressed some concern that changes in the age structure of the population and changes in life style preferences could have a damaging effect on gardening equipment sales.

At a recent meeting, the company's new sales director raised two issues. First, he expressed some concern that the company did not seem to have reliable information about the position of the company's products in its market, how large the markets might be and what the company's share of its markets is. Secondly, he said that he would like to obtain reasonable forecasts of expected sales of a new range of gardening products that the company has designed and plans to launch on the market early next year.

Required:

(a)   Suggest why a company might want to obtain estimates of the total market size, and suggest the methods the Green Company might use to establish the current size of the market and its own market share.   **(15 marks)**

(b)   Suggest the methods that might be used to forecast sales demand for the new range of products.   **(15 marks)**

(Total: 30 marks)

222 RESTFUL HOTELS

Restful Hotels operates a chain of four-star hotels in several countries. Some of the hotels are situated in city centres, but others are in holiday resort centres and on holiday islands. The company's management has been very successful in controlling its operating costs, and the company is profitable. The company is opening new hotels currently at the rate of about three each year.

However, the management are concerned that total sales revenue is growing slowly, and sales income at the new hotels is particularly disappointing. The room occupancy rate is below budget, and there are vacant rooms in most hotels at most times of the year. The quality of service to guests does not appear to have deteriorated, and customers appear to be satisfied with the service they receive.

Two suggestions have been made to increase the rate of revenue growth. One is to use pricing as a marketing tool to attract more customers. The other is to try to attract more customers by focusing on an additional segment of the market.

Required:

(a)   Suggest how the company might use pricing as an element in its marketing mix, as a means of increasing total sales revenue.   **(14 marks)**

(b)   Suggest how market segmentation, and focusing on new segments of the market, might possibly help to increase total sales.   **(6 marks)**

(c)   Suggest why the company has to be careful in using pricing as an element of its marketing strategy.   **(10 marks)**

(Total: 30 marks)

223 CM BREAKFAST FOODS (NOV 06 EXAM)

CM's founder first began producing breakfast food from a start-up unit on a small industrial estate. Now CM is the market leader in Europe and Oceania. Once established in Europe, the company made the breakthrough into Oceania thanks to demand from ex-pats and contacts with a family member who happened to be a director of a supermarket chain in Australia. The company's founder is very 'hands on' and has made all the major strategic decisions to date based on intuition.

CM spends heavily on promoting most of its 20 products on television, normally before and after children's programmes with high viewing figures. Research conducted ten years ago shows that children love small gifts contained within packs and the association of certain of the products to cartoon characters. CM also manufactures its most popular lines and packages them as 'own brand' alternatives for some large supermarket chains. These sell more cheaply than CM branded products, are less costly to produce (as they contain inexpensive packaging and no gifts) but sales remain low.

CM is now facing a more uncertain environment with increasing competition (from a North American firm), sales levels that seem to have peaked and the prospect of the founder retiring very soon. Management consultants advising CM have identified a need to develop a structured marketing strategic plan for the organisation and for greater involvement of other staff in future strategic decisions. As a further complication, CM has recently received some adverse publicity from an international health 'watchdog' body that claims that CM's products contain potentially harmful levels of both sugar and salt.

Required:

(a)   Evaluate CM's situation making specific mention of marketing and ethical issues.   **(10 marks)**

(b)   Explain how CM might develop a marketing strategic plan.   **(10 marks)**

(Total: 20 marks)

224 TROY BOATS

Troy Boats manufactures and sells a range of boats, from small sailing boats up to medium-sized motor cruisers. Sales demand for boats of all kinds is growing at a very fast rate, and the management of the company are very excited about future prospects. Sales growth is expected to continue, as an increasing proportion of the population take to sailing as a leisure activity.

The company's sales director believes that now might be the right time to use brand awareness as a method of establishing Troy Boats as a major producer in the market. Branding is currently not much used, but as the market expands, the sales director believes that branding will be a major feature of the market. He has proposed that Troy Boats should develop a new brand, Argo 0, as a way of positioning itself in this growing market.

He recognises that establishing a brand in a market can be a difficult task, and if Troy Boats is to succeed with a branding initiative, it will need to go through four stages of brand positioning in the market. If the company can do this successfully, it could become extremely successful.

Required:

(a)   Explain the stages of brand positioning for a new branded range of products.

(12 marks)

(b)   Suggest how the company might develop the Argo 0 brand in each of these stages.

(12 marks)

(c)   Suggest why it might be difficult to build a brand for this type of product.   **(6 marks)**

(Total: 30 marks)

225   4QX (NOV 07 EXAM)

4QX is a large exclusive hotel set in an area of outstanding natural beauty. The hotel is a little remote due to the relatively poor transport network. It is located ten miles away from the region's main centre Old Town (the castle ruins of which attract a few tourists during holiday periods). The hotel has attained a high national star rating and specialises in offering executive conference facilities. Unsurprisingly therefore, it caters mainly for corporate guests.

It is a requirement of the hotel rating system that 4QX has, amongst other things, sports and leisure facilities to an approved standard. In order to attain this standard it has, within the last two years, installed a sports and fitness centre ('the centre'), employing fully qualified staff to give instruction and assistance. (Facilities include a small indoor heated swimming pool, an extensively equipped gymnasium, a spa bath and a steam room.) Due to legislation, children under the age of 16 staying in the hotel cannot use the pool without adult supervision or the gymnasium without the supervision of a suitably qualified member of staff. The centre is costly to maintain and underused.

The hotel's manager is currently drawing up a business plan for the hotel and is reviewing all areas of operation. In discussions with sport and fitness centre staff, a proposal has emerged to offer the facility to carefully selected non-guests at certain times of the day in order to bring in some revenue. This could be in the form of annual membership fees (the manager's preferred idea) or a 'pay-as-you-go' charge. The discussions with staff confirm a number of facts:

- The local economy is extremely healthy. The local population is relatively affluent with high levels of disposable income.

- Professional groups are used to paying annual membership fees for the local theatre, a nearby golf club (the manager is also a member and has contacts there), and substantial fees for their children's activities (e.g. dance academies and junior football teams, etc).

- Old Town has a public swimming pool that is dated but almost of Olympic standard. It is used mainly by school children in the day and by a swimming club in the evenings. Taking advantage of government tax incentives to help keep the population fit and healthy, a privately operated, female only, health and beauty facility has recently opened in Old Town. Beyond these facilities, little else in the way of sports and fitness provision exists in the region.

The manager explains that:

- the hotel is unlikely to upgrade the centre's facilities any further in the short term, despite the fact that new, more sophisticated fitness equipment is coming onto the market all the time

- any promotional budget to attract members would be limited

- an estimate of additional revenue potential is needed to complete the business plan.

Required:

(a) Explain the importance of the centre understanding its external (or macro) environment and identify the most significant influences in that external environment that are relevant to the centre. **(10 marks)**

(b) Explain how the centre should undertake market segmentation and describe the most likely segmentation variables that will be identified by such a process. **(10 marks)**

(c) Explain how the centre's income potential can be estimated. **(10 marks)**

(Total: 30 marks)

226 H COMPANY

H Company, a high-street clothing retailer, designs and sells clothing. Until recently, the company name was well-known for quality clothing at an affordable price, but the situation has changed dramatically as new entrants to the market have rapidly taken market share away from H Company.

One marketing analyst has commented that the problem for H Company is that it has never moved from being sales orientated to being marketing orientated and that this is why it has lost touch with its customers.

Required:

(a) Describe the difference between a company that concentrates on 'selling' its products and one that has adopted a marketing approach. Advise H Company on how to develop itself into an organisation that is driven by customer needs. **(10 marks)**

(b) Explain how the management in H Company could make use of the marketing mix to help regain its competitive position in the clothing market. **(10 marks)**

(c) The fashion editor of a national newspaper has offered to feature H Company's clothes regularly in a new 'makeover' article that will appear in weekend editions. In return, H Company will have to agree to running a full-page advert in the newspaper at least once per week.

Explain whether this offer is worth considering. **(10 marks)**

(Total: 30 marks)

227 LO-SPORT LTD

Lo-Sport Ltd (LS) is a manufacturer of sports equipment. It was set up in the south of England in 1988 by two famous, retired professional tennis players Rodney Connors and James Laver, who are the directors and sole shareholders. The company currently produces two types of product – sports rackets and sports shoes.

It manufactures specialist rackets for squash, tennis and badminton, using the latest technology, making them suitable for professional and advanced players. The rackets sell for approximately ten times the average price of rackets available in the high street.

LS also manufactures sports shoes for the mass market. The company's sales of these shoes have, however, been declining for some years, largely due to severe competition from much larger international manufacturers. There has also been a decline in industry sales in recent years. Sports shoes are nevertheless still seen as a fashion item and the large companies support their products with significant advertising.

A friend of the LS directors, Barry Borg, who is a retired research scientist, is employed by LS. Last year he developed a new rubber product, Katex, which he incorporated into a redesigned sports shoe. Early tests of the 'Katex shoe' proved extremely successful, demonstrating enhanced comfort, durability and performance. The product was patented by LS but sales have not yet commenced. However, a major marketing boost was given to the product recently when a prototype shoe was used by an athlete to achieve a world record time for running 400 metres.

Required:

(a)   Describe the main features of the product life cycle ('PLC').   **(8 marks)**

(b)   Identify and explain the strategic position of each of LS's products within the PLC. Assess the implications of this positioning in determining the extent to which LS should invest in each of its products.   **(12 marks)**

(c)   Describe the advantages and disadvantages of penetration pricing over price skimming for the new product Katex.   **(10 marks)**

(Total: 30 marks)

228   SX SNACKS (NOV 05 EXAM)

SX is a growing company that has successfully used local radio advertising for the past few years to raise awareness of its products. It supplies fresh 'quality' sandwiches, home-baked snacks, the finest coffee and freshly squeezed fruit juices for sale at premium prices in petrol filling stations. Products are produced by traditional methods from very early morning by a team of employees at a central depot and are delivered throughout the day by a few casual workers in a fleet of vehicles.

SX has for the first time undertaken a full strategic marketing planning process. One weakness identified was that the number of deliveries required was increasing, while some of the drivers were becoming increasingly unreliable. The owner is worried that this may create an unfavourable image with customers and lead to delays in delivery.

In terms of opportunities, the owner of SX is now aware that, by using technology to a greater degree and identifying customer needs more fully, the firm can grow at an even greater rate. To this end it is proposed that time-saving food preparation and packaging equipment be purchased. This will mean considerably fewer people involved in food preparation but the owner feels that some employees could be redeployed as drivers on a permanent basis. The role of driver would be redefined and, in addition to making deliveries, he or she would be expected to:

- get direct feedback from customers

- persuade petrol stations to take new product lines

- provide intelligence on competitor's products and likely future demand

- hopefully persuade other petrol stations and outlets (such as railway stations and newspaper shops) to stock SX products.

The owner is keen to progress change, consequently:

- The head of delivery and customer relationships has been tasked with developing new job and person details for the driver posts. These will then be discussed with existing food preparation staff.

- A marketing action plan will soon be prepared based on the strategic marketing plan, which will contain immediate marketing issues and actions required. Some detail is already available on people and price so the main areas to consider are product, place and promotion.

Required:

(a) Based on your understanding of the changes proposed by SX, identify the main issues that will be included in the marketing action plan and discuss the implications of these. Your response should consider issues of product, place and promotion only.

(10 marks)

(b) Based upon the information given to you concerning SX, and your own study and experience, produce a draft job description for the redefined post of driver.

(10 marks)

(Total: 20 marks)

MANAGING HUMAN CAPITAL

229   TAXIS AND TYRES (PILOT PAPER)

A year ago, the owner-manager of a taxi service also moved into a new business area of fitting tyres. This came about as a result of the experience of using unbranded tyres on the fleet of ten taxis. Based on several years of use, the owner-manager found that the unbranded tyres lasted almost as long as the branded tyres, but had the advantage of being obtainable at half the price. The set-up costs of the tyre-fitting business were relatively modest and the owner-manager initially fitted the tyres himself. Demand picked up quickly, however, and he was forced to employ an experienced fitter. A few months later, demand accelerated again and he has just advertised for another fitter but, unfortunately, without success.

The tyre-fitting business has produced additional challenges and the owner-manager is finding it increasingly difficult to manage both the taxi service and the new business where he seems to be spending more and more of his time. He already employs one receptionist/taxi controller, but has realised that he now needs another.

As if this were not enough, he is in the middle of extending his operations still further. Customers who buy tyres frequently request that he check the wheel alignment on their car following the fitting of new tyres. He has started to provide this service, but when done manually it is a slow process, so he has invested heavily in a new piece of electronic equipment. This new technology will speed the alignment operation considerably, but neither he nor his tyre-fitter can operate the equipment. The owner feels that tyre fitters should be able to operate the equipment, and an additional member of staff is not required just to operate it.

To add to all these problems, two of his taxi drivers have resigned unexpectedly. Past patterns suggest that of the ten drivers, normally one or two leave each year, generally in the summer months, though now it is winter.

Given all these staffing difficulties, the owner-manager has made use of a relative who happens to have some HR expertise. She has advised the owner-manager on recruitment and selection, training and development. The relative also suggests that the business needs a well thought out human resource plan.

Required:

(a) Prepare an outline human resource plan for the business and explain each aspect of your plan. **(12 marks)**

(b) Discuss the important human resource activities to which attention should be paid in order to obtain the maximum contribution from the workforce.

Note: For requirement (b), exclude those areas upon which the relative has already provided advice to the owner-manager (recruitment and selection, training and development). **(8 marks)**

(Total: 20 marks)

230 T CITY POLICE

The T City Police Force has been subjected to considerable criticism in recent years. The first criticism is from some of the citizens of T City who claim racial harassment and slow response to emergency calls. The second is from a government audit which found that T City Police Force had a poorer record on crime prevention and convictions for crime than any of the other nine city police forces in the country.

As well as a number of other measures the T City Chief of Police has accepted a recommendation from the head of human resources to implement a performance appraisal system linked to a Performance-Related Pay (PRP) system. A spokesman for the Association of Police Officers has objected to the proposed appraisal and PRP systems on the grounds that limited government funding and the poor socio-economic conditions of T City district will make the system unworkable.

Required:

(a) Explain the purpose of performance appraisal. Discuss how the T City Police Force could use the information from the performance appraisal system to improve the performance of its police officers. **(12 marks)**

(b) In the light of comments made by the spokesman for the Association of Police Officers, discuss the potential problems associated with the introduction of the proposed performance appraisal system and the performance-related pay system. **(18 marks)**

(Total: 30 marks)

231 RECRUITMENT

Required:

(a) Describe the process of recruitment. **(10 marks)**

(b) Discuss some of the major problems and issues for firms in selecting the right candidate. **(10 marks)**

(c) Describe the importance of job analysis in the context of recruitment. **(10 marks)**

(Total: 30 marks)

232 CQ4 (MAY 06 EXAM)

CQ4 is a leading European industrial gas production company. CQ4's directors are each responsible for a geographical region containing several small strategic business units (SBUs). SBU managers report in monthly review meetings in great detail to their directors. CQ4 is showing signs of declining profitability and a new chief executive has been appointed and wishes to address the situation. She has complete freedom to identify organisational problems, solutions and strategies.

At their annual conference she tells SBU managers that they hold the key to improved company performance. She has a vision of CQ4 achieving longer term strategic goals of increases in profitability, risk taking and innovation. Under the slogan 'support not report' directors will in future support and provide assistance to their managers to a greater degree, and the frequency and detail of reporting by managers will be reduced.

She announces two new initiatives 'to address the lost years when managers were prevented from delivering truly excellent CQ4 performance':

- Revision of the existing performance appraisal system. Bonuses paid on sales revenue will be replaced by performance-related pay for achievement of individual 'performance target contracts'. Individual SBU managers will sign contracts to deliver these targets. Performance will now be reviewed at yearly rather than monthly meetings with directors. The remuneration and reward package will be adjusted appropriately with the current emphasis on increasing sales revenue shifting to profitability and innovation.

- A structural review to focus the resources and efforts of SBUs on improving net profit. Part of the restructuring will involve SBUs no longer providing their own 'enabling' services such as finance, information technology, and health and safety. These 'distractions from doing the real job' will in future be organised centrally. SBUs will be given far greater responsibility, autonomy and influence over their own profitability.

She tells managers that she is stripping away the things that stop them doing their job properly. In return they must manage their SBU in the way they see most appropriate. They will be better rewarded and 'star achievers' will be fast tracked to senior positions. SBU managers are informed that the HR department has already been tasked with redesigning the remuneration and reward package.

Informal discussions amongst managers afterwards confirm that the new chief executive's message has been well received. Comments such as 'work might be more enjoyable without central interference' and 'for the first time I can do my job properly' were overheard.

Required:

(a) Explain the thinking behind the two initiatives announced by the new chief executive using Herzberg's motivation-hygiene (dual factor) theory as a framework. **(10 marks)**

(b) Discuss the factors that should be taken into account by the HR department when redesigning the remuneration and reward package for SBU managers. **(10 marks)**

(Total: 20 marks)

233 MANAGEMENT DEVELOPMENT

You are required to:

(a) define 'management development' **(4 marks)**

(b) describe the steps that an organisation should take to implement a formal management development system **(16 marks)**

(c) describe the process of succession planning. **(10 marks)**

(Total: 30 marks)

234 REWARD SYSTEMS

Describe and discuss the main features to be included in a reward system. **(30 marks)**

235 DISMISSAL, RETIREMENT, REDUNDANCY

Describe the various processes which lead to employees leaving an organisation, whether planned or unplanned. **(30 marks)**

236 B3 PERSONNEL AGENCY (NOV 06 EXAM)

B3 is a family-run personnel agency. It offers a range of services to both individuals and corporate clients (mainly local medium-sized organisations). The son of the managing director (MD) is currently studying for a specialist university business degree. His course includes a 'management consultancy' module where students are required to analyse an organisation and identify a range of development options for the business. The MD's son's investigations of B3 have led to a consultancy report being produced, extracts of which include:

"B3 should maximise the opportunities offered by information technology to a greater extent. In particular:

- *Opportunity 1.* B3 could develop its recent successful experiment in e-cruitment (the identification of employment opportunities through the worldwide web and the emailing of clients). Currently details of vacancies are collected and matched to individual client's search criteria. When a match is identified clients are emailed and, if they are interested, interviews arranged. This service is not offered by any of B3's main competitors. There is a difficulty, however, in that many companies have barred access to personal emails at work and web access to recruitment sites such as B3's site from their offices. Market research suggests that significant opportunities for m-cruitment (jobs by mobile telephones) also exist. Making use of recent software developments, a text message containing a job title and some contact details could be sent out to individual clients instead of an email, so providing a more convenient and speedy service.

- *Opportunity 2.* Virtually all CVs are currently received in electronic form and a policy decision should be made to develop a paperless operating environment through the development of databases, so upgrading existing office technology.

Analysis of profit indicates that executive searches, corporate 'headhunting' and vacancy identification for individuals (traditional and especially e-cruitment) are all profitable activities.

Involvement in selection processes with corporate clients is unprofitable and should be discontinued. Instead B3 should identify clear guidelines for corporate clients to follow once the short-listing of candidates has occurred."

Required:

(a) Evaluate the opportunities for B3 identified in the consultancy report. **(12 marks)**

(b) Produce guidelines for the selection process that should be adopted by an organisation presented with a short-list of candidates. **(8 marks)**

(Total: 20 marks)

237 HUMAN RESOURCE PLAN

Like many other companies, X has to respond to a variety of pressures for change. Increasing competition has forced company X to reduce costs by downsizing its personnel numbers and reducing the size of the head office. Further measures have included a greater concentration on its core business and processes. To date, these pressures have had a limited effect on the finance department, but the finance director is now under pressure to reduce the number of personnel employed in her department by 30 per cent over the next two years, and by a total of 50 per cent within a five-year period.

In the initial review of the task facing her, the finance director appreciates that she has to take into account a number of changes that are affecting the finance function. These include the ever-increasing application of IT, the increasing financial pressure to outsource transactions and other routine operations to large service centres, and the expectation by the chief executive that finance personnel will play a fuller part in the management of the business.

The department currently employs 24 people divided almost equally between three areas: financial accounting, management accounting and the treasury function.

The age/experience profile is a mix of older, experienced specialist staff, a young to middle-aged group of qualified accountants (many of whom also possess MBA degrees), and a group of trainees with limited experience who have yet to qualify.

Three of the older staff are within five years of the statutory retirement age; two more will move into this category within the time period set by senior management. One or two of the younger qualified staff have been looking for other jobs and one of the trainees has applied for maternity leave.

The finance director has arranged a meeting with the human resources director to discuss the development of a human-resource plan for future staffing, training and development of personnel in the finance department.

Required:

(a) Describe the main stages of the human resource planning process and briefly explain how manpower planning fits into this process. **(12 marks)**

(b) Taking the role of the finance director, prepare a paper by way of preparation for your forthcoming meeting. Explain the key considerations that you will need to take into account in the development of a human resource plan for your department.

(18 marks)

(Total: 30 marks)

238 APPRAISAL

The performance appraisal process is now well established in large organisations.

Required:

(a) Describe briefly the most common objectives of a performance appraisal system.

(6 marks)

(b) Explain why appraisal systems are often less effective in practice than they might be, and advise what management can do to try to ensure their effectiveness. **(14 marks)**

(c) Describe the role of the appraisal interview in determining the success or failure of the appraisal system. **(10 marks)**

(Total: 30 marks)

239 R COMPANY

The finance department of R Company, a large hotel group, has experienced a range of human resource problems following the recruitment of a large number of professional members of staff. Several people have left within the first year and others have not performed as well as might have been expected.

The R Company's human resource management department has suggested that one possible reason might be the Company's lack of a systematic induction programme for new staff.

Required:

(a)   Produce a plan detailing the key activities that need to be covered in a systematic induction programme for the R Company. **(15 marks)**

(b)   Explain how an induction programme can help to overcome the problems experienced by the finance department of R Company as described in the scenario above.

(15 marks)

(Total: 30 marks)

240   CX BEERS (MAY 05 EXAM)

The country Mythland contains several areas of high unemployment, one such area is where CX Beers were produced until recently. CX was an old, family-owned brewery that supplied licensed outlets, including local restaurants, with its beer. CX represented one of the last local brewers of any size, despite retaining many working practices that evolved at least a century ago. Situated on a (now) underused dockside site, the company had, over the years, invested little in plant and machinery and someone jokingly once suggested that much of the brewing equipment should rightfully be in a museum! The company was forced to cease trading last month, despite having an enthusiastic, long-serving, highly skilled workforce and a national reputation for the beer 'CX Winter Warmer' (thanks to winning several national awards). The workforce, many of whom have only ever worked for CX Beers are now facing up to the difficulty of finding alternative employment.

In a press statement the owners said that the brewery's closure was sad for the area, the local workforce and traditionally brewed beer in general. The owners blamed the situation on inefficient and expensive brewing methods, fierce competition from large rival brewers and limited geographical sales. They also mentioned a dependence on seasonal sales that made cash flow difficult (35% over the Christmas period). They concluded that they would like the CX tradition to continue by selling the company as a going concern, however unlikely this was.

It is speculated that property developers may be interested in the site as the dockland area is showing signs of regeneration as a leisure and tourism attraction (thanks to the efforts of the Mythland government). However, two of CX's managers would like to save the business and are drawing up a business plan for a management buy-out. They have three main initiatives that they feel could, in combination, save the enterprise:

- use the site as a basis for a 'living' museum of traditionally brewed beer (with out of date brewing equipment and methods of working as an attraction)

- produce bottled beer for sales in supermarkets

- employ a more flexible but suitably experienced workforce.

One of the managers (your former boss) has asked for your help in advising him how to draft a detailed human resource (HR) plan to inform the business plan.

Required:

(a)   Describe the main issues and stages involved in developing a human resource (HR) plan for the CX buy-out idea. **(12 marks)**

(b)   Discuss how the buy-out team can achieve workforce flexibility. **(8 marks)**

(Total: 20 marks)

241 **COMPANY A AND B**

Company A has acquired Company B. As part of a wide ranging effort to integrate Company B into its operations, systems and procedures, the management of Company A has decided to combine the two existing finance departments. A new finance department will be formed in the headquarters building of Company A. The move by Company B Finance staff to Company A headquarters will mean, for most, a daily road journey of some 20 miles each way.

Required:

(a) Discuss the concerns that Company B finance staff will have as they consider their move to Company A headquarters. Explain why an induction programme is necessary for Company B staff. **(12 marks)**

(b) Produce an induction programme that will help support Company B finance staff in their move to Company A, and which will enable them to contribute productively to the enlarged Company. **(12 marks)**

(c) Explain how Company A should organise its grievance procedures with respect to the integration of former Company B staff. **(6 marks)**

(Total: 30 marks)

242 **ZNZ (MAY 07 EXAM)**

ZnZ is a large government-funded body that employs several hundred staff performing a wide variety of roles. ZnZ is proud of its commitment to people development and is well known for providing equal opportunities for all its employees. ZnZ employs people regardless of race, religion, gender, sexual orientation or physical disability. The organisation invests heavily in training and development and employs a number of trainees who are studying for their professional examinations. It is left to each professionally qualified member of staff to identify their own training needs and then submit requests for support to their department.

ZnZ's human resource plan is currently being reviewed. As part of this process two significant recommendations have emerged from groups and committees considering future human resource issues.

Recommendation one

(From the HR planning group)

The group has recommended that a more systematic approach to the training and development of qualified staff should be adopted.

Recommendation two

(From the Diversity Committee)

The Committee has recommended that every person who is part of a minority or disadvantaged group should have an individual career coach. Under such a scheme, individuals from these groups would be paired with an experienced colleague on a higher grade who would act as their personal individual career coach. The Committee has issued the following guidelines:

• The scheme will not be associated with the appraisal process.

• Coaches should be approachable, suitably experienced and appropriately trained.

• Coaches will not be the individual's own line manager.

• Regular meetings should take place between the two individuals where they should be able to confidentially discuss any concerns and areas for self-development. Inevitably individuals will wish to discuss career-related issues and they should receive appropriate advice from their career coach.

You work for the Director of Human Resourcing who is very sympathetic to the recommendation of the Diversity Committee in particular. (So much so that she feels that the scheme should include all trainees and those middle managers who have been identified as having promotion potential.) She has asked you to investigate both recommendations and brief the management team appropriately.

Required:

(a)   Explain the stages involved in the development for ZnZ of a systematic approach to the training and development of professionally qualified staff.   **(10 marks)**

(b)   Discuss the potential advantages of the individual career coach scheme for ZnZ.

(10 marks)

(c)   Discuss the potential disadvantages of the individual career coach scheme for ZnZ.

(10 marks)

(Total: 30 marks)

243   JANE SMITH

Jane Smith has very recently been made a partner in a medium-sized accounting practice with the requirement that she take charge of the practice's Casterbridge office. The office comprises about ten secretarial, technician and part-qualified audit staff. Jane has never worked at the Casterbridge office and, as part of a first attempt to familiarise herself with the office, she has examined the staff files and associated correspondence. She has been surprised to find that staff turnover and sickness are far higher than in the other practice offices and that there appears to have been a succession of quality problems related to poor client care and operational mistakes.

She has also asked the senior partner if he can explain the reasons for the apparent staff related problems to which he replied 'Well we may have had a number of unavoidable changes in partners responsible for Casterbridge over the last few years but remember, Jane, that we do pay staff above market wage rates and provide good working conditions. What we undoubtedly are looking at here is a case of far too slack management control and supervision'.

Required:

(a)   In the light of relevant theories of motivation and the statement made by the senior partner comment on the apparent staff problems in the Casterbridge office. **(15 marks)**

(b)   Acting in the role of Jane explain how you would proceed in seeking to improve the apparent staff problems in the Casterbridge office.   **(15 marks)**

(Total: 30 marks)

244   NS INSURANCE COMPANY (NOV 05 EXAM)

NS is a large insurance company. The company is structured into four divisions and supported by a small headquarters that includes the personnel function (recently renamed the Human Resources (HR) Division). The post of Head of HR is vacant following the retirement of the long-serving post holder, and the HR strategy is in urgent need of review and revision.

NS has recently announced a new corporate initiative of continuous improvement through the empowerment of its workforce. The Chief Executive explained: "We value our people as our most prized asset. We will encourage them to think, challenge and innovate. Only through empowering them in this way can we achieve continuous improvement. Staff will no longer be expected just to obey orders; from now on they will make and implement decisions to bring about continuous improvement. We want to develop clear performance objectives and be more customer focused."   Your line manager is one of the four Divisional Directors and will soon form part of a panel that will interview candidates for the vacant role of HR Director. She is particularly keen to ensure that the successful candidate would be able to shape the HR Division to the needs of the organisation. She is aware of your CIMA studies and has asked for your help in preparing for the interview.

Required:

Produce outline notes for your Divisional Director which discuss the main points you would expect candidates to highlight in response to the following two areas she intends to explore with candidates at the interview, specifically:

(a)   the likely role that the HR Division will perform in the light of the changing nature of the organisation; and   **(10 marks)**

(b)   the aspects of the HR strategy that will change significantly, given the nature of recent developments within NS.   **(10 marks)**

(Total: 20 marks)

245   NYO.COM

NYO.com was established in February 20X3. Since then, the company, which provides on-line financial advice, has experienced rapid growth and the management has not really had the time to get all management systems and procedures into place.

The company has asked you to look at the way in which the company deals with its disciplinary problems and procedures. The chief executive officer has asked you to do two things.

Required:

(a)   Recommend guidelines for drawing up a disciplinary procedure.   **(12 marks)**

(b)   Explain why NYO.com should have a formal disciplinary procedure.   **(8 marks)**

(c)   Describe the circumstances under which NYO.com would be within its rights to dismiss an employee.   **(10 marks)**

(Total: 30 marks)

Section 4

ANSWERS TO SECTION A-TYPE QUESTIONS

INFORMATION SYSTEMS

1   **A**

These are examples of hardware (equipment) and all are used for the input of data (and so are input devices rather than processing devices).

2   **A**

A local area networks (LAN) is a linked network of computers, terminals and other devices (such as printers) within a limited geographical area. The small geographical area means that the communications links can be provided by cables without the need for modems (unlike wide area networks (WANs), which are linked through an external communications network).

3   **A**

In General System Theory, entropy is a measure of disorder in a system. Left on its own, an open system will tend to break down into randomness and disorder.

4   **B**

An intranet is an internal network within an organisation that makes use of the internet. It can be used for communications to employees and also between employees. However, e-mail is used for communications between employees within an intranet, not chat rooms.

5   **D**

With a database, there is a single set of data files, rather than several different systems, each system with its own separate set of files. A major advantage of a database is avoiding the duplication of data. Data integrity means avoiding inconsistencies between the data used by different computer applications. Having one set of files and avoiding duplication of data (where the duplicated data might not be consistent with each other) therefore helps to achieve data integrity.

Note that databases do not provide unlimited access. Access to some or all of a database can be restricted by the use of passwords. Answer B is therefore incorrect.

6   **A**

An expert system such as a system for law or taxation might be purchased 'off the shelf', but it does not provide a 'powerful software solution' (whatever this means!). Answer C describes a help facility. Answer A is the most appropriate answer: an expert system is a database that contains data obtained from expert knowledge (e.g. in the law or medicine) and experience.

7 A

Re-writing software for an existing system to meet new user requirements is called adaptive maintenance. The re-written software enables the system to *adapt* to meet the changing requirements.

8 B

The old and new systems are run in parallel for a time, until the new system is seen to be operating efficiently and as intended. This is parallel running when the entire organisation switches to operating both systems simultaneously. With a pilot test, one part of the organisation (such as one branch or one region) switches from the old to the new system first, as a test. With phased changeover, the entire organisation switches from the old to the new system one part or phase at a time, until the entire new system is introduced.

9 B

A diagram that illustrates the relationships between 'entities' in a system is an entity relationship model. The relationships are 'one-to-one', 'one-to-many' or 'many-to-many', as indicated by the ends of the lines joining the related entities (which are a single line indicating one or a 'crow's foot' indicating many).

10 C

The PCs in the branches are 'clients' linked to a central server, and the relationship is therefore 'client/server'.

11 D

Decision support systems are used to assist managers in developing forecasts or solutions to problems. They are generally used at middle management level, whereas executive information systems are used by senior managers to obtain information from both internal and external sources. A MIS is a system providing information for management, in the form of reports or file interrogation facilities, but do not offer any decision-making support (such as forecasting model software).

12 C

The controlling software is the database management system (DBMS). A database administrator is an individual who looks after the operation of the database system.

13 B

Entropy represents the disorder or chaos in a system. It occurs when an 'open system', such as a sales system, does not receive new inputs continually from its environment so that it can continue to adapt. Here, the system does not receive new information about customers. When entropy occurs, a system moves into a state of disorder: here, the sales system that made use of the customer file no longer functions.

14 D

In a control system the sensor measures the output of the system.

15 A

Corrective maintenance involves eliminating faults and errors ('bugs') from a system. Although most errors should be identified and corrected during the testing stages of system development, errors might be discovered after the new system has been implemented.

16   D

In broad terms the processing of data is either distributed, centralised or a combination of the two. With **distributed data processing**, as the name suggests, the processing of data is not done by a central computer. Instead, data processing takes place at a 'local' level, remote from the centre. With **centralised processing**, the data processing occurs centrally, by updating central files that are shared by all users in the network.

17   C

An extranet is an extended intranet which links to business partners. Only authorised users are given access and data transmitted across the intranet is secured.

18   D

A network server is a computer (usually high-end, i.e. 'faster', 'bigger') that allows computers in a network to have a shared resource. Most servers in the district are used to share files, to run programs, or to share printers.

19   C

If the sales value is below $5,000 but the customer is not new, the credit granted should be 60 days.

20   B

A standby mainframe (in a different location) can ensure continuity of processing, provided that backup files of the system are continually produced (and also stored in a different location).

21   A

Examples of peripherals are printers and input devices.

22   D

In a distributed data processing system, processing tasks can be distributed to computers throughout the network and shared by those computers. Distributed data processing is an alternative to having all transactions processed centrally.

23   D

A star network has a central computer and all other computers in the network are linked to it directly. In a tree network, also called a hierarchical network, the computers are in three or more layers or tiers. A central computer is linked to a number of second tier computers, and each second tier computer is linked to a number of third tier computers, and so on. Computers in the third tier are not linked directly to the central computer, only to their second tier computer.

24   C

A data flow diagram shows in the form of a chart or picture how data flows through a system.
An entity life history gives details of the different events that cause an entity to be updated.
A decision table is used to show the logic of a process.

25   B

EDI usually involves the transfer of information between different companies and is used for buying and selling.

26   These tools are used by systems analysts to help in designing a new system, and also with the documenting of a new system, for the benefit of:

- themselves, to ensure that they understand the logic of the system

- programmers

- future systems adaptations and maintenance.

The tools enable a systems analyst to draw the logic or features of the system in a form that is more easy to read and understand than a long narrative explanation.

27   The advantages of phased changeover might be as follows:

- It provides better opportunities for testing each part of the new system and resolving any difficulties, before introducing the next part of the new system.

- It gives employees more time to adapt to the new system. This might reduce 'hostility' to the new system.

- It gives more time for re-training and re-deployment of staff whose jobs are taken away by the new system.

28   In-house development of a new system is an alternative to a purchase of an 'off the shelf' software package.

- An in-house developed IS should be designed more closely to meet the specific information requirements of the organisation.

- An in-house developed IS should be designed by means of collaboration between the system designers and the system users. Because the system is designed and tested in-house, users are more likely to accept it quickly and make good use of it.

29   A server is a computer within a computer network. It may be used for:

- holding shared data files for users of the network

- holding shared programs for users of the network

- acting as a 'host computer' for the organisation's intranet system

- operating the organisation's internal e-mail system.

30   (a)   De-coupling means reducing the interdependence between two sub-systems within a system, so that each sub-system can operate independently of the other. Changes in one sub-system do not therefore have an immediate effect on the other sub-system. De-coupling can therefore be useful for controlling sub-systems and for introducing changes into sub-systems.

       (b)   A DBMS and a database provide de-coupling within an information system because the data held on file (the database) is de-coupled from the uses to which the data is put (the applications software). Changes can be made to the data on file without affecting the user software. Application software can be altered without affecting the data on file.

31   System software is software that enables a computer system to carry out basic operational functions so that the computer 'works'. Systems software can be distinguished from application software, which is software that enables a computer user to process data and access information.

The three main categories of system software are:

- An operating system. This directs and controls the basic functions of the computer and its peripheral equipment and the transfer of data within the computer and between the computer and its peripheral equipment.

- Utility programs. These are programs that carry out certain 'housekeeping' routines or functions, such as copying files, sorting data on a file and checking for viruses.

- Communications software. This is used in computer network systems to control the communication links between computers, terminals and other equipment (for example coding, transmitting and receiving data over communications links).

Tutorial note

You might not have identified these three categories of system software, and other solutions – *if correct* in identifying different types of system software – would be acceptable.

---

32   A

For example, Windows XPR.

33   An extranet is an intranet that has been extended to include business partners. The advantages are:

- quicker information flow to/from partners
- makes e-procurement easier as a supplier can check whether or not you need more inventory
- quicker transactions if partners are customers or suppliers
- strengthens relationship with partners due to implied trust.

34   An open system has a high level of interaction with its external environment. Adaptive maintenance is amending the system to adjust to changes in its environment. In a dynamic business environment an open IS system will require regular adaptive maintenance or it will quickly become out of date and irrelevant.

35   A direct changeover from an old to a new system without pilot schemes or parallel running would be used it:
- the managers have complete trust in the new system (for example, an off-the-shelf package that has been used elsewhere)
- the problems for the computer user will be tolerable, even if the system fails to function properly
- none of the other changeover methods are practicable
- as a symbolic gesture – for example, as part of a larger change process.

36   Stages of tests:
- Unit test

  Each module of the programme is tested to make sure it performs the required functions.

- Integration test

  The exchange of information between the modules needs to be examined for correctness.

- System testing

  The system as a whole is reviewed using test data as original input to the system.

- Acceptance testing

Testing by user before introducing it operationally.

Tutorial note:

The following is an alternative approach to this question:

Different kinds of tests:

- Realistic tests

  Uses realistic example of operating environment. Tests understanding and training of users.

- Contrived tests

  System presented with unusual/unexpected events.

- Volume tests

  Uses large volumes of data to check operating and response times.

- Acceptance test

  Testing of complete system by users.

37 Functional requirements are about what the system does:

- user requirements
- data flow
- purpose and frequency of input and outputs
- editing
- file maintenance and backup.

Physical requirements relate to the physical appearance of the system and the way in which its component parts relate to one another:

- outputs – what it looks like
- screen layouts
- data storage
- access to the system
- updating the system
- physical connections and communication
- peripherals
- processing methods – centralised or distributed.

38 A data flow diagram (DFD) is a method of documenting how data is transferred, processed and stored within a system. There are four elements in a DFD:

(1) Data sources. A data source is the source from which data comes or the destination to which data is sent. Typically, a data source is an organisation, department or individual.

(2) Data processes. A data process is a process or activity within the system. A box depicting a data process in a DFD will indicate both what the process is and who carries out the process.

(3) Data flows. A data flow is the movement of data from one element in the system to another, for example from a data source or a data store to a data process, or from a data process to a data process or a data store.

(4) Data stores. A data store is a data file.

39   Data independence is the separation of data from the programs that use the data. The whole concept of a database management system (DBMS) supports the notion of data independence since it represents a system for managing data separately from the programs that use the data. The data can be used by different users for different applications and in different ways.

Flexible data management is thus enabled in the following ways:

- **Less duplication** – data is input once only to update the data on file.
- Less processing – by minimising data redundancy, storage space in the system files is reduced, and **storage space is used more efficiently**.
- Updating is much easier, and data is equally up-to-date for all applications.
- There is **data consistency** (or **data integrity**). All users access the same data and therefore inconsistencies between data in different application systems do not exist.
- **Improving access to data**. Database systems are designed to allow many different users access to the shared files.

40   D

Data redundancy arises when data is duplicated. This could be a sign of inefficiency if storage space is being wasted or it could be a deliberate act to make one or more copies available to speed up access to data or to provide backup (e.g. certain types of RAID mirror data). .

41   A

Network Topology is the study of the arrangement or mapping of the elements (links, nodes, etc) of a network, especially the physical and logical interconnections between nodes.

42   B

Data integrity can be compromised by either malicious acts (such as hacking) or by accidental events (such as transmission errors).

43   C

An entity relationship model is a diagram showing the different entities (anything of significance about which data must be held) in a system and the relationships between them.

44   D

A distinguishing feature of a database system is that, since there is a common set of shared files for all applications, information to update the files is input just once. This means data is held once, and is not duplicated in different files in different application systems. There is also data integrity because all users access the same data and therefore inconsistencies between data in different application systems do not exist.

45   A

Examples of input devices are a keyboard and mouse, a barcode reader and a scanner.

CHANGE MANAGEMENT

46   B

Organisational development solves problems using the diagnostic and problem-solving skills of an external consultant in collaboration with the organisation's management. Typical problems that are the focus of such interventions include lack of co-operation, excessive decentralisation and poor communication.

47   A

Lewin developed force field theory to explain how interactions between human beings are driven by both the people involved and their environment. He was particularly interested in the forces that came into conflict around planned changes.

48   B

The three stages are unfreezing, then change, then refreezing.

49   A

An internal trigger for change is an event or development within the organisation itself, rather than a change that is started by external developments. IT technological change, environmental legislation and demands for a shorter working week are all examples of external triggers for change, caused by technological, political or social change.

50   D

Driving forces are the forces for change, and restraining forces are the factors resistant to change. To achieve desired change, management should recognise what the key driving and restraining forces are. In principle, change can be achieved either by making the driving forces stronger or the restraining forces weaker. Lewin argued that in practice, it is more effective to reduce the strength of the main restraining forces.

51   C

The five component technologies are:

(a)   systems thinking

(b)   personal mastery

(c)   mental models

(d)   building shared vision

(e)   team learning.

52   A

Kanter suggested that change-adept organisations share the following attributes:

(a)   effective leaders who encourage the development of new concepts – imagination to innovate

(b)   leaders who provide competence both personally and in the organisation as a whole – professionalism to perform

(c)   leaders who make connections with and collaborate with 'partners' outside the organisation – openness to collaborate.

53 D

Beer and Nohria argued in favour of a 'balanced approach', combining concern for economic value (such as reducing the size of the workforce, restructuring or incentive schemes) and concern for human capabilities and the learning process. Using one approach followed by the other will be much less effective in introducing change successfully.

54 B

The other changes are all major 'transformational' changes, that affect the organisation's culture and way of operating.

55 A

Unfreezing is the process of both getting employees to recognise that the current situation is unsatisfactory, and also identifying a better way of doing things. Getting qualified staff to accept that some of their work can be done by trained but unqualified people would be a part of the unfreezing process.

56 B

'Diagnostic' refers to identifying the nature of a problem, and the word is perhaps best understood in the context of carrying out a medical diagnosis to identify the cause of a disease. The 'unfreezing' part of the change process involves identifying the existence of an unsatisfactory situation, and gaining acceptance for an improved situation towards which the organisation should move. The 'intervention' stage is presumably the 'change' or movement' phase in Lewin's model. The change process ends with 'refreezing' which is presumably the 'termination' stage.

57 B

Change in most organisations is triggered by changes in their external environment rather than internal developments. The external changes might affect the organisation's culture and will eventually prompt management action (answers A and D). The trigger for change, however, comes from the external environment.

58 D

Perhaps this is the obvious solution. Answer B implies no change at all. Attempts to impose change are likely to end in failure, and answers A and C are both incorrect. A change culture within an organisation has to start with top management, who must give their full support and encouragement to change programmes.

59 D

An OD programme begins with recognising a problem, which is then analysed and diagnosed. A change agent (typically a firm of management consultants) discusses the problem with the organisation's management and agree a programme for change. This is then planned and implemented. After implementation, the changes are reviewed and evaluated. OD is often associated with the work of Warren Bennis.

60 A

The help-line is to assist staff, not to coerce or manipulate them, and has little to do with appointments (co-optation).

61   Senge described a learning organisation in which people are continually learning and being creative and adaptive. In a fast-changing environment, learning organisations will excel because they will respond to the changes in the most effective ways. Senge argued that in a learning organisation, there must be two types of learning:

(a)   adaptive learning, which is learning how to change the organisation in response to changes in the environment, in order to survive

(b)   generative learning, which is learning that improves the ability of individuals to generate new ideas and be creative.

62   **A**

Lewin argued that introducing a driving force toward change often produced an immediate counterforce to maintain the equilibrium. It is often easier to bring about change by removing the restraining forces since there are usually already driving forces in the system.

63   **D**

Organisational development is designed to solve problems that decrease operating efficiency at all levels. It uses the diagnostic and problem-solving skills of an external consultant in collaboration with the organisation's management.

OPERATIONS MANAGEMENT

64   **C**

By definition.

65   **A**

For example ISO 9001:2000 *Quality Management Systems – Requirements* specifies the requirements that must be met by the quality management system within an organisation if it is to meet the standard. Organisations can apply to obtain a certificate for meeting the ISO 9001:2000 quality standards.

66   **A**

By definition.

67   Operations management involves transforming inputs (factors of production such as inventory and labour) into outputs (products and/or services) through a series of operations (manufacturing, assembly, etc).

The technostructure supports effective operations through functions such as Strategic Planning, Personnel Training, Operations Research, Systems Analysis and Design.

68   Companies can obtain competitive advantage through management of the supply chain by:

•   reducing the lead time from suppliers

•   improving purchasing procedures

•   persuading suppliers to improve quality

•   persuading suppliers to provide materials in a form better-suited to production processes so that wastage in production can be reduced

69 Whenever substandard goods are sold, the organisation is likely to incur the cost of replacing or rectifying the items. This will involve additional collection and delivery charges and manufacturing costs.

Selling defective goods may lead to customer dissatisfaction and loss of reputation.

70 **B**

Juran argued that most quality problems are the result of ineffective systems, but poor management is also largely to blame. Although there is some merit in answer A, answer B is more appropriate.

71 **B**

The '5S' practice aims at achieving and maintaining a high quality work environment. Answer B therefore gives the most appropriate answer. The 5Ss are Sort, Straighten, Shine (or Sweep), Standardise and Sustain. Do not be fooled by the five words beginning with the letter S in answer C.

72 **D**

An OPT system is a production scheduling system that focuses on bottlenecks. Production scheduling is based on the capacity of the bottlenecks, and the pace of throughput that these can handle.

73 **D**

The main contribution of Deming to quality management was the use and development of statistical control methods. The quality planning road map was devised by Juran; continuous improvement (kaizen) originated in Japan, and the concept of 'zero defects' as promoted by Crosby.

74 **C**

HO's TQMEX model is an integrated approach to the process of continuous improvement and management of quality which shows the relationship between quality management and other aspects of operations management.

75 **A**

Hammer defined BPR as a fundamental rethinking and radical redesign of business processes. This involves the themes listed.

76 **D**

A Materials Requirements Planning or MRP I system creates a production schedule for end-products from existing and forecast customer demand quantities. It then uses the master production schedule, a bill of materials file, the inventory file and data about production times to produce a detailed schedule for the in-house manufacture of parts and sub-assemblies. It can also produce a purchase requirements schedule for raw materials and components.

An MRP I system is not linked to the computer systems of other functions in the organisation, and answer A refers to MRP II. MRP I schedules production to meet actual and anticipated demand (so answer B is not correct), and is an alternative to scheduling production in economic batch quantities (so answer C is not correct).

77 **C**

A principle of TQM is that commitment to total quality calls for a TQM culture within the organisation, and all employees should be committed to quality improvement (answer A).

The ideal level of defects is zero and there should not be any minimum acceptable level of defects (answer B is incorrect). Statistical quality control is used to monitor defects and provide control reports to management: TQM relies both on employee commitment and statistical quality control – so answer A is not correct. The aim should be to eliminate failure costs, such as costs arising from handling customer complaints, warranties and guarantees, damage to reputation and re-working rejected items. However, some costs relating to quality – prevention costs in particular – have to be incurred, so answer D is incorrect.

78   Cousins suggested that the relationship with suppliers could be defined as a 'strategic supply wheel'. The spokes are different aspects in these relationships with suppliers that should be given due attention:

- organisation structure such as how the different functions are put together
- performance measures including quality, speed, dependability, flexibility and cost
- portfolio of relationships with suppliers
- cost/benefit analysis of any decision made
- skills of staff and competences required of a product.

79   **A**

The seven types of waste are:

- over-production
- inventory and work-in-progress
- transportation
- waste in processing
- motion
- waiting
- making defective products.

80   **C**

Lean manufacturing is closely associated with JIT production. In lean manufacturing, production is initiated by customer demand (demand-pull) and products are made to order. Production should either be a continuous work flow, if there is continuous demand, or in small batch sizes. The ideal batch size is 1 – the customer's order. Large batches are not produced, because these create unwanted inventory. There should be small work cells, with all the equipment needed to make the product and all the necessary labour skills: work cells in a small area that do all the work on a product eliminate waste from motion, transportation and waiting. Workers need to be multi-skilled, so that they can switch from one task to another as the situation requires.

81   **D**

Work flow design, with work organised in small work cells within a small area of the factory floor, can seed up production times and prevent inventory building up. Work flow can be arranged so as to reduce the physical movement of materials and people.

Production should be scheduled to meet customer demand; if necessary, there will be unused capacity. It is better to have several small machines than one large complex machine, because production will be more flexible. The aim should be to reduce set-up times between batches or jobs, because waiting is wasteful.

82   C

With parallel sourcing, Plant A might obtain its key supplies from Supplier 1, whereas Plant B will obtain all its supplies of the same item from Supplier 2 and Plant C from Supplier 3, and so on.

83   B

To meet the objective of adjusting capacity to meet demand, it will be necessary to vary employee numbers or working hours and times, and to hire more or less equipment, to meet changes in demand. Chase demand planning could be appropriate for operations where there are no inventories (or small inventories) and where operations are not capital-intensive.

84   A

BPR seeks radical/transformational change in process (and the processes should be 're-engineered'). In contrast, 5S, 6 Sigma and quality circles are all based on the concept of continuous and incremental improvements.

85   A

'Environment' here relates to green issues.

86   Theory Y identifies a management approach that says that people can exercise self-direction and self-control to achieve objectives to which they are committed. It is associated with managing professional staff.

Theory O is a 'soft' approach to change that encourages participation from the bottom up, motivating through commitment.

When dealing with Theory Y employees, a manager needs to adopt the Theory O approach to change in order to succeed.

87   Quality in manufacturing arises both from the features of a product and also from the elimination of waste and bad workmanship in production. Computer software can assist with the design of new products (computer-aided design) and also with the control of production (computer-aided manufacture). The use of robotics in manufacturing, which helps to achieve error-free production, requires software to control the equipment.

88   Quality control, as the name suggests, is control over the quality of an activity, operation or product. Quality control might involve the inspection of output or the use of statistical techniques by management (quality control charts).

Quality circles are groups of employees from different parts of an organisation, brought together to share ideas and devise ways of improving aspects of quality at work, no matter how small the quality improvements might be.

89   The Six Sigma approach is based on the view that a product (or service) is the end result of a series of processes or operations. If the acceptable rate of error in each process is, say, 1%, the likelihood of error for each unit of end product will be much higher than 1%. In order to control the overall quality of products or services, it is therefore essential to control the quality at each stage in the overall operation to very high standards of rigour.

The overall aim of Six Sigma, conceptually, is to reduce the probability level of defects to the sixth standard deviation (six sigmas) from the norm. If this aim is achieved, total defects will be just 3.4 in one million – close to perfection.

Six Sigma is therefore associated with rigorous risk management and quality control.

90   MRP II is a computer system for the integrated planning of a company's equipment, materials and people in order to meet the business plan, requiring the same information (sales forecasts, actual orders, bill of materials and so on) to be used throughout the company.

An ERP system can be described as an MRP II system with the addition of resources planning for non-manufacturing activities and functions, such as plant maintenance and human resources planning.

91   **D**

Answer D is correct as it is the strong customer focus within WCM that drives all other aspects of the business.

92   **B**

ABC can refer to activity based costing (not mentioned here) or a system of inventory control where more important lines of inventory are given more time and sophisticated sytems to manage them.

93   **A**

The need for correction shows that a failure has occurred, so the answer is A or B. If the corrective work is because a customer has sent the goods back, then it would be an external failure cost. The fact that there is scrap and materials have been lost would indicate that the problem was picked up before goods left the factory, making them internal failure costs.

94   **D**

By definition. Do not confuse with economies of scale, which would be answer C.

95   **D**

Service – activities that ensure that customers enjoy their purchases by providing information systems, installation, training, maintenance, repair and breakdown assistance, etc.

96   **B**

You could argue that all four answers could be involved in why a firm decides to consider its supply chain in more etail. However, only answer B gives a direct cause of supply chain partnerships being established.

97   **D**

This definition of benchmarking comes from the American Productivity and Quality Centre.

98   • Aiming to meet the needs and expectations of customers.

• Application of TQM to all aspects of the organisation's activities.

• TQM should involve everyone in the organisation.

• Seeking continuous improvement (or getting things right first time).

• Developing systems and procedures to support quality and quality improvement.

99   The concept of a quality chain within an organisation is that the operations within the organisation to make a product or provide a service can be seen as a chain of inter-related activities. For each activity or 'micro-operation', there is an internal supplier who does work for an internal customer, who is then an internal supplier to the next internal customer in the chain. The quality of the end-product or service depends on the quality at each link in the chain, and the overall quality is only as good as the weakest link in the chain.

Internal service level agreements (SLAs) can be used in an organisation to ensure the strength of each link in the quality chain. Each internal supplier and internal customer agrees on quality standards and service standards that the internal supplier undertakes to meet. The internal customer is then able to demand that the internal supplier meets the agreed standards.

100 Documentation is required as evidence that the organisation is actually meeting the necessary quality management standards. Without this evidence, there would be insufficient information for external quality auditors to make a fair assessment.

ISO 9001: 2000 specifies that, as a minimum, there should be documentation relating to:

- the control of documents
- the control of records
- the control of non-conformance with standards
- internal auditing of standards
- corrective action taken
- preventive actions taken.

MARKETING

101 B

Attention to customer needs lies at the heart of all successful marketing strategies.

102 C

There is very little point in segmenting the market if segments cannot be identified and targeted.

103 A

By definition.

104 A push policy provides the distribution channel with incentives to promote and market goods, e.g. a manufacturer might give its distributors discounts if they achieve high sales volumes.

A pull strategy involves creating demand, e.g. by a manufacturer advertising heavily so that consumer demand forces distributors to stock the product.

105 C

Selling through the company's website and the internet is a new channel of distribution. Channels of distribution are an element of 'place' within the marketing mix.

106 D

Concentrated marketing means selling a single product to one segment of the market. This is often a suitable marketing strategy for a small business.

107   **Quantitative technique – fitting a trend line** – assumes sales influences fall into four categories:

1   Trends (long-term changes)
2   Cyclical changes
3   Seasonal changes
4   Irregular changes

Uses least squares to determine slope and intercept of a straight line.

Examples:

● DIY retailer: likely home ownership growth.

● Ice-cream producer: temperature forecasts.

Could also give other examples of quantitative techniques:

● **Moving average**: computes the average volume achieved in several periods and then uses it as a prediction for sales in the next period. With a strong trend in the series, the moving average lags behind. With more periods, the moving average forecast changes slowly.

● **'Simple' regression**: try to estimate the relationship between a single dependent variable (Y or sales) and a single independent variable (X) via a straight-line equation. $Y = a + b(X) + e$.

● **Multiple regression**: estimate the relationship between a single dependent variable (Y or sales) and *several* independent variables.

Non-quantitative technique – sales force composite – a bottom-up method consisting of collecting estimates of sales for the future period from all salespeople.

● Salespeople each estimate their territory.

● May consult supervisor.

● Individual forecasts are combined and adjusted for each office.

● Used by 60 to 70% of all companies.

● Need to adjust for bias or over- or under-estimation.

Other techniques which could be given include:

● executive opinion

● market survey

● market testing

● expert opinion

108   **D**

Differentiated marketing involves offering a product in different forms to different segments of the market, and the product offered to each segment is different from the products offered to the other segments. For example, a car manufacturer makes different models of car, and targets each model at a different segment of the market.

109   **A**

Market potential is the size of a market that might exist for a product. Sales potential is the possible volume of sales that an organisation might achieve for its own product. In a competitive market, the sales potential for a product is less than the total market potential for the products of all competitors.

110   A

The price component of the marketing mix includes all aspects relating to the price and purchasing terms offered to customers.

111   B

Answer B provides the most appropriate definition of marketing and what the aim of marketing strategy should be. Marketing strategy should support the overall business strategy, both long term and short term, with a marketing orientation in its approach. Promoting a marketing culture (answer C) is an aspect of marketing strategy, but not its primary aim.

Focusing on sales (a sales-oriented strategy) is more short-term in outlook. With a sales-oriented approach, there is no particular concern whether or not the organisation's products actually meet customer needs. Taking a marketing-oriented view, meeting customer needs is essential for long-term success as well as short-term profit.

112   C

Interactive marketing involves interaction between the seller and the potential buyer. This happens with telemarketing, where the sales person calling a target customer by telephone speaks to the customer. A direct mail shot and a TV advertising campaign are not interactive forms of marketing. Advertising on a web site is also not interactive, although it would presumably be possible to devise some form of interactive advertisement for putting on the seller's web site.

113   A

Market research is research into a market to establish the potential size of the market, the sales potential for an entity's product or service, or to obtain information about customer needs, or customer satisfaction or dissatisfaction with existing products in the market.

Marketing research is research into marketing activities and methods (for example, research into the effectiveness of billboard advertising). Test marketing is the testing of a new product or service in a small, selected market area. A survey of buyers' intentions is carried out to estimate future sales for industrial goods, and the buyers are commercial organisations, not consumers.

114   B

A marketing decision support system is a DSS for use by marketing management. A DSS is used to assist management planning and decision-making, for example by providing sales forecasts. A DSS includes forecasting models, which can produce forecasts from data about past sales.

Answers A and D relate to a customer database and answer C relates to a management information system.

115   A

Answer A gives a definition of differential pricing. Answer C is an *example* of differential pricing (for example, charging different prices for a rail ticket at different times of the day). Differential pricing can also be applied to place (for example, charging different prices for seats in different parts of a theatre), and to market segment (for example, offering lower prices to students or pensioners).

116 D

'Pull' marketing is aimed at persuading end-consumers to demand a product from distributors (such as retailers), which in turn will result in the distributor wanting to stock and sell the item. TV advertising is an example of a promotion that could be intended to have this 'pull' effect.

117 A

An analysis of past sales (answer C) will provide information about total sales, but not about how many customers buy the product, nor in what quantities or how frequently. Observation is useful for looking a customers' buying habits, but does not provide information about the numbers of customers for a product or the frequency of buying. Group interviews can be useful for obtaining information about customer attitudes/consumer attitudes, but the group size is fairly small and so cannot provide reliable estimates of sales measurements.

Sample surveys in different geographical areas – based on interviews with questionnaires – is likely to provide reasonably reliable information about numbers of customers, buying quantities and buying frequency.

118 B

Internal marketing is an activity aimed at getting employees who come into contact with customers (after-sales service staff, counter staff and floor staff in shops, customer service call centre staff etcetera) to recognise the need to meet customer requirements – and training them how to do this.

119 C

The 'classic' life cycle for a product has four phases:

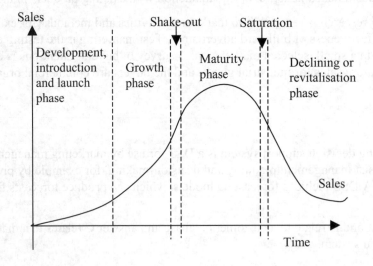

120 C

By definition the answer is C.

121 C

An initiator starts the buying process, usually by identifying a need. The influencer will affect which product is bought, perhaps based on their expertise. The buyer buys it and the user uses it. As such, this terminology could be applied to B2C or B2B marketing:

Example: **Purchasing a child's bike (B2C)**

Member	Role
Initiator	Child pesters parents for new bike
Influencers	Older siblings have an opinion on the choice of bike, once parent recognises child has grown out of present one
Buyer	Parent pays the bill
User	The child

Example: **Purchasing new machinery (B2B)**

Member	Role
Initiator	Machine breaks down, the operator reports it, thus initiating the process
Influencers	User may influence, may also involve supervisor, R&D staff, accountant, sales reps.
Buyer	Buyer handles search for and negotiations with suppliers
User	Operator

However, B2B marketing is more likely to target the buyer only whereas B2C will appeal to each member of the buying group. Overall C is thus the better answer.

122

Tutorial note

You might not have heard of these terms before, but you should try to relate what the terms might mean in the context of the activities of a sales force. The terms should give you a reasonable clue as to what they mean.

(a) 'Hunting' in the context of sales force activities means going out to look for new customers to 'catch'. When the sales force focuses on 'hunting', they are looking for new customers and new business. In contrast, 'farming' means developing existing customers. When the sales force focuses on 'farming', they are looking for ways of selling more to existing customers.

(b) With 'selling', the sales force is concerned primarily with making the initial sale to achieve immediate sales revenue. 'Servicing' refers to the fact that after a customer has purchased products or services, there might be a requirement for after-sales support. With servicing, the aim is to keep the customer satisfied with the product and service, so that he will continue to keep on buying.

123

- The market is homogenous – all customers have similar needs and there is no sensible way of defining distinct segments.

- The cost of targeting specific segments is high and the market is too small to justify the expense.

- The market or the product are in decline and there is not sufficient growth potential to justify the effort.

- Competition in all segments is too strong.

- Analysing the specific needs of different customer groups is too difficult or costly.

124   B2B marketing involves marketing to business buyers, whereas B2C marketing involves marketing to consumers. Business buyers and consumers are often attracted by different aspects of a marketing mix, and make their buying decisions in different ways and for different reasons.

Business buyers are generally more rational than consumers in their buying decisions and are often concerned with the 'commercial' aspects of purchase, in particular price (and credit terms), product quality and specifications and delivery times and reliability.

In business, the person who initiates a buying request (such as an inventory manager or a user department) is not the person who makes the buying decision (for example a buyer in the purchasing department), and for high-value items, a purchase might require special authorisation by senior management.

For marketing purposes, it is usually important to recognise who is most influential in a purchasing decision by a business, the buyer or a technical 'expert', and develop a marketing strategy accordingly – based on price, product specifications, displays at exhibitions and trade fairs, and so on.

In contrast, many consumer goods are fast-moving items, where the customer buys frequently, and often on impulse and in a convenient way. Consumers buy through different channels of distribution: whereas business buyers often respond to direct selling and through established supplier relationships, consumers buy through retail outlets catalogues or the Internet.

For consumers, buying decisions might be affected by advertising and sales promotions more than business buyers.

As a result of these differences, the marketing mix for business customers and the marketing mix for consumers are often very different.

125   The 'traditional' product life cycle goes through the phases of introduction, growth, maturity and decline through the course of its market life. The relevance of the product life cycle to marketing is that:

- marketing might be used to extend a stage in the life of a product

- a different marketing mix might be appropriate for different stages of the life cycle.

(a)   *Introduction stage*. During this stage, the product is new and loss-making, and the task is to gain acceptance by customers. A key element in the marketing mix might be to find suitable and sufficient methods of distributing the product, and price is unlikely to be a significant item for marketing purposes – the product price will be fairly high.

(b)   *Growth stage*. During the growth stage, the total market for the product is expanding, and the product becomes profitable. New competitors enter the market. Within the marketing mix, product design becomes important, and price is also more significant. The growth phase of a product's life might be extended by successful segmentation.

(c)   *Maturity*. During this stage, total sales in the market reach a peak, sales growth ends and total annual sales remain fairly constant. This can be the longest stage in the life of a successful product. The task is now to sustaining profitability, probably by maintaining or increasing market share. Price is likely to be a major element in the marketing mix.

(d)   *Decline*. During the decline stage, total sales of the product fall, and gradually manufacturers and suppliers drop out of the market. It might also be more difficult to segment the market into commercially-viable segments. Distribution (the accessibility of the product to customers) might become a more important element in the marketing mix, and product design innovations are much less important.

126 **B**

Public relations is part of the promotional mix. It involves the creation of positive attitudes regarding products, services or companies by various means, including unpaid media coverage and involvement with community activities.

127 **B**

Loss leaders are frequently used by supermarkets to attract customers into their stores.

128 Physical evidence is the material part of a service. There are no physical attributes to a service, so consumers tend to rely on material cues such as packaging, internet/web pages, paperwork (such as invoices, tickets and despatch notes), brochures, etc.

129 A database offers the ability to generate ad hoc reports quickly and efficiently. This could be of immense use in segmenting or investigating the buying behaviour of customers. For example, a supermarket loyalty card scheme makes it possible to generate reports very quickly on the buying habits of individual customers.

MANAGING HUMAN CAPITAL

130 **D**

Handy's concept states that each of the three leaves of the shamrock is symbolic of a different group of people within the organisation: the professional core of employees; the contractual fringe where all work that could be done by someone else is contracted out; and the flexible labour force includes all those part-time workers and temporary workers.

131 **D**

These are similar in concept to job classifications.

132 **A**

Maslow proposed a hierarchy of needs that can be used to explain human motivation. His work is used primarily in relation to work, but can be applied to customer motivation.

133 **B**

Job analysis and selection occur before the person becomes an employee. Only a rather cynical organisation would aim to manipulate a new employee.

134 **C**

Interviewing is part of selection rather than recruitment, and contract negotiation follow these.

135 **C**

360° degree feedback involves the rating of an individual's performance by people who know something about that person's work. Those involved can include direct subordinates, peers, managers, customers or clients.

136 **D**

A person starting a new job is often given induction and training. Induction is the process of familiarisation with the organisation and training involves the development of the individual's skills in the job. A probationary period (answer A) is a trial period during which the new employee is 'on probation' and has to prove that he or she can do the job well before being offered the job on a permanent basis.

137 D

A key word in the question is 'effective'. Effective appraisal requires a dialogue between the manager and the person being appraised (the 'appraisee'). Any problems with the appraisee's work or performance are identified and should be discussed and resolved constructively. Answer C, in contrast, describes an ineffective appraisal process.

138 C

Vroom developed an expectancy theory model, which suggested that the motivation of an individual to do anything is the result of 'valence' (the strength of the individual's desire to achieve a given outcome or reward) and 'expectancy' (the probability that achieving the given outcome will lead to the reward.) This has nothing to do with knowledge (answer A), satisfaction (answer B) or the quality of work performed (answer D). An individual will be motivated to act in a way that provides the 'best mix' of valence and expectancy.

139 B

Job rotation involves the movement of an individual from one post to another in order to gain experience of all the different tasks or activities in an organisation or a department. For example, an accounts clerk might be moved from the payables ledger to debt collection work and then into cost accounting in order to gain a broader experience of the work in the accounts department. Answer B describes job rotation more accurately than answer D. Answer C describes job enlargement.

140 C

A grievance procedure is a procedure that an individual can follow if he or she feel 'aggrieved' or wronged by something at work, and the problem has not been resolved by the normal channels. It is not a procedure where the employee is assumed to be in the wrong (so answer B is incorrect), nor is it an arbitration procedure or a collective bargaining arrangement.

141 C

An assessment centre brings together a group of applicants for a job or a number of jobs (for example, graduate trainee management positions) and the applicants are put through a variety of intensive assessments in a period of one to three days.

142 B

The correct answer can probably be worked out by common sense. A test cannot be contradictory, although the *results* from tests can be, so answer A cannot be correct. The fact that tests are general in nature does not means that test result will vary over time, so answer C is not correct. This leaves a choice between the tests being unreliable or unstable. If test results vary over time, this means that the tests are unreliable, but there is no reason to suppose that they might be unstable.

143 A

F.W. Taylor was a pioneer of the 'scientific school' of management in the US. He believed that work processes could be analysed and divided into component elements, and that greater efficiency would be obtained by getting employees to specialise in one small aspect or component of the overall process.

144 C

Succession planning involves 'grooming' an individual to take over in a key position after the present job-holder retires or moves on. This should ensure that the person who will take over has been given the necessary training and development programme to take over and do the work competently (answer C). A new person in a key job will not necessarily continue to do things in the same way as his predecessor; therefore answer B is incorrect. Succession planning is connected to promotion policy, where successors are appointed internally: however, the purpose of succession planning should not be to create promotion opportunities and answer A is not correct.

145 B

Recruitment is the process of attracting individuals into applying for a job. Employment agencies do this, usually by advertising or notifying the vacancy to individuals on their books. Screening is the process of vetting applications and removing those that are inappropriate and unlikely to be successful. The remaining applications are then passed to the company, whose responsibility it should be to select candidates for interview and make the selection.

146 A

If the employee's claim is correct, the employer would be liable for constructive dismissal, which is a form of unfair dismissal. A contract with a sub-contractor is subject to contract law, not employment law: the sub-contractor could claim breach of contract. It is probably considered reasonable to dismiss an employee who can no longer perform his job, such as a lorry driver who cannot drive (in the UK, on the assumption that there is no other job that the individual can do). Dismissal on the grounds of redundancy is also legal, although the employer must comply with redundancy procedures and legislation.

147 A

Job evaluation is used to assess what the value of a job is worth to the organisation, and so what an appropriate level of *basic* pay ought to be. With knowledge work, it is often difficult to carry out a reliable, objective job evaluation.

Benchmarking can be used to establish a pay level by looking at basic pay in similar jobs in other organisations (so answer B is not correct). If there is a scarcity of knowledge skills, this will put upward pressure on basic pay levels, but does not create a serious problem for setting pay levels (so answer C is not correct). Performance evaluation is an issue with performance-related pay, but not basic pay (so answer D is not correct).

148 D

A distinguishing feature of a database system is that, since there is a common set of shared files for all applications, information to update the files is input just once. This means data is held once, and is not duplicated in different files in different application systems. There is also data integrity because all users access the same data and therefore inconsistencies between data in different application systems do not exist.

149 D

References from a former employer are notoriously unreliable as a guide to future performance, or the candidate's character and abilities. The former employer is usually unwilling to criticise the individual, and concerned about any liability that might arise. However, a reference (on headed notepaper) should confirm that the candidate did actually work in the job, as stated in his/her job application, and that the employee was not dismissed for bad conduct.

150   D

Job evaluation is primarily a process by which the value of a job is assessed and a suitable rate of pay is decided accordingly. If different jobs are evaluated with the same scoring system, the rates of pay for the different jobs can be set in relation to each other, according to their respective total scores in the evaluation exercise.

151   A

Herzberg argued that the quality of management and working conditions are hygiene factors, and the level of responsibility is a motivator. He also argued that pay is a hygiene factor, particularly basic pay. However, pay can also be used as an incentive/motivator, for example by offering the prospect of a cash bonus for achieving a performance target.

152   D

Lawrence and Lorsch (1967) found that organisations in a stable and predictable environment are most efficient if they have a traditional hierarchical management structure. However, organisations in a rapidly-changing environment or facing rapidly-changing technologies are most successful if they have a flexible structure in which authority is delegated and authority is decentralised. The greater the uncertainty and unpredictability in the environment, the greater is the need for delegation to specialised 'sub-systems' within the organisation.

153   B

Handy argued that the three elements in the motivational calculus for employees together determine the strength of the individual's motivation to put in effort to do the task well.

- Needs consist of the Maslow factors (the hierarchy of needs), together with the individual's character traits and outside influences and pressures.

- Results: an individual will assess what the effect will be of putting additional effort into the work.

- Effectiveness: the individual will then assess the extent to which these results will achieve his/her needs.

Needs, results and effectiveness are therefore all elements in the individual's motivation to put effort into the work.

154   B

In a virtual organisation, more individuals spend more time working from home or other distant locations, linked together by computer networks and (mobile) telephones. There will be fewer meetings between individuals, because informal/casual meetings are not possible. Formal meetings will have to be scheduled and will often be inconvenient to attend.

There is likely to much more team working, with empowerment of employees. This will mean having to give more trust to employees. There will probably also be much greater use of external consultants (outsourcing) and temporary staff.

There is no obvious link between working in a virtual organisation and motivation.

155   C

McGregor's Theory X and Theory Y are attitudes based on social science research, and McGregor regarded them as two distinct attitudes. Theory X is based on assumptions such as the dislike of individuals for work, which means that they have to be controlled and threatened by their supervisors and managers. McGregor believed that Theory Y was difficult to apply in some working conditions, such as mass production operations, and that it was much better suited to the management of managers and other professionals.

156　A

Likert argued that the motivation to work should be supplemented by modern management techniques, not by old systems of rewards and threats.

157　A

Herzberg's main 'motivators' are achievement, recognition, growth/advancement to higher levels, interest in the job and responsibility for the task. Hygiene factors are the company, its policies and administration, pay, security, working conditions, interpersonal relationships, the nature of supervision and status.

158　D

Answers A and B refer to profit-related pay and answer C describes either piece work payment or payment by the hour/day.

159　B

Likert argued in favour of a participative style of management as being the most effective. The least effective, he believed, is 'exploitative authoritative'. Answer D describes the contingency approach to management and leadership: Likert did not belong to this school of thought.

160　C

'Greater emphasis' presumably means that the style of management needs to be used much more. When employees are given more involvement in decision-making, and there are fewer levels of management, the participative style of management is both more appropriate and more necessary. Employees might be empowered, and any form of authoritative leadership will probably be ineffective.

161　C

Answer C should be the obvious and logical answer. In the past, management in some organisations has tried to justify unethical behaviour by saying that it did it in the interests of the organisation. This is an attempt to justify improper behaviour. The argument should not be accepted. However, in some countries, unethical behaviour is justified on these grounds – for example, attempts at bribery or corruption.

162　B

The process of recruitment is the attraction of a field of suitable candidates. Selection is choosing one from that number.

163　B

If you are not familiar with the work of Devanna, you need to identify the solution by means of logic and analysis. An HR cycle indicates a continuous and repetitive process. The components of the cycle need to be in a logical order. It is illogical that job design should follow appraisal, development or performance: answers C and D are therefore incorrect. You might think that both answer A and answer B are possibly correct. However, 'involvement' is an issue for manager and subordinate, not the HR department. On the other hand, the development of individuals through training, job rotation and promotions is an element of HR. Answer B is correct.

164   A

F.W. Taylor was a pioneer of the 'scientific school' of management in the US. He believed that work processes could be analysed and divided into component elements, and that greater efficiency would be obtained by getting employees to specialise in one small aspect or component of the overall process.

165   A

Recruitment agencies are commonly used by organisations, and much training is carried out by external training specialists. For the re-location of staff from one geographical location to another, external specialists are also used. It is much more difficult to outsource staff development, where a detailed knowledge of individuals and their progress and experience within the organisation is required.

166   C

This approach identifies the competences (or 'competencies') that the job holder should have to perform the job well, and the individuals responsible for assessing candidates (such as an interviewer) should be asked to focus on whether each applicant appears to have the required skills or competences. For example, questions in an interview can focus on these areas of interest.

167   A

Answer A is the only one that is comprehensive enough. B is wrong as the assessment centre may be run by an outside firm, C is wrong as the candidate attends the assessment centre and D is wrong because the range of tests includes more than just psychological testing.

168   D

The choice is really between C and D since these issues do not relate to Greiner's model of succession planning. Whilst C seems appropriate and could even be deemed to be correct, D is the best answer. This is because, in a modern interpretation of scientific management, statistical process control would be part of monitoring the one best way of working in an automated manufacturing process, and work analysis is the foundation of work study, a principle feature of scientific management and the real focus for which answer to select.

169   B

Psychological contracts exist between individuals and the organisations to which they belong, be they work or social, and normally take the form of implied and unstated expectations. According to Handy, individuals have sets of results that they expect from organisations – results that will satisfy certain of their needs and in return for which they will expend some of their energies and talents. Similarly, organisations have sets of expectations of individuals and a list of payments and outcomes that they will give to individuals.

170   A

McGregor suggested the ideas of Theory X/Y so the answer has to be A or B. (Self-actualising man is by Schein and hygiene factors are Herzberg's ideas). Answer A is the correct version of Theory X as given by McGregor.

171   C

A is wrong as they are different processes, D is wrong as job analysis may occur before anyone has been recruited to do the job. B has some merit as performance appraisal will be partly based on matching the employee's behaviour with the job analysis. C has more merit as selection would definitely include job analysis and then assessing a candidate's suitability for that role. The performance appraisal could refer to the candidate.

172   A

Outplacement refers to practical support from professional consultants designed to help people who have to leave a company, whether through redundancy or severance, move to the next stage in their careers.

173   B

Taylor developed the idea of 'Scientific Management', which included an emphasis on efficiency and suggested that financial rewards would motivate best.

174   D

Part A section 5.3 of Ethical Guidelines if you're really keen, or commonsense otherwise. None of the other options are reasonable.

175   Analyse objectives – what shape and size should the organisation be?

Forecast demand – what are future staffing requirements?

Forecast supply – what resources are likely to be available?

Develop programmes to deal with any forecast shortages and surpluses.

176   (a)   Job enlargement is the re-design of a job so that the job holder has more responsibilities or a greater range of tasks to perform. Job enlargement might be appropriate where employees are under-utilised, and management are seeking ways of improving efficiency.

(b)   Job rotation is a process in which individuals are moved from one job to another within a department or organisation, in order to give the individual experience in and knowledge of a wide range of jobs. Job rotation is used as part of a training or development programme for individuals.

(c)   Job enrichment means making a job more fulfilling for the individual job-holder. Job enrichment will involve introducing new elements to the work that motivate the individual, and will hopefully encourage him or her to enhance performance.

177   Could include:

- job description
- person specification
- organisation chart
- pay scales
- terms and conditions
- human resources policies
- pre-determined questions
- candidate's application form
- candidate's CV
- references
- covering letter.

178 • Hard HRM stresses the rational and quantitative aspects of managing human resources and improving performance.

• Soft HRM recognises that human relations management must be consistent with the organisation's strategic objectives, but places emphasis on employee development, placing trust in employees, participation and collaboration.

179 To improve the reliability and ensure that the same candidate would be selected by different people:

• use structured interviews not open-ended discussions

• use standard questions to ensure all the interviewee's expertise is explored

• train interviewers

• ensure careful preparation

• use panel interviews to reduce bias.

180 C

Herzberg distinguished motivational factors, such as a sense of achievement associated with doing a job, from hygiene factors, which are more to do with the context of the job rather than the job itself. It is usually more productive to focus on motivational factors because employees will work harder and generally perform better if they are motivated.

181 B

Job enrichment is a deliberate, planned process to improve the responsibility, challenge and creativity of a job.

182 C

An extrinsic reward is a reward that is external to the individual such as money, food or encouragement. An intrinsic reward is one that is internal within the person such as feeling good for a job well done.

183 C

The **Seven Point Plan** devised by Alec Rodger in the 1950s involves the following factors:

• Special aptitudes

• Circumstances

• Interests

• Physical make-up

• Disposition

• Attainments

• General intelligence

184 B

Valence is the value of the perceived outcome: 'What's in it for me?'.

185 A deficiency may be met through internal transfers, promotion, training, external recruitment and reducing labour turnover (by reviewing possible causes). A surplus may be dealt with by running down staff levels by natural wastage, restricting recruitment or, as a last resort, redundancies.

186   Advantages:

- An ongoing supply of well trained, well-motivated people ready to fill posts.

- Defined career paths, helping to recruit and retain better people.

Disadvantages:

- Too long a wait for movement/promotion, potentially resulting in disillusionment.

- Selection of unqualified or unmotivated people for inclusion in the succession plan.

187   Decentralisation pushes responsibility for HR management closer to the point of delivery, in order to improve overall efficiency and to increase the accountability and responsiveness.

Decentralisation can also reduce control over important employment issues, with the potential for different standards in different parts of the organisation.

Section 5

ANSWERS TO SECTION B-TYPE QUESTIONS

188   SPEC

(a)   An IT system should improve the efficiency, effectiveness or economy of an organisation. Efficiency would be achieved if the IT system enables the organisation to accomplish its tasks with fewer resources or in less time. Effectiveness would be achieved if the organisation is able to use the IT system to meet its objectives more successfully. Economy would be achieved if the IT system allows the organisation to operate at lower cost.

The benefits of an IT system for providing information are that it should be able to provide better-quality information so that management are better-informed for decision-making. The information system might be better because there is more relevant information available, or because it is more reliable, or because it is available in a more timely way (for example, available immediately through access to a central data file).

In particular the new IT system could enable Spec to improve the effectiveness of the marketing function as it could be used to collect and analyse marketing information such as product profitability and competitor analysis.

(b)   Diagrams and tables are used by systems developers to analyse current systems and design and document new systems. They supplement narrative descriptions of a system, or provide a more understandable alternative to narrative descriptions.

(i)   A data flow diagram is used to describe the processes that occur within the system. It shows the external sources from which data is obtained or to which data is sent. It also shows how data flows within the system from one operation to another, what operations are carried out on the data and the data files that are used for storing and retrieving data.

(ii)   An entity-relationship model is a static model of the system. It describes the 'entities' within the system, which might be people (eg employees) or objects (eg invoice), places or an activity. The model also describes the relationships between entities in the system, usually as one-to-one or one-to-many relationships. An entity-relationship model should be supported by descriptions of the attributes of each entity. These models are commonly used for database design.

(iii)   An entity life history describes all the events that happen to an entity within the system throughout the entity's 'life'. It is another method of presenting the logic of how a system will operate.

(iv)   A decision table presents the logic of a decision, and indicates what actions should be taken in dealing with a transaction or operation given each possible set of circumstances that might exist. Tables can be used to illustrate aspects of a system's logic, but not the system as a whole.

(c)   Beer and Nohria argued that there are two approaches to the management of change, and managers commonly adopt one or the other at different stages through the change process. They called the two approaches Theory E and Theory O. Theory E focuses on the economic value of change, and management decisions are based on how shareholder value will be increased. It is a 'hard' approach, which shows little or no concern for the employees affected by change. Theory O is a soft approach to change based on 'organisational capability'. It is based on the view that the best way of implementing change is through a learning process of the employees, and with close involvement of employees in making decisions about changes. Whereas Theory E would consider that employees can be persuaded to accept change through offers of financial rewards, Theory O would consider that the effective way of introducing change is through employee motivation.

A significant aspect of the argument of Beer and Nohria is that whereas in many organisations, either Theory E or Theory O is adopted by management at any particular time, the most successful way of implementing change is to apply both approaches simultaneously.

It appears that the Marketing Manager is already keen for the organisation to change, although his staff may be less so. It is important that the marketing staff are fully involved in planning and implementation of the changes to motivate them to support the change. At the same time Spec could consider introducing a reward system which is linked to the success of the changes.

(d)   Mass marketing is marketing to a large 'audience', with the intention that the marketing message should reach a very large number of people. An example of mass marketing is television advertising. Mass marketing is most appropriate for consumer products that are purchased by a large number of households. If Spec sell large quantities of branded sunglasses which it sells through retailers this may be appropriate.

Direct marketing is marketing directly to targeted potential customers. To use this method, it is necessary to have a file or list of actual or potential customers, for example a customer list extracted from a customer database. Examples of direct marketing are face-to-face selling and direct mail. Direct marketing is appropriate where the aim is to target known customers or customers who might be likely to buy, by offering something that might be of interest to them. This approach could be useful when marketing glasses to opticians and retailers.

Interactive marketing is marketing where there is a two-way exchange of information between the seller/marketer and the target customer. An example of interactive marketing is telemarketing, where an organisation telephones customers on a pre-selected list and tries to engage them in a conversation about its products.

(e)   A marketing decision support system is a system that can be used by marketing management to assist them with making decisions. The DSS will include a variety of management aids, such as forecasting models and statistical analysis models.

Market research is crucial to the creation and operation of a marketing DSS. Market research is used to obtain relevant marketing data from a variety of sources, such as market research exercises, test marketing exercises, sales force opinions and external data records. A marketing DSS can be used to analyse the market research data, and provide information that should help marketing managers to reach well-informed decisions.

(f)   Three legal aspects of marketing are as follows:

- Health and safety legislation. There might be requirements for minimum product standards, or legal requirements for providing customers with information about the product. From a marketing perspective, it is important to ensure that customers are aware that any required health and safety standards are met by the products, and where appropriate, information should be provided with documentation or packaging for the products. An example of this could be limits on the level of ultra-violet radiation which sunglasses allow through to the eye.

- Data protection legislation. It is important to ensure that any information held on a customer database is not in breach of data protection legislation.

- Legislation on mis-selling or mis-information. The marketing function should ensure that the selling and advertising/promotion of the company's products does not breach legislation on mis-selling or misleading/incorrect information.

189   NEW SYSTEM

(a)   The main disadvantage of buying off-the-shelf software is that the software is unlikely to provide all the features that an organisation might want, and that could be written into a bespoke system. Consequently, the benefits from an off-the-shelf system might be much less than the benefits from a bespoke system would be. This could have implications for the competitiveness of the organisation. (It might be possible to arrange for the software supplier to write an adapted version of its software for the organisation, but this would add to the cost of the software and delay its implementation, due to the need for writing amended programs and testing them.)

With off-the-shelf software, the user has no control over system amendments and new system versions. The content and timing of new software versions is decided by the software house.

If system support is required for users of the new system, it might be possible to arrange a help desk facility with the software house, at a cost. Alternatively, the software user will have to train its own specialist IT staff in the new system and establish its own help desk internally.

(b)   A prototype is a working version or model, but not the finished item. When prototyping is used for system development, an initial working model is produced and implemented operationally. Experience with the prototype should enable the system user and system designers to identify both weaknesses in the system design and also additional or amended user requirements for the system. Through experience with the system, the user should be able to identify the system requirements more clearly. Another prototype is then developed, incorporating the improvements and amended requirements, and the new prototype is implemented operationally. There is an iterative process, with a succession of prototypes developed and introduced, until the final system version is produced.

Prototyping enables a system to be implemented more quickly, because it becomes operational with the first prototype, before the system development is completed.

Prototyping should also result in better systems, because the system requirements will have been refined and improved with the practical experience and lessons obtained from working with the prototypes.

(c)   Operations strategy is a vital element in the overall strategy of a firm. It concerns how the firm provide its products or services for delivery to the customer. The objective of a commercial firm might be stated as meeting customer needs with products or services, in order to increase the value of the firm over the long-term and the wealth of its shareholders. Meeting customer needs is critically important, particularly in competitive markets.

Operations strategy is concerned with the products or services that are made, and how new products are designed and tested. Product development is an element in both operations and marketing management. It is important that new products should meet customer needs more effectively than competitors' products. Operational strategy for computer-aided design might contribute to this aim.

Operations strategy should also be concerned with how efficiently, effectively and economically products are made or services are provided. Aspects of operating performance include quality, speed, dependability and cost. The management of quality is important because with better quality, customer needs are met more effectively, and costs are reduced. Speed of throughput means that customer needs can be met more quickly. In the case of this company, meeting customer requirements for reliability of delivery is vital to regaining and maintaining market share, so an objective of the operating strategy must be to ensure it meets this particular need. Lower costs mean that the company's objectives of increasing shareholder wealth should also be more achievable.

The way in which the supply chain is managed can also be vitally important for meeting customer needs. Greater value can be obtained by improving the operation of the entire supply chain, for example by creating long-term strategic relationships with suppliers and outsourcing non-essential operations, so that the firm can focus on its core skills.

(d)   The marketing mix 'traditionally' consists of the 4Ps: product, place, price and promotion. 'Product' refers not only to the physical product itself, but also to the services that are provided in association with the physical product. 'Place' refers to the way in which a product is delivered to the customer, and the channel of distribution that is used.

The planned new customer order and delivery system can be used to provide a stronger marketing message to business buyers.

The new computer system could strengthen the 'product' or the 'place' depending on how the benefits of the new system are classified. If the new system is successful, customers will be offered a much more reliable delivery system, where the company can verify immediately whether items are in inventory and provide a 'guaranteed' delivery date to the customer.

The company's customers are all business buyers, and reliability of supply appears to be a key requirement. The sales and marketing team should be able to promote this improvement and make the products appeal more strongly to potential buyers.

(e)   Staff training for a major new system should be organised in stages.

(i)   Initially, the company should ensure that some of its staff are familiar with the new system. The best way of achieving this is to assign a member or several members of staff to the development team, to work with the system developers throughout the entire system development phase. These individuals should acquire a sufficient understanding of the system to prepare user documentation and training materials.

(ii)   It might be appropriate to introduce the new system gradually, so that training in the new system can also be gradual. Selected operational staff should be given some 'class room' training in the new system.

(iii)   Practical training cannot be carried out, however, until the system is sufficiently developed. Typically, this is after system testing, or after the development of the first prototype. Before the system goes 'live', there should be user tests. The purpose of user tests is partially to test the system itself, but also to provide user staff with experience in using the new system. Any operational difficulties that arise can be identified and resolved.

Training should therefore be a combination of formal training, practical training and user instructions (in documentation and/or as a help facility within the software). Operational staff working on the system for the first time should also be supervised carefully. The systems development team might also be used to check output from the system, identify any difficulties that individual members of staff are having with the system, and help to resolve them. This might be described as 'on-the-job' training.

(f)   If staff are to be made redundant, company policy should be to avoid compulsory redundancies if possible. This can be achieved by discussing the situation with staff representatives, with the aim of inviting staff to apply for voluntary redundancy, and finding ways of re-training and re-deploying staff in other parts of the organisation. It might be a legal requirement that staff should be offered suitable alternative jobs within the organisation, if these exist, when their job is no longer required.

If a need for redundancies can be foreseen in advance, the company should try to avoid replacing staff who leave through 'natural wastage' (retiring or moving on to another job). Although this might result in some staff shortages in the short term, it will reduce the need for redundancies in the future.

For the sake of good management-employee relations, it is essential to discuss the need for redundancies openly and honestly with staff and their representatives.

The company should follow all the required legal procedures for making staff redundant, where redundancies are unavoidable.

It might be appropriate for management or supervisors to discuss redundancy one-to-one with the individuals affected, and offer assistance to staff with re-training in new skills for employment in a different organisation.

190   HUBBLES (PILOT PAPER)

(a)   **Slide 1:**

Features of a selling orientation

Focus on selling

Getting customers to buy what we produce

Importance of the sales function

Features of a marketing-led organisation

Focus on customer needs and wants

Developing products to meet those needs

Involvement of all employees

Notes to Slide 1:

A company that 'sells' its products is sales-oriented. The company offers a range of products that it tries to sell to customers, using strong selling techniques, backed by advertising and sales promotions. The philosophy is that a good sales force can sell almost anything.

A marketing-oriented company focuses much more on what customers need and want, and they try to develop products or services to meet those needs in a better way than competitors. A marketing-oriented approach involves all employees in selling, not just the sales force. For example, product design, production quality and customer service all matter, because these are elements on the overall 'package' offered to meet customer needs and expectations.

(b)   **Slide 2:**

Developing the marketing concept:

Focus on customer needs and wants

Re-training of employees

Market research

Identify gaps in the market

Develop a product package to fill the gaps

Notes to Slide 2:

To apply a marketing concept, Hubbles must concentrate much more directly on customer needs and wants. All employees should be trained to adopt this new culture, and the lead must come from senior management. To focus on customer needs, it is essential to find out what customers need and want. This information can be obtained by carrying out market research, and why some consumers prefer the products of competitors to those of Hubble. For example, Hubbles need to know who is buying clothes, and are they interested in buying the latest fashions or classic clothes?

Hubble should use market research to identify gaps in the market, or gaps and weaknesses in its own product range, and it should develop new products or aspects pf the overall 'product package' to fill those gaps and rectify the weaknesses.

(c) **Slide 3:**

Components of marketing mix:

Product

Place

Price

Promotion

People

Notes to Slide 3:

The marketing mix is the mix of activities and product features that make up the approach to marketing a product to customers. The elements of a marketing mix for a product are the product itself, place, price and promotion. People is a fifth element in the mix that can be added.

'Product' refers to the products features, including product quality. 'Place' refers to where and how the product is sold. Price refers to all aspects of sales price, including discounts; and promotion refers to the advertising and sales promotion techniques that are used to market the product. For Hubbles working in retailing, a service industry, 'people' are also significant in the marketing mix, because the company's employees deliver the service and have an effect on customers' perceptions of the service and their satisfaction with it.

(d) **Slide 4:**

Marketing mix and re-gaining competitiveness:

Product: changes in product design

Place: improving sales outlets, developing new sales outlets

Price: use discounting to attract more customers

Promotion: more advertising or sales promotion initiatives

People: train employees in user-friendly service

Notes to Slide 4:

There are many different ways in which a marketing mix can be changes in an attempt to regain competitiveness. Changes could be made to any element in the marketing mix. Changes might be made in the range of products offered, or in the design of products, to make them more attractive to customers. The 'place' could be changed, either by opening new retail outlets, improving the facilities and layout at existing retail outlets, or trying to sell through a completely new distribution channel, such as on the internet. Sales prices could be reduced to attract customers with lower prices. More in-store promotions might be used, or an advertising campaign, to boost promotion. Employees in the stores could be trained in customer-friendly service techniques, to improve customer satisfaction with their 'experience' in visiting Hubbles' stores.

(e)   **Slide 5:**

HR Department contribution

Recruitment

Training

Procedures

Pay and conditions

Notes to Slide 5:

An HR Department can assist the Purchasing Department in the same way that it can assist other departments within an organisation. It can provide services and support in areas where the HR staff have expertise, and take away administrative duties from the management of other departments.

Recruitment. HR can assist with the recruitment of staff, for example by advertising vacancies and using recruitment agencies. HR staff can also assist with interviewing and assessing applicants.

Training. HR staff can develop and implement training programmes for staff in the buying department, to improve their skills.

Procedures. The HR Department can assist other departments by developing a variety of procedures, such as appraisal procedures, grievance procedures and career development planning.

Pay and conditions. The HR Department can assist in the development of rates of pay and working conditions for staff in the buying department, and negotiating with the representatives of employees on terms and conditions.

(f)   **Slide 6:**

Purchasing Department and better performance of the organisation

Purchasing good-quality products

Obtaining better prices

Monitoring delivery times

Efficiency in buying administration

Notes to Slide 6:

A Purchasing Department: contributes to effective organisational performance in several ways.

Professional buyers can ensure that products obtained from suppliers are to a satisfactory specification and quality.

A central Purchasing Department should be able to negotiate lower prices for bulk purchasing.

The Buying Department can monitor delivery times, and ensure that suppliers are chased if they fail to deliver on time.

The Buying Department should apply better administrative techniques to improve the efficiency of buying, such as Electronic Data Interchange or Just in Time purchasing.

191   STAND PRODUCTS

(a)   Kanter argued that in order to build a creative organisation, management should have a change culture and develop a change strategy, based on participation by employees and empowerment of employees to make decisions for change. She argued that the following guidelines should be applied by management:

(i)   to develop an acceptance of change (a change culture) within the organisation

(ii)   to encourage new ideas from employees at all levels within the organisation

(iii) to enable employees and different groups within the organisation to interact and share ideas

(iv)   to be tolerant of failures, because not all innovations will succeed

(v)   to give recognition to creative activity and reward employees for innovation.

(b)   An external trigger for change is an event or a change in circumstances or conditions that prompt an organisation into making changes. It is often helpful to categorise external triggers for change as:

- political change triggers, which are significant political events or developments

- economic change triggers, which are changes (possibly long-term changes) in economic conditions

- social and cultural change triggers, which are changes in social conditions or cultural outlook, such as a greater expectation of retiring at an older age

- technological change triggers, which are significant changes in technology such as improved systems for communications or transport

- environmental change triggers, such as a diminishing inventory of key raw materials

- legal change triggers, which are significant changes in the law affecting what a company may or may not be allowed to do.

(c)   Greiner identified five stages of growth for an organisation. Each successive stage in an organisation's growth is triggered by a crisis affecting the efficiency of the organisation's management.

- The first stage of growth occurs when the organisation is small. A successful organisation grows by being creative and innovative. The leadership is entrepreneurial. However, as the organisation grows over time, the established methods of control and decision-making used by the entrepreneurial leadership cease to operate efficiently, and there is a growing need for management systems for organisation, planning and control. This leads to a crisis of management.

- The crisis of management results in a move to new growth stage, which Greiner called growth through direction. There is an organised structure with formal management systems, and a management hierarchy develops. However, as the organisation continues to grow, these simple management structures cease to be effective. 'Local' managers feel that they understand the business better than their bosses, and can run the business better if they are given more authority. This results in a crisis of autonomy.

- A crisis of autonomy triggers the next stage in growth, which is growth through delegation. More authority is delegated to local managers, and a decentralised management structure emerges, for example with profit centres. As the organisation grows, and more authority is decentralised however, senior management begin to lose control over the organisation, and a crisis of control occurs.

- The crisis of control leads to the fourth stage in growth, growth through co-ordination. During this growth stage, central management reasserts control over the organisation as a whole through internal reporting systems and communication systems. Central management co-ordinates the activities of the different local management structures. However, formal reporting systems eventually result in a culture of bureaucracy in central management, which local management resists. This results in a crisis of red tape.

- The fifth stage in organisation growth, which overcomes the crisis of red tape, is growth through collaboration. Structures are less formal, and there is greater emphasis on collaboration between head office and local management in problem-solving, and there is a strong culture of participation in decision-making and team-work.

The fact that the managing director feels that the head office is now losing control of its operations and marketing strategies and that there is a need to bring back more power and influence to head office suggests that Stand Products is at the stage where a crisis of control is occurring.

(d) Compulsory redundancies occur when (1) the employer no longer requires any employees to carry out work of a particular kind (or work of a particular kind in a particular geographical area) and (2) the employer therefore ceases to employ them and puts them out of work, against their wishes.

Compulsory redundancies might be avoided by:

- voluntary re-deployment of employees to other jobs in the organisation

- a voluntary transfer scheme to re-deploy employees to another part of the organisation in a different geographical location

- re-training arrangements so that employees can do other work requiring different skills

- voluntary early retirement arrangements

- a job share scheme, so that two former full-time employees might share a job, each working part-time.

(e) The concept of the supply wheel, developed by Cousins, is based on the view that organisations are moving away from managing the flow of goods into the organisation (traditional purchasing) towards the management of the supply process and the overall supply chain. A company is only as strong as the weakest link in the supply chain. For some companies, such as companies that are moving towards a virtual organisation, most or all of the supply chain is outsourced.

Corporate strategy and supply strategy are at the centre of the supply wheel. Depending on the strategies that are adopted, there are implications for several connected items:

- the structure of the organisation and its supply chain: for example, to what extent will the company concentrate on design and innovation and how much of the supply chain will be outsourced?

- developing a portfolio of supply relationships, and managing them. This appears to be an important issue for Stand Products as the company has already identified problems with suppliers.

- developing the required skills and competences to manage the supply chain: for example, the need is now recognised for professional purchasing staff

- cost-benefit analysis to assess the benefits of supplier relationships: for example, some suppliers agree to an 'open book' approach to sharing information on costs

- developing performance measures for the assessment of purchasing and the collaborative relationships with suppliers: for example, having jointly-agreed measures of performance for the supplier and the supply relationship, and using a balanced scorecard approach that includes performance measurements for supply.

(f) The operations director could consider performance measures relating to a range of elements of performance:

- A quality objective. Quality standards can be set for an operation, which can then be judged by measures of quality, such as wastage rates, defective items, customer complaints, and so on.

- A speed objective. This is concerned with how quickly an item should be delivered to the customer after receipt of an order. Actual performance can be measured, and compared with an objective or target.

- A dependability objective. This is the objective of delivering an item to the customer (internal or external) exactly when promised, and without delays or cancellations.

- A flexibility objective. This is the objective of being able to adapt operations to meet variations in customer requirements or operational circumstances.

- A cost objective. This is the objective of performing the operation without exceeding a target cost level, and measuring actual costs against the target. This is the current focus of the company's performance measurement.

192 HILO CONSULTANCY

(a) A customer database is a file containing data about a company's customers. It can be used by a company to build relationships with its customers, by identifying their needs and buying characteristics. When a company understands the characteristics of its customers, it can design different ways of communicating with (marketing to) different types of customer, in order to sell more successfully.

The information held for each customer on a database might be, in addition to name and address, demographic data obtained from order forms, warranty cards, enquiries and responses to surveys. Information about a customer can be built up over time, from both customer service contacts and market research activities.

Customer databases can then be used to make decisions about:

- when to contact the customer (for example, a car dealer should contact a customer before the due date for an annual service and check-up)

- which products should be marketed to the customer (so that direct mail shots, for example, can be targeted more efficiently)

- which benefits should be stressed to the customer (on the basis of the product attributes that the customer seems to find the most important).

A customer database can therefore be used to create customised marketing programmes, that should be more cost-efficient and effective. For example, a customer database can be used to develop a customer loyalty rewards scheme, or for promoting new products.

(b) A high performance work arrangement might be defined as an arrangement which relies on all members of the organisation for their ideas, intelligence and commitment to making the organisation successful. It is particularly important for a knowledge-based company like Hilo Consultancy.

The arrangements will include some or all of the following features:

- more job complexity

- multi-tasking and multi-skilling

- the continual development of employee skills

- a minimum hierarchical structure of management

- a distribution of responsibility to employees, often through work teams

- much more use of horizontal communications (direct communications between employees or work teams)

- pay incentives for performance and for acquiring new skills

- more focus by the organisation on 'core activities'

- greater use of outsourcing or sub-contractors.

A high performance work arrangement might be given another name, such as 'employee empowerment'.

(c) A project-based organisation is often seen in consultancy companies. It is one that is structured mainly as a large number of projects, many of them inter-related, using knowledge workers in project teams. The management structure is small and many of the project teams might use external consultants and temporary workers.

The main problems for the HR management in these organisations concern the relationships between the organisation and its knowledge workers. Particular HR problems are as follows.

- Career development. Since the management structure is small and flatter, the organisation cannot offer prospects of promotion as career development to most of its employees.

- Competence development. HR management need to ensure that their knowledge workers sustain and develop their knowledge and skills in a changing environment. This is very important for a consultancy company which is selling the expertise of its staff. However, personal development and training needs might be more difficult to identify.

- Pay. There are often problems in establishing a fair and satisfactory pay scheme for knowledge work.

- Trust. There are potential problems for management, who need to trust employees to a very large degree, since the organisation 'empowers' its employees.

- The HR management will also need to negotiate short-term contracts with external workers and temporary workers.

(d) Schein argued that if a manager wants to motivate employees successfully, the way that the manager thinks that employees behave should match they way that they actually do behave.

The four types of employee behaviour he identified were as follows.

- *Rational-economic man.* This individual's prime motivator is self-interest and maximising personal gain. The implication is that this type of person will be motivated by a pay system that rewards employees for performance.

- *Social man.* This individual's prime motivator is to satisfy social needs through relations with others at work. The implication here is that this type of employee will be motivated by a 'task culture' and teamwork.

- *Self-actualising man.* This individual's prime motivator is similar to the self-actualising needs identified by Maslow. This type of employee is motivated by demanding, challenging and rewarding work.

- *Complex man.* The motivation of these individuals is even more complex. Managers need to identify the motivators of each individual in order to get the best out of them.

(e) The International Standards Organisation (ISO), which is a network of national standards institutes, developed the ISO 9000 series to encourage the achievement of high quality standards within organisations. Organisations obtaining ISO 9000 certification are those which can demonstrate that they:

- fulfil the quality requirements of customers

- where appropriate, meet regulatory requirements with regard to quality

- enhance customer satisfaction

- achieve continuous improvement in pursuit of these objectives.

The quality principles on which the ISO 9000 series is based are:

- customer focus: the focus of the organisation should be meeting customer needs and giving customer satisfaction

- leadership: management should give a lead to all employees in creating a quality culture within the organisation

- involvement of people: the quality improvement process should involve everyone

- process approach: the approach to improving quality should focus on an analysis of processes

- system approach to management: management should recognise that processes within an organisation are integrated, and a systems approach to process management is required

- continual improvement: there should be a continual search for ways of improving

- factual approach to decision-making: management decisions should be made wherever possible on the basis of factual evidence

- mutually beneficial relationships with suppliers.

(f) The ISO 9001: *2000 guidelines* are designed to enable an organisation to establish a management system that provides confidence in the conformance of its products or services to established or specified quality requirements or standards.

The approach required is a process-based approach.

- The first step in a quality management exercise should be to establish the processes that will be investigated. The processes might be processes for managing the organisation, for managing the resources of the organisation (inputs), its realisation processes (processes that produce the output of the organisation) and its processes for measurement, analysis and improvement.

- The next step is to identify the processes within the organisation. This should begin with defining the purpose of the organisation and its policies and objectives. Having done this, the individual processes should be identified, and the sequence in which they occur or the inter-relationships between them. For each processes, there must be a 'process owner' and specified process documentation.

- Having identified the processes, each process should be planned according to the required quality standards. For each process this involves:

  - defining the process activities (inputs, outputs and activities to convert inputs to outputs)

- defining the monitoring and measurement requirements (for measuring effectiveness and efficiency for items such as supplier performance, waste, failure rates, the frequency of incidents, on-time delivery, customer satisfaction and conformity with requirements

- verifying the process and its activities against the planned objectives.

- When plans for each process have been made and verified, the planned process should be implemented.

- The process should be subject to continual analysis, comparing actual performance with the defined requirements. Where possible, statistical methods of analysis should be used, because these will be objective. Weaknesses in the process or opportunities for improvements should be identified.

- Corrective action should be taken and process improvements should be made.

193   PMK MANUFACTURING

(a)   Taylor argued that the objectives of management should be as follows:

- the development of a science for each element of an employee's work (based, for example, on time and motion study)

- the scientific, selection, training and development of workers

- the development of a spirit of co-operation between managers and workers, so that scientifically-devised procedures can be applied to work practices

- the division of work between workers and managers in almost equal shares, with each group doing the work for which it is best-suited. This implies a formal, hierarchical organisation structure, systems of abstract rules and procedures and impersonal relationships between staff.

The managing director may see scientific management as old-fashioned because, although Taylor's principles have a certain logic, most applications of it fail to account for two inherent difficulties which are recognised by more recent approaches:

- it ignores individual differences: the most efficient way of working for one person may be inefficient for another

- it ignores the fact that the economic interests of workers and management are rarely identical, so that both the measurement processes and the retraining required by Taylor's methods would frequently be resented and sometimes sabotaged by the workforce.

(b)   Feedback is information that is collected from a system (as 'measured outputs' of the system) and reported back to a system controller. The feedback is compared with a standard or target, and if the measured results differ from the standard by more than a tolerable amount, the controller takes appropriate control action to adjust the 'inputs to the system'.

- Negative feedback is information indicating that actual performance of the system is worse than the standard or target, so that corrective action might be needed.

- Positive feedback is information indicating that actual performance of the system is better than the standard or target, so that it might be appropriate to take measures to ensure that the favourable results continue or are made even better.

An example of a feedback system in management is a budgetary control system. Actual results of a business or operation for a given period are measured and information is fed back to management comparing actual results with the budget. Where the differences are considered significant, suitable control measures might be taken by the managers responsible.

(c) The ISO 9004 quality standard defines continuous improvement as an eight-step method:

- Involve the entire organisation.

- Initiate quality improvement projects or activities.

- Investigate the possible causes of quality problems.

- Establish a cause-and-effect relationship for quality problems.

- Take corrective or preventative measures to deal with the problem.

- Confirm the improvement.

- Sustain the gains.

- Continue the improvement.

(d) BPR was defined by Hammer and Champny (1993) as 'the fundamental re-thinking and radical re-design of business processes to achieve dramatic improvements in critical, contemporary measures of performance such as cost, quality, service and speed'.

They argued that organisations should re-organise their operations in a radical way. Instead of having separate departmental functions, for sales, engineering, machining, finishing and so on, operations should be organised around business processes that meet customer needs.

Hammer identified four main principles of BPR:

- Re-thinking business processes in a cross-functional manner, and structuring operations around the *outcomes* of the process rather than on functional lines (the tasks that go *into* the process).

- Seeking improvements in operations through a radical re-design of processes.

- Where possible, organise operations so that the people who use the output from a process should also be the people who perform the process, because they will then be more concerned with high standards of performance for the process. This means reducing the number of internal suppliers and internal customers.

- Giving the authority to make decisions to people where the work is done, so that those who do the work also control it.

In order to achieve the full potential of BPR, these principles should be applied to the entire organisation, not just to parts of it. If implemented effectively, BPR should help PMK to address the problems identified with workflow and co-ordination between different parts of the organisation.

(e) The operational requirements for a system of JIT production are as follows.

- Zero inventories. Producing output to meet customer demand as and when it arises.

- High quality and reliability. If items are defective and rejected as sub-standard, production will be disrupted and sales to the customer delayed, since there will be no items available to supply from inventory.

- Speed of throughput-production. JIT relies on fast throughput in the production process in order to meet customer orders quickly.

- Flexibility. Production operations must be flexible, with very small batch sizes, so that production can be switched from product to product as customer demand arises.

JIT also has the objective of reducing costs, by eliminating the costs of holding inventory, by avoiding defective output and by achieving fast throughput in production.

(f)   Reck and Long (*Purchasing: A Competitive Weapon* (1988)) promoted the concept that close relationships with a small number of key suppliers, all carefully selected, gives purchasing a strategic relevance that adds to the competitiveness of the firm. Purchasing should not be concerned with getting the lowest prices from suppliers. Instead, it should be about developing strategic relationships with suppliers in order to add value to the supply chain. The most effective firms in a competitive market are therefore those that have strategic relationships with their key suppliers.

Reck and Long identified four stages of development that purchasing must pass through to become a 'strategic weapon' for the firm.

- Stage 1 is a passive stage. Purchasing has no strategic direction, and the purchasing function simply reacts to demands from other departments or functions within the firm. Suppliers are selected on the basis of price and stability.

- Stage 2 is an independent stage. The purchasing function adopts the latest purchasing techniques, but purchasing strategy is still independent of overall corporate strategy. However, the firm recognises the need for more professional purchasing staff, and that there are opportunities for the purchasing function to contribute to profitability.

- Stage 3 is a supportive stage. During this stage, the purchasing function supports the competitive strategy of the firm. Suppliers are considered a resource to be developed and used, and the purchasing function continually monitors markets, products and suppliers.

- Stage 4 is an integrative phase, when the purchasing function becomes fully integrated into competitive strategy. Relationships with key suppliers are mutually interdependent. Purchasing contributes to the development strategy, and possibly has representation at board level within the firm.

194   SOFT DIVISION

Tutorial note

Kanter listed 'ten rules' for discouraging innovation. You are not required to know what these are, but your answer should list ideas that are similar to those suggested by Kanter.

(a)   Many of the following ways of discouraging innovation are common with an authoritarian style of leadership and therefore are likely to have been seen in Soft.

- A senior manager might treat any new idea from a subordinate with suspicion, both because it is new and because it comes from a 'lower' person.

- A senior manager might insist that when a subordinate needs approval for something requiring the manager's personal approval, he must go through several different layers of management first, and obtain signed approval from each of these managers.

- When an individual or department suggests a new idea, the senior manager might invite other individuals or departments to criticise it. Everyone is therefore given an opportunity to criticise everyone else's ideas.

- The manager is critical of many things and does not give praise.

- The manager regards problems as a sign of failure: this discourages subordinates from reporting problems in their area of responsibility and suggesting ideas to resolve them.

- The senior manager controls everything strictly.

- The senior manager makes decisions about reorganisation in secret, and springs them on employees without warning.

- The manager makes sure that requests from employees for information are fully explained and justified.

- The senior manager, in the name of delegation of authority, gives subordinates unpleasant management tasks such as making other employees redundant.

- The senior manager never forgets that he is the boss, and as the boss, he knows everything important about managing a business.

(b)   Demand forecasting of employee numbers and skills might use any or several of the following methods.

- Management's judgement about the likely future requirements for each category of employee.

- Trend analysis. Future employee requirements might be forecast by projecting historical employee numbers and growth rates into the future, using statistical analysis. (Adjustments can be made for any expected improvements in productivity.)

- Ratio analysis. Employee numbers might be calculated as a ratio or proportion of another key figure in the business plan. For example, the forecast growth in employee numbers might be linked to the expected growth in sales revenue.

- Work study methods. These use estimates of the standard times to do certain work and estimates of work volumes. Staff numbers can be calculated from these standard times, allowing for expected working hours, idle time, holidays, absenteeism, and so on.

(c)

- Natural wastage. The company might decide not to recruit replacements when one of the employees leaves (retires or resigns).

- If any of the employees are on fixed-term contracts, the company can decide not to renew the contracts when (and if) they expire.

- A voluntary early retirement scheme might be offered.

- A scheme for re-training the employees to do other work might be devised.

- If these arrangements fail to avoid the need for some redundancies the company may begin the redundancy programme by looking for individuals who are willing to take voluntary redundancy (on favourable terms), rather than making compulsory redundancies.

(d)   Psychometric tests are tests, often using questionnaires, that assess the mental abilities and aptitudes of an individual (verbal, numerical and spatial reasoning) and also personality traits and the individual's interests and values.

The main advantages of these tests are that:

- many are well-established, and have been tried and tested over time

- they provide an objective assessment of an individual, based on the individual's own responses to questions

- they can be validated, by comparing a recruit's scores in a psychometric test with his or her performance in the job.

The main disadvantages of psychometric tests are that:

- there are some doubts about the value of personality testing for recruitment and employee assessments

- psychometric tests do not directly test an individual's competencies for a particular job

- individuals taking a test in a language that is not their first language could be at a disadvantage

- experts in psychometric tests are needed to analyse test results properly, and they can be expensive.

(e) (i) An appraisal system is used to assess the performance of an individual in his or her work. The purpose of the appraisal might be either:

- to consider the future training and development needs of the individual, or

- to assess performance with a view to rewarding the individual, in a performance-related pay scheme.

(ii) There are several potential problems with a performance-related pay scheme. These are:

1 deciding what aspects of performance should be used for the assessment

2 identifying performance measures that recognise longer-term as well as short-term benefits for the organisation

3 preventing employees from focusing on targets linked to pay-related performance, to the exclusion of all other aspects of performance

4 making the scheme fair for everyone

5 deciding *how much* to pay for performance.

(f) Corporate social responsibility refers mainly to the issues a company might (or should) consider with regard to employees' rights, human rights, the environment and sustainable growth, contributing to the general welfare of society and acting in an ethical way in business.

The marketing department of a company with a CSR policy needs to consider the positive or negative consequences of the products or services the company sells, how the products have been made, to whom they are sold and how they are advertised or promoted.

For example:

- products should be manufactured to the required legal standards for health and safety: where appropriate, health and safety facts should be displayed on the packaging for the products or on the product itself

- packaging should be 'environment friendly', for example consisting of bio-degradable materials

- the company might need to consider how its suppliers manufacture their goods: for example, a well-known brand of footwear suffered damage to its reputation from reports that the shoes were supplied by manufacturers using child labour

- advertising should be honest

- sales promotions might be linked to charity donations or charity events.

Public awareness and investor awareness of CSR is growing, and marketing departments will probably need to give increasing attention to this area, and its consequences (positive or negative) for their company's reputation.

195   CHAPTERLAND (NOV 06 EXAM)

(a)   'Better cost control' is likely to mean cutting budgets, which will never be a popular act in any organisation. Attempting such a change would require considerable finesse, but the CEO appears to have acted in a very clumsy manner and has not attempted to carry the other managers with him.

The CEO should not have been so dismissive of the external performance measures. While these are bound to be flawed, they have been adopted for use throughout the country and must have some value. Some attempt should have been made to perform well in these terms because the bad rankings mean that the unit is perceived as inefficient and ineffective, which will demotivate staff and harm their long-term career prospects.

(b)   Human Resources should ensure that progress in terms of the dimensions of any change is reflected in staff appraisal schemes. This will give an incentive to embrace the changes and work towards their implementation.

HR can also ensure that any new appointments are made with the needs created by the changes in mind. This might mean recruiting more experienced or better qualified staff, or ensuing that new recruits are willing and able to contribute to the process of change.

(c)   Outsourcing can reduce costs, sometimes through efficiencies and sometimes because service-providers are able to recruit staff at a lower rate of pay than was given by the client company for the same grades of staff. If outsourcing reduces costs then the budget deficit might be addressed to some extent.

If Q2 outsources its services then it will be able to pass some of the responsibility over to the outsourcing company. This might be particularly advantageous in the area of cleaning because Q2 does not appear to have a great deal of expertise in managing cleaning services. An expert third party should be able to improve matters.

(d)   Internal benchmarking might be used to identify good/best practice within Q2. For example, different clinical specialisms within the hospital might be very similar in terms of their staffing and administrative profiles. It should be possible to compare performance on areas such as cleanliness, staff absenteeism and so on.

Competitive benchmarking would be useful provided a suitable basis for comparison can be identified. Publicly funded hospitals are not in competition with one another and so there should not be a major problem in finding another hospital or group of hospitals with which to share information.

Process benchmarking might be worth considering for areas such as patient catering in case it is possible to learn something useful from other types of organisation.

(e)   It should not be too difficult to create a caring culture within an organisation such as a hospital. Arguably, there will be a desire to work towards this type of change and this could be the basis for an action plan.

Lewin's planned change process might be a suitable model for this process.

- Existing practices and behaviour needs to be 'unfrozen'. The need for change needs to be communicated and understood.

- The change itself should aim to encourage participation by staff at all levels and support should be sought. The change process should be adequately resourced.

- Once the process has concluded, the new behaviour patterns need to be 'refrozen' in place. This might be accomplished in part by using the staff appraisal and reward system.

(f)   There are many ways in which performance might be measured. Given the complexity of the organisation, along with the fact that it does not have a single measurable criterion, it would probably be useful to adopt a balanced scorecard approach. This would gather information on four main perspectives:

- Customer – including measures of clinical results, cleanliness, etc.

- Learning and growth – the extent to which staff are being developed and kept up to date, particularly in terms of new clinical matters.

- Business process – are there any ways in which the systems can be made more efficient?

- Financial – budgeted v actual income surpluses/deficits and expenditure.

196   GOURMET COMPANY

(a)   Contingency theory states that:

- there is no single best way to organise and manage a business organization; and

- the most appropriate way to organise depends on the circumstances.

The termed 'contingency theory' was originated by Lawrence and Lorsch in 1967. They argued that the development and structure of an organisation depends on the amount of uncertainty and the rate of change in its environment.

Different parts of an organisation may face different environmental uncertainties and changes. For example, the manufacturing and food stores divisions in Gourmet Company are in very different business areas. To deal with these various different environments, an organisation creates specialised sub-units, each with different structural characteristics. For example, sub-units might have different levels of formalisation in the management structure, and different degrees of centralisation/decentralisation of authority. The greater the differences in the environments of each sub-unit, the greater the extent of differentiation in their structures needs to be.

Lawrence and Lorsch also argued when an organisation develops separate sub-units or departments to deal with differing environmental circumstances, problems arise with effective co-ordination between the sub-units. They therefore argued that the efficiency and success of an organisation depends on a combination of:

- the extent to which they are able to create sub-units to the level required by the environment; and

- the success with which these different sub-units can be integrated effectively.

(b)   (i)   A continuous inventory management system involves maintaining a continuous record of current inventory levels. Materials and parts are re-ordered when the quantity held in inventory falls below a specified reorder level or when there are insufficient items remaining in inventory to meet the expected future requirements for production.

A periodic inventory system involves checking inventory levels from time to time (periodically) and placing orders for fresh quantities to bring the inventory level back up to a specified maximum amount.

An ABC system of inventory management classifies inventory items into categories A, B and C, according to their importance (volume of usage and cost). Closer control is applied to the most important items (probably using a continuous management system) and least control is applied to the minor, low-value items.

(ii)   MRP I schedules production and materials purchasing requirements on the basis of actual and expected demand for the firm's end-products. Materials are purchased to meet production requirements when there are insufficient quantities in inventory. MRP I therefore requires a continuous inventory management system for major inventory items. However, an ABC approach is also consistent with MRP I.

(c)   The JIT philosophy can be applied to the provision of services as well as to manufacturing products. The aim should be to provide a service to the customer immediately, when the customer wants it. This requires:

- avoiding waste in providing the service

- eliminating wasteful effort

- getting the service 'right first time' so that it does not have to be done again

- holding minimal inventories of materials needed to provide the service

- avoiding unnecessary movements (motion) in providing the service.

A key aim of JIT in service provision should be to reduce queues to zero. Waiting is wasteful, inactive time. All time spent waiting in a queue in wasteful. To meet customer needs, it is important not to waste the customer's time.

(d)   A user-friendly computer system is a system with a Human-Computer Interface (HCI) that makes the system easy to use and understand. The main aspects of the HCI in a system are the methods of input for data, and the interaction between the human user and the computer when the system is in operation. For many systems, the interaction works through on-screen dialogue and prompts.

A customer will very little experience of computer systems should be expected to operate the system without difficulty.

The most user-friendly input method will depend on the nature of the system. The choice of input method or methods should be made on the basis of convenience speed and, as far as possible, avoiding input errors. For customers in a food store, checking out their own purchases and making their payments, the main input methods will probably be a bar code reader for pricing the purchases, and some form of plastic card reader for payments. Some form of key pad or touch screen might also be appropriate.

A user-friendly interface should also be provided by the user's screen. The screen should display clear instructions and where necessary prompt the user into the next step of processing. It will also clearly display the cost of the purchases.

(e)   Concept screening is the process of vetting a new product idea, to assess whether the product is likely to meet the standards required to give it a chance of success in the market. Product ideas are generally screened from three perspectives.

- *A marketing perspective*. This considers the features of the product, and the customer needs or requirements that the product will meet. This leads on to a consideration of the probable size of the market, the market share that the firm might achieve and whether sales demand is therefore likely to be high enough.

- *A financial perspective*. A new product idea should be evaluated financially, and the expected returns should exceed the costs. The assessment might use investment appraisal techniques, notably DCF analysis and risk analysis.

- *An operations perspective*. The screening process will also consider the implications for operations, and in particular whether the firm has the production capacity to make the new item, and whether significant change swill be needed in operational systems and procedures.

(f)   Branding is an element of both the 'product' and 'promotion' elements of the marketing mix. It is used for several purposes.

- It helps to differentiate the products of one manufacturer (or retailer) from those of competitors. Customers can identify with a brand, and associate each brand with a particular price/quality mix.

- Consumers might develop a loyalty to a particular brand. A company might be able to take advantage of brand loyalty to extend its product range to new products with the same brand name.

- Customer loyalty to a brand can give a manufacturer more control over its marketing strategy, and in its negotiations with distributors.

- Retailers might be more willing to display products with a recognised brand, rather than lesser-known brands.

- Branding can be used to reduce the importance of price in the marketing mix. Customers might be willing to pay more for a 'quality' brand.

- Advertising is made easier, because advertisements can focus on selling the brand rather than the product itself. Where rival products do not differ significantly from each other (for example, in the case of many basic food items), this can be important.

- Branding helps with the self-selection of products by customers in supermarkets and other retail stores.

197 V COSMETICS (MAY 05 EXAM)

Examiner's comments

Most sub questions were handled will by candidates. Several candidates illustrated their answers with examples drawn from well known companies (for example, Virgin).

Common errors

- Responses exceeding the limit required.

- A lack of understanding of the concept of ethics and its relationship to the proposals.

- Unclear understanding of direct marketing.

(a) Using the 4Ps marketing mix, the approach can be explained as follows:

Product

- Range of cosmetics.

- Strong brand name, implying a quality product at a competitive price.

Promotion

- V typically spends little on advertising relying instead on the strength of its brand name.

- The cosmetics associates will also promote the products to friends at cosmetics parties.

- Internet and mobile telephone technology will also be used to communicate details of the products to potential customers.

Price

- Competitively priced against high street brands.

Place

- Will not be on sale in shops.

- Customers can order using the Internet and their mobile telephones.

- Customers can also buy from the cosmetic associates.

- Little information given about distribution.

In all of this it is key that the marketing mix variables are blended to satisfy customer needs.

(b) The human resource implications of using 'cosmetics associates' are as follows:

- Selection and recruitment: applicants must be trustworthy, presentable, engaging and reflect the image of the company. This is particularly important, as the company brand name is the main aspect of the marketing mix.

- Training: associates need to be trained in:

    – features of the product range

    – how to organise and run the parties

    – sales techniques

    – the firm's administrative procedures for handling orders and payments.

- Remuneration: the usual method for associates would be commission (e.g. 25% of sales revenue generated) but V may have to offer a basic salary as well to attract suitable candidates.

- Retention: having built up contacts, V does not want associates leaving to work for themselves or a competitor.

- Supervision: there needs to be a system so V can check that associates are not damaging the firm's reputation by hard selling or poor customer care.

(c) The main features of direct marketing are as follows:

- 'Direct' means that there are no intermediaries – V would deal directly with the end consumer.

- Often claimed to be cheaper as no need to share profits with intermediaries.

- Should enable better control of the sales process.

- Very common with internet companies e.g. Amazon.

(d) The advantages of the internet are:

- Potential to reach huge numbers of people.

- Will reach the right sort of people – V's customers are likely to be younger, more affluent and thus more used to buying online.

- Cheap as avoids the costs of a physical site.

- Can use existing websites.

- Facilitates e-commerce so customers can buy online.

- Speed of communication.

- Convenient for customers.

- Allows a customer to compare products easily.

- Can build up information database about customers.

(e) V might use the internet and mobile phone technology as follows:

The internet

- The website should be engaging and have competitions.

- Promotion could involve banner ads, *sponsored search engine results* and affiliate websites.

- Competitive price approach *will fit with people's expectations* when shopping online.

- Customers can order online.

- Customers can buy using credit cards via a secure server.

- Details could be passed onto associates.

Mobile phones

- The method again fits with the sense of fun associated with V's image.

- Promotion via text messages and alerts

- Details could be passed onto associates.

(f)   The main ethical issues are:

- Are associates being treated fairly, especially with regard to remuneration if it is commission only?

- Is it ethical for associates to visit people's homes to sell the product?

- Will associates feel under pressure to sell to their friends even though they might not want to use the products?

- (Mis)use of customer database.

- Is it ethical to 'cold call' people on their mobiles?

- Whether the product has been or will be tested on animals.

- Does the manufacture of the product use non-renewable resources like oil?

- Where will the product be manufactured – if in a third world country then V will have to ensure local workers are treated fairly and not exploited.

198   XX (MAY 07 EXAM)

Key answer tip:

The question only asks for comments on two issues – all four are given below for completeness. The issues are interrelated so there may be overlap between the answers to different issues.

(a)   **Weakening position relative to competitors due to inappropriate strategies**

- Carry out analysis of the company and the environment to identify appropriate strategies and objectives.

- E-commerce strategy is not improving position because customers prefer traditional methods – need to refocus effort into other areas.

- Need to direct effort into innovation in product range and return to previous strategy of differentiation through innovation. New initiatives in place should address this.

Poor management at all levels and a neglect of core business and products

- Changes in management team and proposed reorganisation should begin to address this.

- As part of proposed reorganisation, undertake thorough workforce planning and review requirements for central staffing.

o   Make unsuitable staff redundant (note this will incur additional cost in the short term).

o   Retrain remaining staff (this is also proposed).

- Refocus performance management systems:

  o   targets relating to key products and businesses

  o   reward innovation and creativity.

Weak financial control and management accounting information

- Review requirements for staffing (as above) and recruit new finance staff with appropriate skills and experience. Retrain existing staff where possible.

- Make improving financial management a priority for the new management team.

- Review budget priorities and relate them to critical success factors.

- Reinstate or increase budget for financial management.

- Redirect funding from e-commerce to new management information system (may already be included in plans for new software solutions for manufacturing).

- Develop new reporting to reflect key success criteria and changes to performance measurement requirements.

Inappropriate marketing practices and a failure to manage the company's product portfolio leading to unprofitable lines and few new products

- Market research and analysis to identify customer requirements.

- Analyse profitability of existing products and eliminate or improve unprofitable lines. This should be included as an ongoing requirement in the new management information system.

- Redirect resources from e.g. e-commerce to fund research and development of new products.

- Change culture to encourage creativity and innovation.

(b)   Downsizing is the scaling-back of the size of operations and closing uneconomic businesses in order to refocus the organisation to concentrate on core, profitable businesses.

- It should also involve rationalisation to reorganise operations in a way that makes them more logical, efficient and effective.

- Is likely to involve redundancy of significant numbers of employees.

- Delayering is the removal of middle layers of the organisational hierarchy to develop a flatter structure.

- This will involve a reduction in the numbers of staff who are not directly involved in relating to customers.

- Should result in a faster decision making and a flexible organisation which is more responsive to customer needs.

- Delayering is more appropriate for XX for the following reasons:

- The problems facing XX relate to an ineffective management structure rather than being in the wrong business.

- The company has already recognised that there is a large central staff which is not meeting the needs of the business.

- The company needs to become more responsive to customer needs and empower the front-line staff lower down the organisation who work more closely with the customers.

(c)   **Disadvantages of using the internet as the sole marketing tool**

Loss of customers

- Exclusive use of the internet completely rules out customers without access to the technology.

- Customers who prefer to use traditional means will be put off – and all competitors use traditional methods.

- Using e-commerce demands that the site is secure. Concerns over security could deter existing or potential customers.

- Customers who prefer a traditional approach may be put off by what they see as a more impersonal company which is less interested in their needs.

Resource issues

- Effective use of e-commerce requires a high level of IT skills and good web designers to ensure site is user-friendly and has high impact – XX staff may not have the required skills so the company may need to recruit or retrain staff.

- The website needs to be kept up-to-date which means an ongoing requirement for staff which XX may not currently have.

- The use of e-commerce requires a high investment in software and support systems to link the website to other operations, which reduces the funds available for other activities that may be more important strategically.

- All the above have cost implications.

(d)   **Factors to consider when deciding whether to invest in a product**

The demand for the product

- The size of the market for the product over its lifetime.

- The stage in the product life cycle will give an indication of the growth potential of the product and whether it merits investment. Products in the maturity and decline stages probably do not.

- The competition:

    o   whether there are substitute products from competitors

    o   whether competitors are investing in or developing similar products

    o   the likely response to XX investing in a product.

XX's product portfolio

- The product's priority within the product portfolio when compared in terms profitability, market share and market growth.

- Interrelationships between products – is having a particular product important to ensure sales of other products?

Financial aspects

- The amount of investment required, the funds available and other demands on resources.

- The profitability of the product and the returns over the life of the product.

Risks

- Any risks associated with the product in terms of the market reaction.

- The likelihood of not receiving expected returns on the investment.

(e) **Software applications**

There are a number of different systems which could be introduced that will bring different benefits.

Manufacturing resource planning (MRP I/MRP II)

These are applications which are designed to manage the work flow and inventory levels. Advantages include:

- reductions in inventory

- improved used of facilities

- improved work flow and delivery times, leading to improved customer satisfaction.

Optimised Production Technology (OPT)

A system designed to identify and help remove bottlenecks in the manufacturing process. Advantages include:

- reduction in costs

- fewer defects and improved quality

- more effective use of limited resources

- improved workflow and shorter delivery times.

Computerised economic machine loading

Advantages include:

- more efficient use of machinery

- cost reduction.

Computer aided design and manufacture

Advantages include:

- improved product quality

- fewer defects in production – less scrap and reduced costs of quality

- lower costs pre-production.

(f) **The benefits of XX resuming its investment in training**

Strategic implications

There are a number of strategic benefits which have the potential to lead to an improvement in the efficiency and effectiveness of XX and improve the company's competitiveness.

- Ensure that staff have the skills and knowledge required for the company to meet its objectives – a gap in skills has already been identified.

- Improve the effectiveness of the workforce.

- Improve the flexibility of the workforce.

- Find a more cost-effective way of filling skills gaps than replacing existing staff or using consultants or contractors.

- An improvement in the image of XX as it is seen as a company which invests in people.

Other benefits

- Training could lead to an increase in morale of staff and improved motivation.

- Good training provision for staff is seen as part of the remuneration and reward by employees.

- Improved career development for employees.

199   MOTIVATION ASSUMPTIONS

(a)   (i)   *Maslow's need-based theory* – Maslow developed a model of human motivation which was composed of five levels of distinct human needs, arranged in an hierarchical order. These are:

- physiological needs (food, water, air, etc)

- safety needs (security, stability, freedom from physical danger)

- social needs (belongingness and love)

- esteem needs (achievement, recognition)

- self-actualisation needs (self-fulfilment or realisation of one's potential).

According to Maslow these needs exist in a hierarchy, whereby human behaviour is motivated by the attempt to satisfy that need which is most important at a particular point.

Furthermore, the strength of any particular need is determined by its position in the hierarchy and by the degree to which any lower-order needs have been satisfied. The lower-order needs (physiological and safety) are dominant until satisfied, whereupon the higher-order needs come into operation.

(ii)   *Herzberg's motivation-hygiene theory* is also known as the two-factor or dual-factor theory. The motivation-hygiene theory explains human motivation in terms of factors which act as satisfiers and dissatisfiers. According to Herzberg, those factors that act as satisfying agents, and therefore are motivating forces, include achievement, recognition, advancement and growth in the job. These are known as job contentment factors or satisfiers in that they lead to job satisfaction, but not job dissatisfaction should they be absent. These motivating factors stem from the performance of one's work.

The second group, referred to variously as the maintenance or hygiene factors, include money, status, job security, supervision, company policy and administration and working conditions. Unlike the first group, these hygiene factors are not motivators, but their absence leads to job dissatisfaction. Thus for Herzberg human motivation should be viewed in a two-dimensional way, with the presence or absence of certain job factors leading to satisfaction and dissatisfaction.

(iii)   *Theory X and Theory Y* – McGregor identified that managers have a rule of thumb to describe how people can be motivated to work.

Advocates of Theory X would view their subordinates as an 'untrustworthy, money-motivated, calculative mass' who have an inherent dislike of work and will avoid it wherever possible. This rational-economic view of man was adopted by classical theorists such as Taylor and Fayol.

If there are subordinates with these attitudes then they would have to be driven, threatened and coerced to get them to expend adequate effort towards the achievement of organisational objectives. Economic incentives including payment by results and group and individual bonuses would be the only form of motivation and workers would be exhorted to 'work hard, obey orders and we will look after you'.

At the other extreme, followers of Theory Y believe that people like and gain satisfaction from work – it is as natural as play or rest. This self-actualising concept of man is that adopted by the behaviourists who claim that even the unskilled, occupied in the most menial tasks, seek self-actualisation and a sense of meaning and accomplishment in their work, provided that their basic needs are more or less fulfilled.

McGregor did not put this forward as a theory of motivation as such, but as a description of how managers think in the lack of a more scientific understanding. Each theory has implications for management style – Theory X suggests close supervision and control; Theory Y suggests delegation.

(b) The effect that the changes at R Company will have on the sales people could be as follows.

(i) *Commission consolidated into higher salary* – if someone has been doing particularly well out of the previous incentive payment system, he/she will not like this change – it may even demotivate them. Less effort is now required by them to make the same amount of money. Those who will be motivated by this change are those who work in a sales area where commission was low; they may see the system as fairer overall.

The effect of the change will depend on the staff's individual needs. Those who are starting out in their career may find more money motivates them – they are aiming to satisfy their basic needs. Those who are wanting to fulfil their self-fulfilment needs may not necessarily be greatly affected by a salary change. Younger people and those who also have a mortgage and family to consider are usually motivated by money. They will react either positively or negatively to this change depending on the effect it has on their pay packet.

Herzberg argued that salary was a hygiene factor, so the change will only motivate if staff felt underpaid before.

The salary change is more likely to increase motivation for McGregor's Theory X employees than Theory Y.

(ii) *Non-contributory pension scheme* – this would seem to satisfy an individual's security needs. However, a younger person who sees old age as a long way off is less likely to be motivated by this offer. An older person seeing their working days coming to an end may find it more rewarding and feel grateful to the R Co for providing it. However, because they are older they do not have so much time left in employment and will receive less pension than the younger members.

One could argue that a pension would be a hygiene factor, using Herzberg's ideas, so the change will only motivate staff who felt aggrieved at the previous policy.

Theory Y staff are more likely to have a long-term perspective on their careers so will value the pension change more.

(iii) *More prestigious cars* – this is a status symbol and shows the member of staff and other people how highly they are regarded by the R Co. It should help to fulfil their ego needs. We must remember that for each section the extent to which the individual is motivated will depend on his/her own needs. For example, if someone already has a Porsche of his/her own, being given a company Rover is not likely to motivate them.

It is debatable whether a company car would be seen as a motivator, conveying status and recognition, or a hygiene factor, regarded as a "right".

Increased holidays – this seems a good offer except for those people who live and breathe work. Young single employees who are looking to make a name for themselves will find this less attractive than employees with a family who want to spend more time with their children.

Theory X staff will definitely value not having to work as much!

200   S & C (MAY 06 EXAM)

(a)   The two main options are to change the software (i.e. have it adapted to give a better fit to S & C's business processes) or to change the business processes themselves so that they fit with the software.

It may be possible to revise the software, although the vendor will have to agree to this because access to the underlying source code will have copyright implications. The actual revision to the software could be quite an involved and expensive undertaking. The changes might lead to problems later on. If there are bugs then the vendor might blame the company for making changes. Any future revisions and upgrades might also be more difficult to install.

S & C's staff might be unhappy about changing their systems in order to meet the requirements of a software package. However, it will generally be much easier to adapt the manual processes involved in a computerised system than to rewrite the software. In addition, it is unlikely that the software would have become an industry standard if it were significantly out of line with the processes and procedures of a typical user. It is, therefore, unlikely to require a great deal of change to create the fit.

(b)   A phased approach reduces the extent of the upheaval associated with the change, albeit at the cost of having this upheaval extended over a longer period. Seeing the new system come online in phases will be motivating because the partners and staff will see progress towards an end. The fact that the project manager is absent means that a series of small-scale changes might be easier to deliver and each step can be checked for integrity before moving on to the next.

The 'big bang' approach requires much greater confidence in the new system. If it works then it will allow for a clean change from the old to the new, but if there are problems then there is a danger that they will be difficult to rectify. The fact that this is a standard package reduces the risk of it going wrong, although there will always be risks associated with converting files to the new system and the interface with other parts of the organisation can go wrong.

(c)   The **partners** must demonstrate their commitment to the new system. If they are not clear in their enthusiasm for the change then their employees are unlikely to be keen.

The **project steering group** must set the pace for the change, particularly if it is to be implemented in phases. Deadlines should be set and a set of tasks and responsibilities assigned to users.

Middle management must ensure that their staff are trained in the new sub-systems as they come online and that any checks and balances that are used to ensure correct implementation are in place.

Users have to be keen to make the change work. If they are not willing to learn and adapt then the new system is likely to fail. Staff in the 'front line' are more likely to have a feel for things that are going wrong and they should ensure that any concerns are dealt with promptly and efficiently.

(d)   Users should have been consulted throughout the design stage of the project. Once it has reached the implementation phase then it should be clear to them what they need to do in terms of checking the output from different parts of the system and also in evaluating their own need for training and staff development.

Individual users might undertake specific responsibilities for testing the conversion of data and checking the output. It is generally too expensive to run the old system in parallel with the new for any length of time and so users should aim to test each phase as quickly and efficiently as possible.

Users who become proficient with the new system in the early phases might be able to mentor colleagues when it is their turn to make the change. Some users will have a greater affinity for IT than others and they might be selected for training in the initial stages.

(e) Training needs to be pitched at an appropriate level of detail:

- Partners need to be aware of the strategic implications of the new system, such as its ability to provide information and contribute to control.

- Managers need more detailed training so that they can use the system to monitor their areas of responsibility and supervise those members of their staff who input data into the system.

- Users need detailed knowledge of operating procedures, menu structures, error correction and so on.

Training might be conducted in-house or it may be possible to buy training in from the software vendor or a third party training company.

(f) The company needs to know whether the system meets its needs. Any shortcomings should be addressed as quickly as possible and remedied.

The cost and timing of the change needs to be reviewed to ensure that the project was completed on budget and on time. Any serious deviations from plan should be analysed to ensure that they are avoided in the future. It may also be possible to claim some compensation from the vendor or any consultant who was involved in the project.

The review will give the company a better idea of its strengths and weaknesses in managing projects of this type. This might affect the manner in which future projects are undertaken – perhaps future projects will be given to external consultants.

201   TF7 (NOV 07 EXAM)

(a) TF7's database contains information relating to:

- product specifications

- product availability

- delivery times

- price information.

As this information is available to employees at their desks, who should therefore be able to search for the information relating to any product, the company should gain the following advantages:

- Any employee should be able to respond to queries from customers with prompt and reliable information.

- Employees should be able to investigate customers' problems relating to product specifications, availability and delivery.

- The company should be able to use the information on the database to monitor and improve performance in areas such as speed of delivery and price.

- The company should be able to highlight problems such as product shortages at an early stage to enable issues to be resolved promptly.

- The customers will be able to use this information independently, thereby reducing the workload on TF7's staff.

(b) The purpose of a *management information system (MIS)* is to provide information to management to enable it to make timely and effective decisions for planning and controlling the activities for which it is responsible. The value of an MIS should be that it helps management to make better and more effective decisions than it would if it did not have the information.

Today MISs are becoming more flexible by providing access to information whenever needed (rather than pre-specified reports on a periodic basis). Users can often generate more customised reports by selecting subsets of data (such as listing the products with 2% increase in sales over the past month), using different sorting options (by sales region, by salesperson, by highest volume of sales) and different display choices (graphical, tabular).

An *executive information system (EIS)* is a purpose-built system for senior executives. It gives them access to information from a variety of sources, both inside and outside the organisation. A key feature of an EIS is that it provides information to the executive in a summarised form, but also gives the executive the option to 'drill down' to a greater level of detail.

Typical features of an EIS include:

- the ability to call up summary data from the organisation's main systems (e.g. a summary profit statement for the month and related balance sheet)

- the ability to 'drill down' to a more detailed level (e.g. to call for a breakdown of the stock figure in the balance sheet)

- the ability to manipulate the summary data (e.g. re-arrange its format make comparisons with similar data, etc)

- built-in graphics, charts and other presentational aids

- the ability to set up templates so that information from different areas is always summarised in the same format

- the provision of analysis tools, similar to those found in spreadsheets, to enable the computation of ratios, identification of trends and 'what-if' analysis.

(c) TF7 has been undertaking business-to-business trading to wholesalers and now plans to sell direct to consumers. The following issues need to be considered:

- The company will have a very large number of small customers rather than a small number of large ones. This will require a different approach to selling, using a large team of customer relations staff rather than a team of salespersons. Relationships with customers will be much less personal.

- In order to cope with the large volume of small orders, the company will need to develop order processing systems and facilities to pack and distribute small orders. The company will also need to develop information systems to process orders, record interactions with customers and respond to queries. This will be aided by linking to the existing database.

- Success companies who deal directly with customers through websites and call centres depend on efficiency – stripping out overheads or unproductive running costs such as bricks and mortar outlets, sales forces, dealer margins and stockholding. This will need to be a focus for TF7.

- The company will need to use new methods of communicating with customers and potential customers. Rather than increasing sales by improving relationships, the company will need to attract customers through different channels, such as:

  - the website

  - print and television advertising

  - direct marketing through mailshots and email

  - print and online catalogues.

- The company will need to consider how it will sell to the general public, for example through the web, telephone or postal orders and then develop appropriate systems to handle orders through each channel.

- The company will need to determine which customers it is going to target and whether it is appropriate to segment the market. This will influence the way in which it promotes its products and the means by which it sells its products – for example, older customers may be less likely to purchase over the internet, instead preferring to order over the telephone or by post.

- Customer satisfaction will be very important to ensure repeat business and sales growth. With the move to selling direct to consumers this will depend on aspects such as response to queries, efficiency and accuracy of order processing, and speed of delivery. The company will need to adapt its processes and performance measurement to reflect this.

- All of the above issues have implications for the staffing requirements of the company and the training and development of employees who will need to fulfil a new role and work with different objectives.

(d)   It is important for TF7 to evaluate the effectiveness of the training events. To do this the organisation needs information about the training arrangements such as the content, objectives and assessments. TF7 must also be clear about the criteria by which it will evaluate the training programme. If the evaluation is to be used to improve training, then the organisation will also need machinery for feeding the evaluation into the training design activity so that courses and programmes can be adjusted as necessary. Where criteria relate to measures of performance, it is important to measure before and after training to assess the impact.

There are a number of questions which TF7 needs to ask at the end of staff training events:

- Was the training effective?

- Did the employees acquire the knowledge and skills that the activity was intended to provide?

- Can the employees do the job, which requires the knowledge and skills that they have acquired?

- Was it worthwhile in terms of return on expenditure incurred in giving the training?

- Is there some other way that the organisation can secure a suitably skilled employee that is less expensive, such as effecting different training arrangements or buying-in the skills?

Hamblin suggests that there are five levels at which evaluation can take place:

- *Reactions* – of the trainees to the training, their feelings about how enjoyable and useful it has been, etc.

- *Learning* – what new skills and knowledge have been acquired or what changes in attitude have taken place as a result of the training?

- *Job behaviour* – at this level, evaluation tries to measure the extent to which trainees have applied their training on the job.

- *Organisation* – training may be assessed in terms of the ways in which changes in job behaviour affect the functioning of the organisation where the trainees are employed in terms of measures such as output, productivity, quality, etc.

- *Ultimate value* – this is a measure of the training in terms of how the organisation as a whole has benefited from the training in terms of greater profitability, survival or growth.

(e)   Once the training needs are collated, the training funds are made available, and the priorities are established in relation to the urgency of the training, the training decisions must be made. These include decisions on the scale and type of training system needed, and whether it can best be provided by the organisation's own staff or by external consultants. Training methods, timing and duration, location and who is actually going to be conducting the training also need to be decided. Training may be carried out 'in-house' or externally.

There are a number of advantages to TF7 of using specialist providers as well as its own staff in delivering training programmes:

- In times of change, such as TF7 is about to experience if it adopts a new approach to business, there will be an increased short-term demand for training. By using external trainers TF7 will be able to provide additional training without having to increase its training staff or facilities in the long term.

- The new direction being considered by TF7 will require new skills which the company does not currently have. This means that the company's training department is unlikely to have the necessary expertise to train others in these new skills. Specialist providers could be found who bring knowledge and experience which TF7 does not have.

- If the company's own staff work alongside specialist providers, then this may result in a transfer of knowledge and expertise to TF7 training staff which will equip them to deliver training in the future.

- Specialist providers may have facilities that could be used to provide off-site training courses. Training can be more effective if it takes place away from the workplace as this enables employees to step back from their everyday responsibilities to concentrate on their training.

- Specialist providers can offer alternative approaches to training which may be appropriate to TF7's needs and which the company itself does not have the facilities or expertise to provide, such as outdoor leadership training for managers.

(f)   A quality circle is a small group of employees, usually five to eight people, who come from the same area of work, but with a range of skills from those of the factory floor up to management. They meet voluntarily on a regular basis, to discuss work-related problems, identifying and analysing the problems and trying to find a practicable solution. Although they discuss mostly issues relating to quality, they might also talk about health and safety issues and productivity. Putting the idea of quality circles into practice can be very difficult, particularly in organisations where the management hierarchy is firmly established and 'bottom-up' decision making is alien to its culture. There are a number of ways in which TF7 can encourage the development of the use of quality circles:

- ensuring that there is high profile executive commitment to support the initiative

- ensuring that staff members have the training in problem solving and analysis which they need to identify problems and develop workable solutions

- ensuring that staff members who are involved in quality circles are free to spend the time necessary away from their day-to-day responsibilities to take part in meetings and activities; this may have budgetary implications

- reviewing the information system in the organisation to identify the information needs of quality circles and to ensure that any data required to assess performance and identify problems is available to them

- demonstrating that the senior management of the organisation takes the process seriously and takes any action to resolve problems which is identified as necessary by quality circles; this will encourage more staff to get involved

- developing a culture in the organisation that allows possible changes to be tested out, allowing for the possibility of mistakes

- providing training for all staff to increase awareness of the importance and value of quality circles.

202   ROUND THE TABLE (NOV 05 EXAM)

Key answer tip:

The question asks for guidance notes, so avoid lengthy paragraphs and use bullet points.

(a)   Why a level capacity strategy might be difficult for a firm wishing to adopt a just-in-time (JIT) strategy

Level capacity

- With a level capacity strategy, the aim is to maintain processing capacity at a uniform or level amount throughout the planning period, regardless of fluctuations in demand.

Just-in-time

- JIT systems aim to hold minimal inventory, producing goods just in time to be used or sold.

Problems

- At times of low demand, a level capacity strategy will result in increasing inventory levels, contradicting the JIT aim of minimal inventory.

- At times of high demand, a level capacity strategy will result in falling inventory levels – possibly to zero. If the demand continues to be high, then production will have to be increased to meet customer requirements on time. The level capacity approach would prevent this happening, thus the JIT system will fail to deliver.

- These problems highlight the fact that JIT is a pull system responding to demand, whereas a level capacity strategy is a push system focusing on production.

Conclusion

- Unlikely to be compatible unless demand is very steady.

(b)   The impact of demand strategies on marketing

Demand strategy ('demand management')

- An organisation might attempt to 'manage demand' with the aim of stabilising demand and making it more predictable.

- If demand is fairly stable and predictable, capacity levels can then be planned accordingly.

Implications for marketing

- An aim of demand management is often to encourage customers to use a service in an off-peak period rather than at peak times. Examples of demand management are:

   - on the railways or buses, offering off-peak tickets at much lower prices

   - lower prices for 'off-season' holidays

   - lower prices for telephone calls at off-peak times.

- A company might use advertising to boost demand during low demand seasons, such as encouraging consumers to eat more ice cream during the cold months of the year.

- In some cases, an organisation might seek to boost demand in low-sales periods by offering a completely different product or service with the same resources. For example, mobile vans used for selling ice cream in the hot months might be converted to selling hot meals such as burgers and hot dogs during the colder months.

(c) Chase strategies and flexible organisations

Chase strategies

- With a chase demand plan, the objective is to match capacity as closely as possible with demand. If demand increases, capacity is increased, and if demand falls, capacity is reduced.

Flexible organisations

- Flexible organisations seek to build in the ability to change rapidly in response to changing market conditions.

Relationship

- In order to achieve a chase demand strategy, resources must be flexible.

  – Staff numbers must be easily increased or reduced in numbers, possibly by hiring temporary and part-time staff, overtime or sub-contracting.

  – Variations in equipment capacity must be achievable by methods such as equipment hire.

- In capital-intensive operations, a chase demand plan is unworkable, because equipment cannot be easily increased or decreased at short notice.

(d) Differences between service organisations and manufacturing organisations

The main difference between service and manufacturing organisations is that the former cannot hold inventory to act as a buffer between demand and capacity. This has the following implications:

Level capacity strategies

- If demand is less than capacity, there will be idle resources – management must accept that there will be idle resources for much of the time. This is often evident in operations such as retailing, and the hotels and restaurants business.

- When demand exceeds capacity, the operation will have to turn away some of the customers.

Chase strategies

- Trying to match capacity with demand is often very difficult for service industries, especially if staff are highly skilled.

- Additional capacity can be gained by the use of temporary staff or freelancers, but at the risk of quality suffering.

Demand strategies

- Many service operators try to manage demand to increase staff utilisation. This can include price discrimination to attract customers to quiet periods when staff would otherwise be sitting around with nothing to do.

- Many restaurants offer special menus mid-week and at lunchtimes.

(e) Software to improve inbound logistics

What are inbound logistics?

Inbound logistics are the activities concerned with sources of funds (working capital, investment), relationship with suppliers, supply sources and costs, receiving, storing and distributing the inputs to the organisation system (materials handling, inventory control, transport, etc).

Software applications

Inbound logistics can be improved by use of the following:

- MRP I applications – Materials Requirement Planning (MRP 1) is a computerised system for planning the requirements for raw materials and components, sub-assemblies and finished items. It is a system that converts a production schedule into a listing of the materials and components required to meet that schedule, so that adequate inventory levels are maintained and items are available when needed.

- ERP applications – Enterprise Resource Planning (ERP) was developed from MRP. In an MRP system, the effects of any change in sales demand are calculated by the system, and new schedules for manufacturing and materials procurement are produced. An ERP system performs a similar function, but it integrates data from all operations within the organisation.

- JIT applications – to help manage inventory.

- E-procurement software to speed up the buying process and thus reduce the need for buffer inventory.

- Allowing suppliers access to an extranet, where they can see scheduled production and ensure that items are made and delivered in time.

- Warehouse management applications to speed up finding and delivering inventory items.

- Delivery and distribution applications to improve the efficiency of delivering raw materials and components to where they are needed in operations.

- Software applications to assist in quality control checking of bought items.

(f)   Computerised assistance that could be used by those selling cars and wanting improve demand

The following computerised assistance could help boost demand:

- Website-based selling that could reduce the overheads associated with a traditional showroom and allow the firm to offer lower priced vehicles. A website has the additional advantages of always being open and being able to show more detailed information, involving product reviews and comparisons.

- Viral marketing – the recent Citroën advert with a car performing a Justin Timberlake-style dance routine was originally a small video file that the firm hoped people would email to their friends as it was very original when it first came out.

- Maintaining a database of previous customers so they can be contacted directly to encourage them to replace their old cars with a new one.

- Use of emails to advertise ('spam').

- If 'computerised assistance' extends to enabling greater flexibility in the production process, then the sales staff can offer customers a greater range of choices without significantly delaying delivery times.

- The company can ensure that its inventory is listed on various car search websites to enable customer and dealer to find each other. This is particularly useful for secondhand and rare cars.

Section 6

ANSWERS TO SECTION C-TYPE QUESTIONS

INFORMATION SYSTEMS

203 PROJECT MANAGEMENT

(a) Project management differs from functional management in that it is the management of resources which are attempting to achieve specific objectives within set timescales and budgets. Functional management, on the other hand, is concerned with providing an on-going service.

A project has boundaries and it is one of the activities of the project management team to set and keep the project within those boundaries.

A project will be initiated to develop or try something new and accurate costs are therefore difficult to estimate. It is also difficult to estimate benefits or eventual outcome and projects must therefore be carefully controlled and monitored.

The project management team would need, first of all, to identify the standards for:

(i) the organisation of the project, including any user involvement

(ii) estimating, resourcing and scheduling the project including drawing up a project plan

(iii) quality control

(iv) the activities performed and their assessments

(v) the end product produced or developed.

Each project will be different, but it is still necessary to identify suitable technical standards relating to what is being developed.

The development of a computerised administrative system is used to illustrate an approach to project management. The stages are as detailed below.

Organisation

Creating a project board who will be responsible for the project and who will have authority over it. The board will be responsible for:

(i) approving plans

(ii) monitoring progress

(iii) allocating resources

(iv) assessing results

(v) recommending continuance or termination.

A project manager will be in charge of the project itself and he will report back to the project board.

The project manager is responsible for:

(i)   defining individual responsibilities

(ii)   preparing state or phase plans

(iii)   setting objectives

(iv)   collating information from project teams

(v)   controlling team activities

(vi)   reporting to the project board.

The project manager would have a number of project teams with team leaders reporting back to him.

Planning

At the beginning of a project outline technical plans will be needed to identify the major technical activities.

When the technical plans have been produced, identification of required resources can then take place. These resources include 'expert' staff who may be required at particular times or for particular activities.

The project itself will be broken down into a number of stages, with each stage being monitored and then assessed at its completion. In this way identification of deviances from the expected plan can be fully analysed.

Controls

At the end of each stage the project manager will report to the project board, who will compare the actual achievements against the expected achievements.

These comparisons will allow the project board to estimate the likelihood of the project being successful, completed within the specified timescale, and completed within the specified budget.

Activities/end products

The activities of the project should result in the end project being quality assured, as each activity is fully monitored throughout.

A quality assurance test would be performed before each stage or before the final project was deemed to be completed.

Review

At the completion of the project the management of that project would be reviewed. Although no two projects are the same, experience gained throughout the course of the project should be fully assessed and documented in order that similar types of projects may benefit in future.

(b)   The management of a project is very complex. Activities need to be scheduled and planned in order to make the most effective use of the resources available.

Some activities are reliant upon other activities having been completed before they themselves can be started. All activities therefore need to be properly planned to assess the order in which they need to be undertaken. A critical path will exist throughout the project. Network analysis identifies the dependence of one activity on another.

Computer-based packages now exist which aid the project manager to identify the critical path. If activities differ in their actual time from their estimated time, these differences can be entered into the computer and a recalculation of the critical path takes place.

Project evaluation and review techniques (PERT) allow for probability and risk assessment to be input and resource requirements to be more accurately estimated.

PERT packages aid project management because they allow for fast recalculation of the critical path. Project managers may also perform 'what if' calculations in order to assess possible outcomes for alternative assumptions.

Computer aided software engineering (CASE) is another tool of the project manager. CASE tools incorporate the use of products such as 4GLs which automate part of the programming function. 'Case tools' is the generic term for this support.

Project management is also aided by the use of standard packages such as word-processing, desktop publishing, etc. These packages prove most useful in the rapid preparation of clearly laid out reports and manuals.

(c)   It might be less expensive to use in-house staff. A third party vendor would add a margin to the costs of the programming time. Provided in-house staff are available there would be no net cost to using in-house staff.

In-house staff should have a clearer insight into the needs of the organisation and the manner in which its systems are organised. This might mean that the resulting software is superior to that which might be produced externally.

Writing the software in-house means that the organisation has control over the documentation and source documents. These can be filed and will be available to assist with upgrades and developments. If a third party supplier retains any of these files then it might become difficult to maintain the system in the future.

Writing a new system will be a major undertaking. Most organisations would find that this would overwhelm their in-house resources. The ongoing maintenance of existing systems would be set aside during this period, possibly causing problems elsewhere in the organisation.

204   E-MAIL

(a)   Communication by e-mail impacts on work practices in a number of ways. It affects the speed of communication, it adds to the choice of media to use when sending messages or conducting meetings and it accommodates teleworking to suit different lifestyles. There are also negative aspects to the communication channel. It encourages 'chatting' and other non-essential communications and some people use a type of shorthand, which does not seem very business-like.

The **speed of communication** with e-mail is one of the major impacts on work practices. There is an almost instant delivery of messages, documents, reports or letters. The technology allows the same message to be sent simultaneously to a group of people, such as a committee, and there are no significant time delays, whereby one person receives the information before another. This particular feature reduces ambiguities and helps facilitate co-ordination.

Because people receive their messages as they are sitting at their computers working, there is also a tendency for them to **reply more quickly** than they would to a circulated hard copy. This means that delays in waiting for information can be reduced or eliminated and time can be spent doing more productive work. Unfortunately, when people send messages that require a response, there is an expectation that it will be instantaneous. When there is a delay it generally creates a certain amount of impatience and frustration.

Another impact of e-mail on work practices is that it **increases the choice of communication channel**. Many tasks can be completed more quickly and effectively than would have previously been the case without e-mail facilities. It has advantages over traditional forms of communication. Documents no longer need to be despatched by courier. It is more economical than sending letters because it costs less to send an e-mail than the cost of a postage stamp, especially when fast delivery is required. It can be more secure than sending a letter or memo because access can be denied by the use of passwords. Electronic delivery and read receipts can be requested, and a record can be kept of messages, which gives it an advantage over telephone calls.

Because e-mail allows information to be disseminated more readily via circulation lists, bulletin boards and discussion databases, **the need for meetings is greatly reduced**. Until quite recently companies had regular committee-type meetings just to distribute information. These types of meetings can be very costly and do not always achieve what is required. The use of e-mail can be a far more efficient and reliable way of keeping everyone informed. There are still some types of meetings which it is not possible to replace by e-mail, but the arrangements for them e.g., the distribution of agenda, can all be distributed more efficiently with e-mail.

The downside to all this is that it has obvious implications for employment and the requisite skills of the work force. There can be a tendency for employees to become attached to their computer screens and avoid social contact. This could be undesirable if employees are unable to work together.

The Internet, with its e-mail facilities, is a part of many people's lifestyle and is no longer considered a form of communication for business only. It has enabled teleworking, with many more people working away from the office environment, changing the entire focus of work. The **virtual organisation** allows individuals to work on a project or task and communicate with other members of the team, using e-mail, as though they were sharing an office. It no longer matters where people are located or what time suits them to be working. The Internet allows e-mail messages to be sent anywhere in the world at any time of the day or night for the cost of a telephone call. The message is sent to a mailbox and this can be accessed when the recipient logs on to their computer.

There are bound to be **some disadvantages** associated with communication by e-mail. Because it is very easy to use there may be several messages going backwards and forwards between individuals in a short space of time. People are tempted to use their e-mail facility as a chat line for social as well as work purposes. They can also waste time by distributing items that are not related to work, such as screen savers and games.

Another disadvantage is that messages sent via e-mail tend to be much more informal than traditional hard copy letters and can also be more informal than a telephone call. They are inclined to be very short, without any frills such as salutations. Certain groups have developed a type of language that is only used in e-mail communications. This language uses keyboard characters to denote certain words or phrases. Unfortunately, this trend will have an impact on the language used at work. Employers have been complaining for a long time that school leavers have poor literacy skills and cannot write a business letter. With fewer reasons to practice these skills because of new technologies, formal letter writing will become redundant.

(b)   Like all forms of communication, e-mail has its place and is very useful and efficient. However, there are a number of occasions where it would not be an appropriate form of communication. They include interviews and meetings of a personal or confidential nature, group discussions and training sessions.

E-mail messages are inappropriate for interviews of a personal or confidential nature. One-to-one interviews for a job or an appraisal could not be conducted without the parties to the interview being together. Part of the interview technique is to see how people react to different types of questioning and this could not be handled by e-mail. Disciplinary and grievance interviews are similar but raise sensitive issues, which do not lend themselves to being reduced to short e-mail messages. Some messages are so sensitive that even face-to-face communication is difficult. No one would want to find out some bad news via an e-mail.

Although there are ways of making messages secure and delivering them to the right person, there can be security problems associated with sending messages over a computer network. Within an organisation, messages can be delivered to the wrong person via the internal e-mail system because they have a similar name to the intended recipient. Messages sent via the Internet may pass through several servers en route to their destination and at any of these servers the messages could be read, intercepted or copied.

Discussion groups, conferences, meetings and training sessions are all occasions when e-mail would not be a suitable method of communication. It would only take ten people in a discussion group, using e-mail to send items to each other to be discussed, for the messages to become very confused. People participating in the discussion could soon lose track of how it is progressing. Because there is a mixture of oral and visual communication involved in some conferences and training sessions, they are unsuitable for e-mail. It is very difficult to show the subtleties of body language other than at face-to-face meetings.

(c) Use of company email for personal correspondence could create serious problems for the organisation. If a member of staff sends a message that is deemed offensive or defamatory, then it may leave the organisation open to adverse publicity or even legal action.

The receipt of personal emails may involve staff receiving files from unrealiable sources. These could contain viruses that could cause systems crashes.

Personal use of company email may put a strain on the organisation's communications bandwidth, slowing down legitimate correspondence.

Reading and replying to personal emails may be a distraction from employees' duties unless they restrict such activities to breaks.

205 SMALL CHAIN

(a)   Essentially, there are four approaches from which to choose:

Direct changeover

The existing system is abandoned for the new at a given point in time. Prima facie this seems an economical approach, but this is balanced by the risk that the new system will not work perfectly. Furthermore, there will be no safety net, in terms of existing procedures and staff, with which to recover the situation. It is not suitable for large systems crucial to the well-being of the organisation. If the new system bears little or no similarity to the old, this may be the only route. In the context of the department store, it should be obvious that this is not a viable option; if the new system collapses, then the store potentially loses all sales until it is remounted.

Parallel running

This involves the running at the same time of both old and new systems, with results being compared. Until the new system is proven, the old system will be relied upon. A relatively safe approach, which also allows staff to consolidate training in the new system before live running commences. It is expensive, however, because of the extra resources required to run two systems side by side. Parallel running is necessary where it is vital the new system is proven before operation. In the case of the Point of Sale (POS) system, this would be the most suitable method of changeover.

Phased changeover

Here the new system is introduced department by department, or location by location. This is less drastic than direct changeover, and less costly than parallel running, although each department may still be parallel run. For the department store group it might well be a sensible approach to introduce the new POS system into just one store, initially, and parallel run at that store first, before switching to phased changeover, and subsequently to implementation at all other stores.

Pilot changeover

This is another compromise approach, involving the running of the new system, or functions/subsystems thereof, on a sample of users, transactions, files, etc. in parallel with the new system. This might be followed by full parallel running, or a switch to phased changeover. Care must be taken with the choice of sample. The nature of the new system here, makes it unlikely that this approach could be adopted.

Whichever approach, or combination of approaches, is adopted, good management control, including thorough monitoring, will be essential if the new system is to be successful.

(b)   **Checklist of implementation** activities should include:

- development of a changeover timetable
- involvement of all affected personnel in planning
- advance notification to employees, followed by periodic progress bulletins
- development of training programme
- consider possible needs for external resources
- delivery of Point-Of-Sale (POS) equipment
- testing of equipment
- installation and testing of software
- completion of documentation
- training for systems operators
- system trials
- changeover period
- acceptance of new system
- operational running.

(c)   **Systems evaluation**

This is a vital and important part of system implementation. Its objective is the systematic assessment of system performance to determine whether the established goals are being achieved.

A number of criteria are commonly used to measure the performance of the systems:

Time, i.e. the time required for a particular action to be performed. Response time is the time that elapses before a system responds to a demand placed upon it; for the POS system, this must be measured in seconds. Turnaround time is the length of time required before results are returned; for a POS system, little processing is done, and this may not be significant.

Costs, sometimes the only measure applied, are used to determine whether the various parts of the system are performing to financial expectations, and include labour costs, overheads, variable costs, maintenance costs, training costs, data entry costs, data storage costs, etc. For the POS system, all of these should be considered.

Hardware performance should be measured in terms of speed, reliability, maintenance, operating costs and power requirements. The performance of the POS devices in the various store departments, the central computer servicing the POS system and any networking components must be evaluated.

Software performance should be measured in terms of processing speed, quality and quantity of output, accuracy, reliability, maintenance and update requirements. Again, this is necessary for all software involved in the POS system.

Accuracy is a measure of freedom from errors achieved by the system and can be measured in several ways; but it is important that the type of errors as well as volume is analysed to ensure that serious errors are quickly identified. In the POS system, it is essential, for example, that the prices charged to customers are accurate.

Security means that all records are secure, that equipment is protected and that unauthorised or illegal access is minimised. It is important that the central database containing product prices is not corrupted, for example.

Morale is reflected in the satisfaction and acceptance that employees feel towards their jobs. Absentee rate and employee turnover are two factors that can be used to assess morale of the POS operators in the stores.

Customer reactions are an important factor in the context of the POS system; large numbers of complaints from customers would indicate that the system is not performing satisfactorily.

All the data gathered from the various components of evaluation should be studied to assess the success or otherwise of the system and, if the latter, to help pinpoint the reasons why performance is not reaching expectations.

(d)   The new system might offer the opportunity to reduce staffing. The fact that information is being gathered automatically and in real time from the POS means that there will be less need for clerical analysis in support of inventory control, preparation of sales reports, etc. The prospect of such changes may be a source of uncertainty and unrest in the period leading up to the change.

Sales staff could find the introduction of the new system unsettling. In the short term they will need to adapt to the technology. This could prove stressful if it leads to delays in serving customers. In the longer term, the system could speed up the flow of customers, reducing the need to employ as many sales staff.

The new system will pemit far more accurate and responsive inventory management. Staff theft is a serious problem in the retail industry. The new system will make staff theft far more transparent and obvious. Detection and prevention of theft is desirable, but it can also lead to poorer staff relations, with honest staff feeling aggrieved if intrusive measures are taken to reduce the extent of any detected problem.

206   IN-HOUSE SOLUTION

Developing a large in-house computer system calls for a large investment of resources. The major risk is that the investment is a failure, and the system fails to deliver the expected performance or provide the expected benefits. There have been reported instances, for example, of major new computer systems for government departments simply failing to function as intended.

A key requirement is good project management. A responsibility of the project manager should be to ensure that the system requirements are properly specified and that the system is designed to meet its requirements. The system should also be implemented on schedule and within its budget.

(a)   The specification of the requirements for an in-house system is a critical element in the system development. Unless the requirements are fully and accurately specified, the developed system will fail to provide complete user satisfaction. There are two ways of dealing with this problem. One approach is to take extreme care when the system requirements are specified prior to starting the system design work, and to ensure that the computer user agrees with the formal system specification. A problem with this approach is that it may be difficult to specify system requirements completely at such an early stage, especially when the new system will be large and complex. A second approach is to develop the new system by an iterative process, using prototypes. Each successive prototype of the system can be implemented and tested in practice, and the user can use the experience with each prototype to review and revise the system requirements for the next prototype. Prototyping should therefore help to ensure that the final system meets the user's actual needs as closely as possible.

(b) There is a risk that the system will not be designed properly, and that the designers will fail to meet the system specifications. The systems analysts should be required to demonstrate their understanding of the current system, and that their new system design will meet the users' requirements. The project manager should therefore ensure that the process of analysing the current system and designing a new system is documented clearly. Techniques such as data flow diagrams and entity-relationship models can be used to demonstrate the logic of the system, so that the user can confirm that the current system has been properly analysed and the new design appears appropriate.

An in-house system development should also involve representatives of the computer user. For example, individuals employed by the computer user may be assigned to the project development team. A responsibility of these individuals should be to check the new system design and discuss detailed operating features with the systems analysts.

The new system should also be thoroughly tested before it is implemented. Each individual program should be tested individually, to confirm that the program logic is correct and the program has been written correctly. A systems test should then check to ensure that the individual elements or programs within the system are compatible with each other, such that the output of one program can be read as input to another program.

(c) The project manager should have responsibility not only for ensuring that the system is designed properly, but also that it is completed on schedule. There are techniques to assist with project scheduling control, such as critical path charts or Gantt charts (which can be produced with standard project management software). Critical path analysis allows the project manager to monitor progress on the system development activities, and identify those that are time-critical and those that can be delayed without affecting the overall completion time for the project.

The computer user might want to introduce a new system as quickly as possible, and there is a risk that completing a finished system will take too long. A solution to this problem would be to develop the new system in an iterative fashion, using prototypes. An initial prototype can be designed and implemented much more quickly than a fully-finished system. The user can therefore use the new system operationally before it is completed.

(d) There is also a risk that the new system will cost more to develop than planned. Higher-than-expected costs might affect the financial justification for the new system. The project manager should therefore exercise effective cost control. An appropriate method of doing this would be a simple budgetary control reporting system, with regular reports of actual costs to date against budgeted costs, for each phase of the development. Ideally, the regular reports should also include re-assessments of the remaining costs to complete the project. When the project costs appear to be exceeding budget, the project manager should take appropriate control measures.

(e)   The computer user might have difficulty in learning how to use the new system, and there might be strong resistance from employees who are reluctant to use it. Successful implementation of a major new system requires the close involvement of everyone affected. At an appropriate time during the system development, employees of the computer user should be introduced to the system, trained in how to use the system, and asked for their opinions on how the system might be operated in practice. The choice of system changeover method might also affect the ease of implementation, and the extent of user acceptance. A pilot test or phased implementation of the new system might give the users more time to familiarise themselves with the change.

(f)   A system development should not end with its initial implementation. There is a strong likelihood that some features of the system will not operate as intended, and that the users' requirements will continue to change. There might also be serious errors in the programs that do not become apparent until after the system is in operation. These problems will affect the efficiency of the system unless arrangements are in place for system maintenance. IT staff should be designated to provide post-implementation for the system, assisting with the post-implementation review and providing whatever maintenance and updating is required.

207   DATABASE

(a)   A database is a file of data, or several inter-related files of data, structured in such a way that the data can be accessed, used and updated by different applications. A database is therefore a common set of data files for multiple users.

A database management system is software that manages and controls a database. It controls access to the data files from multiple users and provides data security. A DBMS can be defined as software that stands between data files and the applications using those files. A DBMS therefore de-couples the data and the applications.

As a result of de-coupling, it is possible to write amendments to individual application programs without having to make amendments to the data files. Similarly, it is possible to make changes to the data on file independently of any changes in applications. The physical layout of data on the database can be altered without having to change the application programs that use it.

(b)   Three benefits of a database management system, compared with separate application systems, are:

- centralised data management

- data independence

- systems integration.

In a database system, the data is managed by the DBMS and all access to the data is through the DBMS. This contrasts with conventional data processing systems where each application program has direct access to the data it reads or manipulates.

When applications are designed as separate computer systems, the programs written for each application are usually based on a detailed knowledge of data structure and format in the data files. Any change of data structure or format would therefore require appropriate changes to the application programs as well as to the files. If major changes are made to the data, the application programs would probably have to be rewritten.

In contrast, in a database system, the DBMS is an interface between the application programs and the data. When changes are made to the data representation in the database, the data maintained by the DBMS is changed but the DBMS continues to provide data to the application programs in the same way as before, transforming the data as necessary for the application program. This provides data independence. Every time a change is made to the data structure, the programs already using the data before the change will continue to work.

With a database and DBMS, all files are integrated into one system. This reduces data redundancy (unnecessary duplication), making data management more efficient. In addition, a DBMS provides centralised control of the operational data.

Databases therefore have several distinct advantages over separate data files for different computer applications:

(i)   The data is input once only, and is available to all applications. If separate files are maintained for each application, data that is common to more than one system must be input once into each system. Single input is quicker and the number of input errors will be fewer.

(ii)   Databases also avoid the duplication of data on files, thereby saving storage space in the computer system.

(iii)   A database provides data integrity. All users of data for any computer application use the same data. This provides consistency, and avoids the possibility that different computer applications might use inconsistent data.

(iv)   Access to data on file is available to a wide range of users, simply by specifying the data required.

(v)   A database provides flexibility for computer users. Since there is a common set of data, new computer applications can be written more easily, without having to construct new files.

(vi)   A large database can provide opportunities for in-depth analysis of the data ('data mining') to extract new information by identifying patterns in the data that were not previously apparent.

(vii)   The cost of system maintenance should be lower, since data is updated only once, not several times for different applications.

(viii) The data on a database has to be structured (modelled) logically. Modelling should help to give system designers and users a better and clearer understanding of the data that they use.

(c)   An EIS provides senior executives with the means to prepare ad hoc reports in order to identify opportunities and to evaluate proposals. Ideally, it will offer a decision-maker the means to 'drill down' through a report to obtain increasing levels of detail as and when required.

A database will offer the means for an organisation to provide the data required by its EIS. The flexibility inherent in a database design will make it easier to use the EIS to its full potential.

For example, management might wish to prepare, say, a set of accounting statements for a particular segment of the business even though this had not been anticipated in the design of the routine reporting system. Once the statements have been prepared then the managers will be able to call for more detail (e.g. an analysis of a particular category of sale).

Offering data in this flexible way means that it will be relatively easy to produce reports and documents, including graphs and charts, to assist in discussion and analysis.

The overall system will make it far easier for managers to ask 'what-if?' questions. It will be relatively easy for managers to evaluate the implications of potential changes arising from brainstorming meetings or proposals from consultants.

CHANGE MANAGEMENT

208 ZED BANK (PILOT PAPER)

(a) Lewin suggested that a process of change within an organisation should go through three main stages of: 'unfreeze', 'movement' and 'refreeze':

- The process of 'unfreezing' involves persuading employees that the current situation is unsatisfactory and that change is desirable. Unless employees believe that the current situation is unsatisfactory, they will not want to change anything. However, in addition to persuading employees to be dissatisfied with the current position, it is also necessary to offer an attractive alternative that employees will prefer, but which can only be reached by means of change.

  It is therefore essential at this stage of the change process that management should have a clear idea of the new situation they want to create, so that they can explain it to employees and convince employees that the new situation is desirable.

- The process of movement or change cannot happen until employees are willing to give up the existing situation and know what they would like to have instead. This is the process of continuing to win the support of employees, whilst implementing the planned changes. It is generally argued that in order to make the process of change easier to implement, employees should participate in the process, by contributing ideas and suggestions about what should be done. Employees should also be kept fully informed, so that they know what is happening, and do not feel that unwelcome changes are being imposed on them.

  The movement process also requires management to identify the areas where resistance to change is strongest, and to take measures to reduce the resistance and obtain greater acceptance for the changes.

- The final main stage in the change process is 'refreeze'. Having achieved the desired changes, management should try to ensure that the new situation survives, and the organisation does not revert to its old ways and old systems. The refreeze process is therefore designed to reinforce the change. This might be achieved by close supervision and management but the most effective way of sustaining change is to keep the support of all employees. One way of doing this might be to offer cash bonuses or other incentives that are linked to achieving target performance levels.

(b) (i) Incremental change means step-by-step changes over time, in small steps. When incremental change occurs within an organisation, it is possible for the organisation to adapt to the change without having to alter its culture or structures significantly. Employees are able to adapt to the gradual changes, and are not unsettled by them.

In contrast, transformational change is a sweeping change that has immediate and widespread effects. The effect of transformational change is usually to alter the structure and culture of the organisation, often with major staff redundancies and the recruitment of new staff with new skills.

The spokesperson for the bank has argued that the change will be incremental. Since the change will take place over a long period of time, staff will have time to adapt to the new structure. There will be no compulsory redundancies and staff will be re-trained in new skills. Although some branches will close, others will remain open, and customers will be offered additional facilities through on-line banking.

The trade union leader believes that the change will be much more dramatic. He might believe that many employees will leave the bank because they are unable to adapt to the new service, or because they are unwilling to re-locate from the branches that are closed down. The bank might push through the branch closure programme more quickly than it has currently proposed, and staff redundancies could be made compulsory if there are not enough individuals willing to take voluntary redundancy.

Essentially, the two individuals take differing viewpoints because they are looking at change differently. The spokesperson for the bank wants to persuade employees to accept the change, and even welcome it. The trade union representative wants to warn employees about the potential consequences, and has therefore stressed the risks.

(ii)   Participation might make the changes appear less threatening to employees because they will know that their views will be taken into account in the transition process. The fact that they will be able to enter into a dialogue will reduce the risk of them refusing to cooperate with the proposals.

Involving the employees will, ideally, create a sense of ownership on the employees' part. That will enable Zed Bank to draw on their insights and experience of the company in making the changes as effectively as possible.

There are, however, drawbacks to participation. It can slow the rate of change because time must be allowed for consultation and feedback.

Participation will only work if there is a sense of mutual trust and loyalty. If staff members are distanced and resentful then their input to the transition will have little or no value. If management is not willing to trust staff and take their input seriously then there will be 'pseudo-participation' which will tend to create greater resentment than failing to consult.

Employees have to be willing to engage with the changes and work towards bringing them about. Otherwise their participation in the process might be used to delay or disrupt the changes rather than bring them into effect.

In this case, the fact that some members of staff will be affected more than others might create the possibility of some groups of employees feeling alienated by both the bank and their colleagues. For example, staff in the branches that are due to be closed may be more likely to lose their jobs or have to make significant changes to their working patterns than those employed in large, city-centre branches.

209   ORGANISATIONAL DEVELOPMENT

(a)   Organisational development (OD) emerged in the 1960s and is commonly associated with the work of Warren Bennis. OD is concerned with change in organisations, and Bennis believed that to implement change, a major educational programme was necessary to change the attitudes of employees 'so that they can better adapt to new technologies, markets and challenges, and to the dizzying rate of change itself.'

OD is also associated with management consultants, who act in the role of 'agents for change'.

The basic approach begins with the recognition that the organisation is having difficulty in adapting to change, and employees are generally hostile to the idea of change. Management consultants, in their role as change agents, diagnose the problems.

Another feature of OD is that to educate employees into accepting and welcoming change, it is essential to involve them in the identifying what the problems are, what is causing them and how the problem might be resolved.

It is essential that during the diagnostic phase, trust is built up between individuals and groups within the organisation, and with the consultants. In the case of B Company, for example, trust needs to be re-established between operations staff and quality control staff; therefore it is essential to bring them together in the diagnostic and problem-solving exercise.

A number of different ideas might be considered about how each problem might be dealt with. Agreement then needs to be reached about which ideas should be tested, and how the tests should be carried out. It might be decided, for example, to implement a suggested solution on a trial basis, and monitor the results before trying to extend the solution to the rest of the organisation.

The actual techniques of carrying out diagnostic and problem-solving exercises, and the types of 'solution' favoured by OD experts, can vary considerably.

(b) The approach described above can be applied to the B Company. However, the company is facing a large number of problems, and each will have to be diagnosed.

The management consultants hired to assist in the programme should carry out an initial survey of the situation. It appears that the company has a variety of problems arising from environmental change. Even the demands from staff for higher pay might be linked to high pay rises in the economy generally.

All the 200 employees in the organisation should be involved in the programme, and having carried out their initial study, the consultants, together with senior management, should probably hold a general meeting with all staff and explain the perceived problems and the purpose of the programme.

An immediate concern has to be the low morale and lack of co-operation between departments. This has not been a problem in the past, and there may well be particular reasons why the deterioration occurred. In discussing the company's problems with staff, these motivational issues need to be recognised and considered.

The consultants might begin by trying to identify and analyse the company's problems on a departmental basis, trying to win some trust and obtain some co-operation from all the individuals. The investigation needs to consider what the problems are in implementing the new hygiene regulations, why changes in consumer tastes have had an adverse effect on business, what problems are being caused by the activities of competitors, what has been the perceived reasons for and impact of the material price increases, and why employees feel the need for higher pay.

As trust develops – which it needs to do if the programme is to succeed – the issues of low morale, and poor inter-departmental relations can be considered more openly. When the time is appropriate, the consultants should bring together people from different departments so that they can discuss and diagnose the problems they have experienced.

Since the key issues seem to be internal, getting employees to recognise the nature of these problems and their causes will be a critical element of the OD programme.

The consultants should make sure that at all times during the OD programme, all employees feel that they are a part of the exercise and that their views will be heard. Since it is difficult to listen to the views of 200 individuals face-to-face, opinion surveys might be used, and the results of the surveys reported back. It is also important, as the programme progresses, to keep everyone informed about ideas that are emerging and solutions that are being proposed.

The lack of faith in management is also another problem that has been identified and that is probably a fundamental issue. The OD consultants need to use a method of persuading management to recognise their failings, and to consider how they should be acting instead. A series of face-to-face interviews with management, in which they are informed about the negative feedback from employees about their abilities, might be a useful method of bringing the problem into the open for discussion and resolution.

The problems arising from the environment will not be resolved until the problems of morale, co-operation and conflict are resolved. Working towards solutions to the external problems can provide a way of recognising and resolving the internal problems. The conflict between operations and quality control might be very difficult to resolve, and the consultants will have to make sure that the two sides discuss their grievances freely with each other. (The consultants should be well-trained and experienced in conflict resolution.)

The consultants should also keep in view the goal of educating the work force into recognising the need for change and welcoming the idea of change in order to get better.

The consultants might consider that the problems of poor co-operation between departments calls for a radical solution, and a solution might be encouraged that is based on a radical re-organisation of operations around processes rather than functions. (This would be a form of business process re-engineering.)

(c)   The company should ask several consultants to tender for the contract. Consultants should be approached on the basis that they have a reputation for being experienced in the area of organisational development.

Tenders should be scrutinised for relevant indicators that the consultants will bring about successful change, such as:

- prior experience of the food industry

- a logical and sensible proposal for the approach to be taken to B Company

- a realistic timeframe and budget.

The shortlisted firm should be asked to meet with the board in order to discuss the proposals. This meeting should include the senior members of the consultancy team who will participate in the project. The board should not finally grant the contract unless it is satisfied that there is a rapport with the consultants.

210   EVERLAND BANKS (MAY 06 EXAM)

Requirement (a)

It is always dangerous for a business or even a whole industry to focus on the products that it wishes to provide rather than the needs of its customers. The banking industry may have enjoyed an artificial protection in the past because customers have been forced to take banking services from a limited number of providers who have tended not to differentiate themselves in terms of their products. If customers do not feel that their needs are being met, then they will be willing to consider alternative offerings once the rules are relaxed to permit a wider range of business.

The prospect of a change, should motivate the banks to re-examine their business models and make the effort to develop a deeper understanding of what their customers actually wish from a bank. It will take some time to develop new types of account, train staff in the provision of new services and recruit new employees with the necessary skills to fill any gaps in the present complement.

If banks do not change, then experience from Utopia indicates that complacency could prove disastrous. The banking industry there had to adapt to the business methods used by new entrants to the industry. By implication, standing still was not an option. If they had left things as they were then they would have run the risk of losing significant custom to the new businesses and they would also have missed out on the new opportunities offered by the opportunity to sell new services.

The relaxation of banking law should be seen as an opportunity rather than a threat. The existing banks need not necessarily lose ground to newcomers provided they establish what services their customers need and plan to offer these as soon as it becomes possible to do so legally.

Requirement (b)

The banks should consider adopting a change in their overall strategy to emphasise marketing:

Strategic analysis

- The banks should identify their strengths and weaknesses, their core competences and the resources that they have available to them.

- The prospects for change in the external environment should be analysed. What sorts of banking will new institutions be permitted to offer? What additional services will be opened up to the banks?

- How are the banks currently perceived? Can perceptions for integrity and security be built on to retain customers while still offering room to innovate?

Strategic choice

- Can the market be segmented in any way?

- If so, which segments should the banks seek to retain?

- How should each target segment be approached? How will the banks compete with one another and with any new entrants?

Strategy implementation

- What resources need to be acquired? Does this require new staff with additional skills?

- How should the banks promote both existing and new services?

- What targets should be set and how will progress be monitored and controlled?

- How will the changes be managed without alienating those existing staff whose skills and enthusiasm will need to be harnessed?

211 K COMPANY

(a) Learning organisations are those that encourage questions and explicitly recognise mistakes as part of the learning process. Edler, Burgoyne and Boydell define the learning organisation as 'an organisation that facilitates the learning of all its members and constantly transforms itself'.

Peter Senge identifies five core competences for any company that wants to become a 'learning organisation':

- Building a shared vision or common sense of purpose, so that all members of the organisation are pulling together all the time, instead of only being brought together by an external crisis.

- Achieving personal mastery of the issues to be learnt through continuous self-development and learning, and passing this learning onto others through the organisation's cognitive systems and memories. In this way, the organisation maintains and develops it own norms, values, behaviours and mental maps over time, even though the individuals who first 'learnt' them are no longer there.

- Utilising mental models, so that individuals can both identify the assumptions that they bring to a situation, and develop alternative ways of doing things which will have a significant impact.

- Team learning, so that not only individual team members but the team collectively learns how to tackle difficult situations and decisions without losing the benefits of team working.

- Systems thinking, so that a situation is analysed for how it fits together as a whole, rather than just as a set of separate problems to be solved separately. In particular, this involves an understanding of how the organisation as a whole fits together and functions, so that the effect of an issue which impacts on one part of the organisation can be analysed in terms of its impact on the whole.

Building up a learning organisation should be undertaken in stages. Initially the emphasis will be on bringing all the organisation's workers round to an understanding of the importance of such matters as continual improvement, quality and benchmarking as ways to achieve improvements in 'how we do things round here'. Bureaucratic brakes on such improvements should also be removed at this point.

In the next stages the organisation's managers in particular can be encouraged to think of new ways in which the organisation could function – for instance, new technology, new markets, and new ways of delighting the customer.

The final stage is achieved when the processes undergone in the first two stages have become a way of life for everyone involved in the organisation. The important point about this stage is that it should be maintained in the long term so that the organisation can benefit fully from all the effort that has been put in. In other words, building a learning organisation is a continuous process rather than a project which can be implemented and then left. This is of particular importance for K Company as it operates in conditions of permanent, rapid change.

The implementation of the ideas implicit in the learning organisation is a significant effort which K Company probably feels it cannot afford to fail in. The company should also be aware that cultural changes will be required.

(b)   The idea of the assessment centre is part of a philosophy that grew out of the obvious shortcomings of the application, interview and references alone as selection techniques. Assessment centres allow assessment of individuals working in a group or alone by a team of assessors, who use a variety of assessment techniques depending on the requirements of the client.

The first step towards setting up an assessment centre is to make sure that the jobs on offer have been fully analysed into a set of competences, against which a set of criteria can be developed. The assessment centre activities can then be designed so as to test these competences against the criteria. The activities can include, as well as interviews and 'psychometric' tests, hands on simulations, in-tray exercises, role-play and presentations. There may even be outdoor, team-building exercises.

Since assessment centres became a more widely used technique it has been shown that they are much better at predicting a successful match between the selected candidate and the employer. The wider the range of techniques used, the more successful the result in terms of a good match.

Because there is such a wide range of assessment methods used at an assessment centre, it is argued that the approach is more thorough and therefore more successful than the more traditional approaches. If nothing else, the process takes longer and allows the potential employer to see the candidates over a longer period of time, and therefore 'get to know them' in a number of situations. This contrasts well with the very time-constrained, artificial interview situation. The methodology must be rigorous however, or else there is the temptation to select the person who just seems the most sociable etc.

The big disadvantage of assessment centres is the cost of setting them up, administering them, staffing them and producing the results. Many smaller companies simply cannot afford them , although recruitment consultants can stage them on behalf of a client if there is a one-off, very important appointment to be made. If this is the situation for K Company then selective use of assessment centres will probably be very beneficial.

(c) Vision statements are often a source of cynicism and alienation. Organisations frequently pay lip service to an idea but do not really mean it.

If there is a genuine vision and shared culture then the members of an organisation will work together in that direction because they want to, not because they have been told to or are responding to some artificial stimulus.

It is extremely difficult to impose a leader's convictions on an orgabisation, no matter how heart-felt and sincere those convictions are.

A successful vision has to be shared by everyone. Achieving this needs to involve everyone. The leadership challenge is to uncover and define a shared picture of the future that fosters genuine commitment rather than mere compliance.

212   R & L (MAY 05 EXAM)

Examiner's comments

This was a popular question and most candidates answered (a) in particular well. Some candidates drew purposeful examples from similar organisations including the recent MG/Rover experience.

Common errors

*   A large number of candidates described change management theories in part (b) without relating them to the scenario or addressing the central issue of how resistance might be overcome.

(a) R & L has built up a reputation as a good employer and will want to preserve this strength while still reducing the size of the workforce. To do this it can take the following initiatives:

Consultation

If there is a trade union at the firm, then union officials should be involved from the very beginning in designing a programme to reduce the size of the workforce. Once the union agree that job cuts are needed now to protect jobs in the future, then their help should be forthcoming.

Even if there is no a union, then employees should be consulted at all stages of the process. This will reduce hostility from workers and will be seen by the outside world as the firm acting more reasonably than imposing changes on the workforce.

Initial steps

One of the first steps R & L should take is to review future staff turnover or 'natural wastage' to see how much of the 50% reduction can be met by staff leaving anyway and/or retiring. Experience could indicate figures for the former and a review of HR files should indicate the numbers for the latter.

An immediate halt on recruitment would also reduce future job losses.

Reducing labour hours without reducing the number of workers

R & L can protect some jobs by reducing the hours people work rather than losing employees. This can be done by a mixture of the following:

- job sharing schemes

- part-time working

- a shorter working week

- reducing the amount of overtime offered.

Reducing the number of employees without compulsory redundancy

R & L's reputation will be damaged most by forced, compulsory redundancies, so the firm will wish to keep these to a minimum. Worker numbers can be cut without redundancy by the following:

- 'encouraging' anyone over retirement age to retire

- offering early retirement to workers over a certain age

- outsourcing non-core functions to outside suppliers who agree to employ some R & L workers as part of the deal.

Retraining

It may be that there are areas of the firm where more staff are needed. Rather than recruiting from outside the firm, training should be offered to existing staff so they can be moved within R & L.

Support

Employees who are affected by the changes should be offered support. This could take a number of forms:

- counselling and support for those facing early retirement or redundancy

- retraining offered in new skills necessary to get jobs in other firms

- training and help in preparing a CV, how to fill in application forms and interview techniques to help workers find new jobs

- offering redundancy payments that are higher than the legal minimum.

(b) **Kotter and Schlesinger** identified six main methods of dealing with resistance to change. These can be applied to the situation facing R&L as follows:

1   Education and communication

Resistance to change is often fuelled by rumours and suspicion so improved communication can help by clarifying the situation. It is rarely sufficient on its own unless the rumours were totally unfounded. For example, knowing that you will be made redundant takes away the anxiety whether or not you will lose your job but does not take away resistance to the cuts.

Given R & L's desire to continue to be and be seen to be a good employer, this would be a suitable strategy and would involve meetings with employees to explain why job losses are necessary and the different options available (as discussed in part (a))

2   Participation and involvement

Key stakeholders who have both significant power and significant interest in the changes should be involved in the change process. This will facilitate better acceptance of the changes and commitment to work through problems together.

In the case of R&L this is another highly suitable method and should involve consulting trade union representatives and workers generally and incorporating their ideas. The union for example, may promise to stop workers going out on strike if the firm promise to keep compulsory redundancies to an absolute minimum and agree to generous redundancy payments.

3   *Facilitation and support*

Facilitation and support are designed to reduce employee anxiety and involve counseling and training. It is particularly appropriate when employees are going to have to adjust to fundamental changes.

With R&L this is also a highly suitable strategy given the major changes envisaged and the desire to be a good employer. All of the initiatives discussed under the heading of 'support' in section (a) would be appropriate here.

4   *Negotiation and agreement*

There is frequently an element of compromise in change management so each party feels that they have gained something from the process. For example, if employees feel that they have kept their jobs, then they might be willing to accept reduced hours and pay.

This is another suitable strategy for R&L as it appears to have had good employee relations in the past so could count on goodwill in negotiations rather than outright hostility.

5   *Manipulation and co-optation*

This can involve misinformation, keeping employees in the dark about changes and buying off key players, usually to drive changes through more quickly.

For R&L this would not be a suitable strategy as workers would feel used and tricked, creating significant ill-feeling. Ultimately this would affect R&L's reputation may result in more staff leaving and does not fit with R&L's desire to be a good employer.

6   *Explicit and implicit coercion*

In extreme cases some firms resort to force and the threat of force to push through changes. This could involve sacking any workers who could cause problems, intimidation and threats. This is a particularly dangerous strategy when a strong trade union is present, as it will usually result in confrontation.

This is not suitable for R&L as it does not fit with the stated aim of continuing to be a good employer and may be both illegal and unethical.

213   T COMPANY

(a)   **Triggers for change**

Organisational change can be driven by both external developments and/or internal organisational factors. The key triggers for change in T Company are as follows:

External triggers	*Internal triggers*
• Government decisions to deregulate the telecommunications industry	• Senior management decisions to enter the mobile telephone market and, later, broadband internet services
• Technological developments in wireless technology (mobile phones!)	
• Development of broadband Internet technology	• Managers' decision to sack workers
• Shift in consumer tastes away from fixed line telephones to mobile phones	• Workers' decision to take industrial action to preserve jobs
	• Trade union's decision to support the actions of T Company employees

The key difficulties that the T Company is likely to face in making all the necessary changes are as follows.

Existing culture

The inherited bureaucratic culture of the organisation with its rules and procedures is likely to act as a barrier to change.

Employees' resistance to change

Employees will resist change due to:

- fear of being unable to cope with the new technology
- unwillingness to throw away existing skills and learn new ones
- fear of job losses
- fear that new jobs will be more specialised and more boring.

Action of trade unions

The threat of action by the trade union will make change even more difficult.

(b) **The change process**

Success to date

T Company has had a mixed record of success in the management of change to date.

The main success is that it has managed to change from being a provider of only fixed line telephone services to one that now also provides mobile and broadband Internet services. This is despite the old bureaucratic culture and structure.

The main failures have been as follows:

- Attempts to downsize the workforce resulted in industrial action that cost T Company many millions.
- The current implementation of broadband services is also meeting with resistance. Engineers have threatened industrial action in support of a large pay rise.

Managing future change

There is no universal plan for the successful management of change as each situation is different. At best, there are useful models and principles to help in the design of the change process. One such model was developed by Lewin.

Lewin argued that some (usually external) forces are outside management's control and so management should concentrate on the internal forces driving change and those resisting change. Lewin suggested a three-step process to then manage the change as follows:

1   'Unfreezing' – which involves reducing forces that resist change. This involves providing people with an understanding of why change needs to occur so that they can more easily accept it.

2   'Changing behaviour' – in such a way that new attitudes, values and behaviour become part of employees' new ways of thinking.

3   'Refreezing' – introducing mechanisms, such as reward systems and structures, to ensure that the new behaviour pattern is maintained.

In the case of T Company, many of the forces for change are outside the control of the senior management. Management needs to accept the changes in the market place and adopt strategies to deal with the threats and opportunities the changes present.

Unfreezing

Management can use the threat of competition to persuade employees and the trade union that, unless changes are made, the very survival of the company and, therefore, the jobs of employees, are at risk. This should create dissatisfaction with existing methods.

Changing behaviour

Changing behaviour is difficult and will require a range of methods:

- effective communication of what needs to be changed and why
- regular meetings involving all employees
- negotiation with unions to ensure their participation in the change process.

The directors may be tempted to force changes through regardless of the reasons for resistance. The danger of this approach is that employees often return to the old ways of working once the pressure is removed.

Refreezing

- To consolidate changes made appropriate incentives and penalties must be put in place.
- Rather than sitting still there should be an emphasis on constant improvement to raise levels of productivity even further.

(c) The most obvious mechanism is the control and manipulation of organisational resources. Senior management can allocate resources in such a way that managers and departments are encouraged to embrace the new culture. This might be combined with the development of revised internal reporting systems so that resistance to change is highlighted and penalised in terms of performance measures.

Management might publicise its desire to change the culture within the company. Amongst other things, this could be raised as an issue by board members who are participating in interviews for promoted posts. Middle management might, therefore, be encouraged to align itself with the interests of this elite.

The company's systems need to be consistent with the whole process of change. If reporting and decision-making systems are based on the outmoded culture then it will persist and will, indeed, be viewed as the board's preferred approach.

The board might even resort to symbolic devices. Creating positive messages in support of those who embrace the changes and adapt to it will speed implementation more quickly.

214 CHAPTERLAND (NOV 07 EXAM)

(a) **Tutorial note:**

There are a number of approaches which you could take to this question and different models which could be used to frame an answer – the following answer uses one such model as an example. You do not need to quote a particular model but should cover similar points in your answer.

There are a number of reasons why employees resist change. Kotter and Schlesinger (1979) suggested that there are four reasons which explain why certain people resist change:

- parochial self-interest (some people are concerned with the implication of the change for themselves and how it may affect their own interests, rather than considering the effects for the success of the business)

- misunderstanding (communication problems, inadequate information)

- low tolerance to change (certain people are very keen on security and stability in their work)

- different assessments of the situation (some employees may disagree on the reasons for the change and on the advantages and disadvantages of the change process.

In the case of SW1, there is resistance to change from the university lecturers. Any of the above factors may be involved, as it is not clear how much has been explained to lecturers about the need for change and how much communication has taken place. There may well be misunderstandings and different perceptions of the need for change and the effect on the services provided within SW1. In particular, although it is not clear exactly what the proposals are, they may well have greater implications for the lecturers than for other groups. This will be discussed further in part (b).

The six change approaches set out by Kotter and Schlesinger is a model to prevent, decrease or minimise resistance to change in organisations. It suggests different possible approaches, all of which could have been used by the management of SW1:

- Participation – involving employees, usually by allowing some input into decision making, even designing their own jobs, pay structures, etc. There is no evidence that this method has been used.

- Education and communication – usually used as a background factor to reinforce another approach and based on the belief that communication about the benefits of change to employees will result in their acceptance of the need to exercise the changes necessary. There is nothing to suggest that SW1's management has attempted to educate the workforce about the benefits of the changes. It does not appear that there has been any direct communication between the management of SW1 and the employees either during negotiations or to resolve the current problem. If there had been, it is possible that there would have been more support for the proposals from the lecturers.

- Facilitation and support – employees may need to be counselled to help them overcome their fears and anxieties about change. Again, there is no evidence that this has been used.

- Manipulation and co-optation – covert attempts to sidestep potential resistance. Management can put forward proposals that deliberately appeal to the specific interest, sensitivities and emotions of the key groups involved in the change. Co-optation involves giving key people access to the decision-making process.

- Negotiation – enabling several parties with opposing interests to bargain. This bargaining leads to a situation of compromise and agreement. This is the main method which SW1's management has chosen to use to implement the changes; it has instructed a negotiating team to work with the unions to gain agreement to the proposals. The advantage of a negotiation strategy is that it offers the company the opportunity to note possible conflict and allows it to be dealt with in an orderly fashion. This hopefully prevents such problems as industrial action. Also, when an agreement has been made, the outcome can be to encourage commitment, preserve morale and maintain output. The main disadvantage is that this approach may be time-consuming and, should opposition be strong enough, the management might choose to adopt a power strategy instead. This appears to be what has happened in Chapterland – as the management of SW1 believe that negotiations are taking too long, they have reverted to the use of coercion (see below).

- Power/coercion – implementing change by compelling employees to agree. The advantages of this method are that changes can be made with speed and adhering to management's requirements is easy when opposition is weak from the workforce. The disadvantages include the lack of commitment of the workforce and determination to reverse policy when times change and also poor support resulting in weak motivation, low morale and performance. This is the main method being used in the wake of resistance to the change from the lecturers. In

the absence of any other softer approach, this may well cause alienation of
employees and low morale.

(b) The main ethical issues associated with the regional management's attempts to alter
pay and conditions are:

- fairness and consistency in dealing with staff

- legality of its actions

- responsibility to customers and clients

- issues related to morale of the staff.

Fairness

Changes to the pay and conditions need to be fair and consistent, and seen as such by
staff. Employees need to feel that the pay and conditions are fair and equitable, not
just in relation to other staff in the same organisation, but also in comparison with
pay received by others undertaking a similar role in other regions.

There may well be good business reasons for wanting staff in all areas to share
similar terms and conditions – however, this may not be seen as fair to the lecturers
in particular. They are likely to be looking at comparisons with staff in other
universities and other parts of the education sector, where fixed holidays and not
working at weekends is likely to be the norm. It could appear to staff that the
management is imposing the same arrangements on everyone even if this is not
required for the specific service – in this case, for example, it would be expected that
teaching would stop at certain times of the year in university vacations.

Another reason why the lecturers may feel that they have been treated unfairly is that
changes to the holiday arrangements and the introduction of weekend working will
have a significant impact on the lecturers' quality of life, which they may see as
much greater than the impact on traffic wardens of losing an allowance for
laundering their uniforms. Indeed, for other groups it appears that the benefits they
are losing are financial, and these are being replaced by financial compensation. In
the case of the lecturers, however, the benefits that they appear to be losing are not
financial and financial compensation may seem unfair.

It is also important that the management deals with all groups of staff in a consistent
manner – however, the lecturers appear to be the only group threatened with the sack
if they do not agree. Staff are also likely to see the threat as unreasonable and a
disproportionate reaction.

Legality of actions

The management of SW1 needs to ensure that its actions are legal. Depending on
employment law in Chapterland, it is possible that the actions proposed in terms of
considering that lecturers not accepting the new terms have resigned could constitute
unfair dismissal. It is likely that forcing employees to sign a new contract in this way
is illegal.

Responsibility to customers and clients

SW1 has a responsibility to provide a service to the community. The regional
management needs to consider the effect of its actions on its ability to provide this
service. For example, if the university loses a large number of its lecturing staff, this
will have a significant adverse impact on the students and their studies.

Impact on the morale of staff

The final issue which the management needs to consider is the effect on the morale
of its staff. The action towards the lecturing staff will inevitably have a detrimental
impact on their morale. However, it is also possible that, even if other staff are not

directly involved, their morale will be affected once they see the actions taken towards another group of employees, as this will convey a message about how the regional management values its staff.

(c) The performance management system will have a number of purposes, i.e. to recruit, retain and reward performance in order to motivate the staff. If it is to do this effectively, it is important that it is seen as:

- fair

- equitable

- comparable with internal and external comparators.

There are a number of challenges facing SW1's management in achieving this:

- The elements of any performance-related payment system are the pay – basic and bonus – and the benefits. The balance between each of these components will depend on the particular circumstances and requirements of the organisation. The first difficulty will be to decide this balance for SW1, which ensures that the basic salary is sufficient to attract staff, but that the proportion linked to performance is large enough to provide an incentive to perform well.

- Designing a system that works equally well across all parts of the organisation will be difficult. The different services will have different objectives and are likely to operate in different ways. The system will need to be sufficiently flexible to ensure that it can be adapted to respond to different requirements. The management will also need to have a clear understanding of what these requirements are.

- A further difficulty in designing the system will be deciding whether the system will be purely based on individual performance, or whether there is an element which should be based on the performance of groups or teams who need to work together to achieve objectives.

- If the system is to encourage performance in line with organisational objectives, it will be particularly important to ensure that the targets are based on objectives cascaded down from the strategic objectives.

- Different staff and staff groups will be motivated by different things – money may be more important to some kinds of employees than others. Understanding what motivates individuals can be difficult but needs to be done to ensure that the system does indeed encourage improved performance.

- To be effective, a performance-related reward system needs to be supported by an effective appraisal system. This may be difficult to establish, especially in areas of the organisation which have not traditionally taken this approach.

- It is often difficult to evaluate staff performance when the qualitative rather than the quantitative indicators are considered, such as in case of the lecturers. The emphasis on quantity, such as mark achieved, may have a negative effect on quality, such as knowledge acquired, as it will encourage lecturers to up the results or to focus on the examinable topics rather than the subjects as a whole.

- The system needs to be supported by employees. To ensure that this is the case, communication and involvement of staff in designing the scheme is important. This may be a challenge, particularly in the wake of the conflict which is likely to result from the adversarial approach taken to changing terms and conditions already.

OPERATIONS MANAGEMENT

215   YO (MAY 07 EXAM)

(a)   **Managing suppliers as part of a value system**

Most products reach the customer through activities carried out in more than one organisation. According to the value chain model developed by Michael Porter, within each organisation the physically and technologically distinct activities that an organisation performs form a value chain in which total revenue minus total costs of all activities undertaken to develop and market a product or service yields value. Porter argued that competitive advantage arises out of the ways in which firms organise and perform activities. The value chain describes how an organisation uses its inputs and transforms them into outputs, which customers are prepared to pay for.

All organisations in a particular industry will have a similar value chain, which will include activities such as obtaining raw materials, designing products, and building manufacturing facilities, developing co-operative agreements, and providing customer service. An organisation will be profitable as long as total revenues exceed the total costs incurred in creating and delivering the product or service. It is therefore necessary that organisations should strive to understand their value chain and also that of their competitors, suppliers, distributors, etc. These companies form a value network or system where value chains of individual companies are connected. In this case, the value chains of YO and MX are connected as part of a wider value system, with YO downstream of MX. YO interacts with suppliers of fabrics and other materials and MX interacts with the final customer.

It is important that the value system is managed to maximise performance and competitive advantage for the companies involved, which is what MX is trying to achieve. The reliability of its suppliers and the quality of their goods is key for the success of any retailer such as MX.

It appears that, in the past, the strategy that MX has used is to buy from many suppliers and to ensure that the 'company' is not dependent on any single supplier. This has probably enabled MX to keep the costs down as part of the strategy to sell high volumes at low process. If MX is to move 'upmarket' and sell a better quality range of goods at higher prices, the company now needs to work more closely with a smaller number of suppliers to ensure that clothing meets the higher quality requirements.

MX has therefore identified the need to concentrate on working with a smaller number of suppliers and to work more closely with YO, particularly with the designers, to ensure that the clothing which YO manufactures meets the requirements of MX's customers. In turn, as 80% of YO's sales are to MX, YO has an incentive to implement a TQM approach to secure a position as one of MX's preferred suppliers and receive higher prices for its goods. If MX manages the relationship with YO effectively and the two companies work together well, there is potential for improved value in the entire value system and improved competitive advantage, with both companies benefiting.

(b)   **Total quality management**

Ken Holmes *(Total Quality Management)* has defined quality as 'the totality of features and characteristics of a product or service which bears on its ability to meet stated or implied needs'. Quality is also normally seen in relation to price, and customers judge the quality of a product in relation to the price they have to pay. Customers will accept a product of lower design quality provided that the price is lower than the price of a better quality alternative.

Total quality management (TQM) is the name given to programmes which seek to ensure that goods are produced and services are supplied of the highest quality. Its origin lies primarily in Japanese organisations and it is argued that TQM has been a significant factor in Japanese global business success. The first definition of TQM in the US was given by Armand Feigenbaum in the 1950s in *Total Quality Control*. TQM is 'an effective system for integrating the quality development, quality maintenance and quality improvement efforts of various groups in an organisation so as to enable production and service at the most economical levels which allow for full customer satisfaction'.

- Total – means that everyone in the value chain is involved in the process, including employees, customers and suppliers.

- Quality – products and services must meet the customers' requirements.

- Management – management must be fully committed and encourage everyone else to become quality conscious.

As MX is its major customer, YO is heavily dependent on MX and has no choice but to focus on quality rather than its current price focus or lose the contract. There are a number of principles of quality management that YO needs to apply and which have requirements on the organisation. The following principles are set out in the ISO 9000 series of quality management standards.

Customer focus. There must be a customer focus. This means understanding and measuring the customer's, i.e. MX's, requirements, not just measuring customer satisfaction. This will come from YO's sales staff and designers working closely with MX.

Leadership. YO's management must take an active role in implementing and sustaining quality improvement and demonstrate that they are committed to it.

Involvement of people. YO's management must ensure that all employees are aware of how their activities contribute towards the achievement of quality objectives – not just the designers who will be more aware of MX's requirements, but the production staff as well.

Process approach. There should be a process-based approach to quality management. In a process-based approach, the business is seen as a series of individual processes, with outputs from one process sometimes being the input to another process. Management should seek to define and improve the interaction and linkages between the different processes. The entire company needs to work together to meet quality standards.

There should be a **system approach to management**. Management should not think departmentally.

- **Continuous improvement**. Total quality management demands continuous improvement of processes to maintain and improve performance and quality. This may involve the training of staff and equipping them with the skills to make improvements to their individual activities as well as developing a culture which encourages staff to identify problems and highlight issues which need to be resolved.

A **factual approach to decision-making**. Decisions affecting quality should be based on data about work processes that has been gathered and analysed.

Mutually beneficial supplier relationships. As with the relationship with MX, the relationship between YO and its suppliers needs to be based on openness and mutual trust, with a sharing of information about quality.

(c)   The result of MX's new strategy is that YO needs to focus more on quality rather than cost and this has implications for the way in which the people in the company approach their work.

Changes in the human resources practices

- Staff need to be trained in order that they develop an awareness of the need for quality and the importance of this in everyone's role. Employees may also need to be trained in specific quality-related skills such as problem-solving and analysis.

- Recruitment practices need to change to ensure that new staff have the skills required for improved quality and that new recruits appreciate the importance of quality. This may mean paying higher salaries to attract the right staff.

- In addition YO may have to recruit new designers who have the creativity to design more upmarket clothing.

- The company needs to introduce performance measures and reward systems which reflect the need for improved quality, rather than cost control and quantity of output (although this should not be ignored completely).

- Attention should be paid to the retention of staff who produce quality goods – this may mean developing new pay structures and increasing salaries of the best staff.

The attitude and behaviour of employees

In general, staff will need to work in different ways and with different priorities.

- Production staff (machinists and tailors) will need to focus on getting the product right the first time. They will also need to be continually aware of any issues relating to their part of the manufacture which prevent them producing quality clothing and be prepared to resolve the problem or report it.

- Designers need to work closely with MX and incorporate MX's ideas and requirements in their designs. They will need to be more creative as they are designing for a different market where the design itself is more important and cannot just be a copy of another designer's clothes.

- Buyers need to look for different suppliers who can supply better quality cloth and trimmings. This will be more important than cost which has been the priority in the past. They will also need to ensure that the materials meet MX's needs. The buyers will need new targets which reflect the new priority of finding reliable suppliers of quality materials.

- Sales staff will need to develop a closer working relationship with MX. They will also need to find new customers, for the proportion of YO's output not bought by MX, who are also looking for better quality clothing but are prepared to pay more for it.

- Managers need to lead from the top and support the staff in changing the way in which they work, demonstrating that high quality work is valued within YO.

216   PRODUCTION SCHEDULING

(a)   When batch production is based on economic batch quantity sizes, each batch size for a particular product is the same. The batch size is the quantity that minimises total annual inventory costs, which are assumed to consist of inventory holding costs and batch set-up costs. However, the Economic Batch Quantity (EBQ) formula is based on the assumption that the demand for the item is constant each day, week or month, and in addition there are no costs from stock-outs.

A levelled scheduling system is based on different assumptions. It is assumed that demand is fairly predictable, over the short term at least, but might vary from one period to another. In the case of VB Production, weekly demand for each product is forecast to vary over the next four weeks. Production is therefore scheduled as a constant amount each week over the planning period. In the case of VB Production, this means that if the next four weeks are taken as the planning period, weekly production would be 4,750 units of Product A, 9,500 units of Product B and 6,000 units of Product C.

An advantage of a levelled scheduling system is that it may be possible to operate a continuous production process, with no lost time between batches (because the production process is continuing all the time). However, whether or not this is possible will depend on the output capacity of the production process, and whether or not the three products are made on the same machines or on different machines.

If the company moved from production of the three products in economic batch quantities to a levelled scheduling system, management would have to consider the following issues.

- With an EBQ system, there is usually an inventory re-order level, and a new batch of items is produced as soon as the inventory quantity falls to this level. With levelled scheduling, a system is required for ensuring that there is adequate inventory available to meet demand (unless stock-outs are acceptable). This could be a particular problem when the scheduled production quantities in any week are less than the expected sales demand. For example, if the scheduled weekly production of Product A is 4,750 units each week, 9,500 units will be produced in weeks 1 and 2, when total sales demand is expected to be 11,000 units.

- There should also be a good practical or economic reason for switching from batch production in economic batch quantities to levelled production scheduling. One potential reason is to achieve a continuous production process for all three products, with no down times between batches. However, if the three products would still be manufactured in batches, it is not clear whether levelled production scheduling would bring any benefits. Management needs to recognise that the most appropriate production scheduling system will vary according to circumstances.

(b) With a levelled scheduling system, production is scheduled at a constant rate in each period to meet anticipated demand. It is a volume-based system of production scheduling, where the focus of attention is on quantities manufactured in each period. With JIT production, in contrast, production is initiated by actual demand rather than anticipated demand, and the focus of attention is on the rate at which items can be produced. Whereas levelled production scheduling is a volume based scheduling system, JIT is a rate-based system.

It is by no means clear how a JIT production system would benefit VB Production. Sales demand for each of the three products varies each week, but demand quantities seem fairly large. This suggests that sales orders for each product are received regularly. When orders for a product are received regularly, such that production has to be regular, some of the goals of JIT production become unachievable. For example, JIT production has an ideal batch size of one, and production is scheduled for specific orders as they are received.

To achieve JIT production when sales demand is fairly continuous, but sales volumes vary from week to week, there would need to be a system of regulating the production flow up or down in response to demand, so that sales demand can be met quickly without having any inventory from which to meet the demand.

JIT production involves more than simply responding to customer orders, eliminating inventory, production flexibility and speed of throughput. It is also concerned with quality and reliability in production and the elimination of waste. As with continuous improvement, the success of a JIT system requires the participation and involvement of employees, and a change of culture within the organisation, towards one of eliminating waste, flexible work practices and ensuring speedy throughput. A change to JIT would therefore need careful planning, the total commitment of senior management, and full co-operation from all the employees affected. This is likely to require some time to achieve.

217 PIPE DREAM

(a) The main features of TQM are as follows.

(i) The primary aim within a system of TQM is to meet the needs and requirements of customers and achieve full customer satisfaction. Juran argued that having identified its customers' needs, an entity should develop products that meet those needs and it should seek to optimise the product features so that they meet the needs of the entity as well as those of its customers. The entity should then develop a process for making the product, and should optimise the process.

(ii)   TQM should be applied to all aspects of an entities activities, not just to production operations, and to all employees, whatever their job.

(iii)   TQM must involve everyone within the organisation, and there must be a commitment to quality from everyone. To achieve this commitment, there must be committed leadership and a change of organisational culture. The concept of empowerment of employees is very closely associated with TQM: management must give more power to employees to make their own decisions, and should learn to trust them to do what is best.

(iv)   All quality-related costs should be measured and managed. These costs can be classified as prevention costs, inspection costs, internal failure costs and external failure costs. An aim should be to minimise the total of these costs. In TQM, the view is that by investing in prevention, total quality costs will be minimised. In the long-run, it is cheaper to prevent poor quality than to look out for it or rectify the problem when something goes wrong. Crosby developed the concept of 'getting things right first time', so that failures do not happen.

(v)   An entity must develop systems for monitoring quality performance and to support quality improvements. Deming is associated with developing systems of statistical quality measurement and statistical quality control. Establishing quality standards and monitoring actual performance against those standards has also led to the development of international quality standards (for example, the ISO 9000 series).

(b)   The main problems with introducing TQM into operations are likely to be getting the total commitment of senior management and the willing support of employees. A radical change is needed in culture and in attitudes towards the customer and quality. For management, the changes must involve greater empowerment to employees and greater trust.

Since the cultural changes required are so large, it might take time to introduce a system of TQM successfully.

A starting point should probably be to win the enthusiastic support of management. Managers should be given training in TQM concepts and practices, so that they understand what TQM is about and what they, as managers, should be expected to do. Without the full support of management, employees are unlikely to be persuaded that TQM is worthwhile.

Although TQM and continuous improvement are not the same, it might be appropriate to adopt some of the concepts of continuous improvement. In particular, the entity might introduce '5S practice', to improve the quality of the work environment.

Employees need to understand the importance of meeting quality standards, and the entity should establish quality standards for its operations. Employees should be encouraged to achieve the quality standards, and actual performance should be reviewed against the targets. The principles of Six Sigma might be introduced, so that statistical quality control is applied throughout the production process, and the levels of waste and defective output are reduced to minimal levels.

Quality should perhaps be written into all of the entity's procedures and systems. A criticism of TQM is that it might become too bureaucratic and procedure-led. Nevertheless, the entity might benefit from reviewing its management of quality systems, in accordance with the ISO 9001: *2000 guidelines*.

(c)   The emphasis in TQM is on the prevention of mistakes. Arguably, it could be almost as wasteful to incur additional costs on manufacturing goods to an unnecessarily small tolerance as it would to waste money on correcting defects or scrapping waste products. For example, if Pipe Dream's customers require pipes of a particular length, plus or minus two millimetres, there is no need to aim to manufacture pipes that are within a tenth of a millimetre of the specification. Making pipes that were that close to the target might offer advantages if there were no cost associated with doing so, but otherwise the company should develop processes that are intended to get all output to within the intended standards of output.

TQM is essentially about understanding the needs of customers (both internal and external) and working towards meeting those needs. For example, a motorist who wishes to purchase an inexpensive car might be prepared to tolerate the use of cheaper materials in trimming and decorating the interior of the car, but might still prize durability and reliability in the car itself. There is no need for a car manufacturer who is aiming at the cheaper end of the market to produce cars that are built to the same standard as those produced by the manufacturers of premium markets.

Tutorial note

It can be a matter of some confusion that concerns for customer requirements and for quality/no waste are common to several operations management approaches – notably TQM, JIT and continuous improvement. The question here asks about TQM, and the answer therefore does not mention continuous improvement, introducing a system of quality circles, kanban systems and the control of production flow, or lean manufacturing. Before you take the examination, it would probably be a good idea to establish clearly in your own mind which operations management practice you associate with each 'ideology'.)

218   URBAN DANCE

(a)   There are three types of benchmarking that the company might consider: internal benchmarking, competitive benchmarking and activity benchmarking.

Internal benchmarking is based on the assumption that within an organisation, there are several different units performing very similar activities. In the case of Urban Dance, the company operates a number of dance schools. It is also assumed that some units will perform better than others, at least in certain respects.

The internal benchmarking process therefore involves comparing the performance of the different units with each other. The aim is to identify 'best practice', and the ways in which one unit is performing better than the others. It should then be possible to apply the best practice in the other units, and so improve the performance of the company as a whole.

In order to carry out any benchmarking exercise, it is important to identify key aspects of performance for measurement, and having done this, to establish one or more suitable measures. The benchmarking exercise involves measuring these pre-determined aspects of performance, and analysing the differences and their causes.

A limitation of internal benchmarking, however, is its assumption that best practice can be identified within the entity itself. In practice, this might not be the case. All the schools of Urban Dance might use similar sub-optimal practices and achieve sub-optimal performance. Comparing their performance might therefore fail to reveal any information of value.

Competitive benchmarking is based on similar general principles as internal benchmarking, but with the significant difference that one or more competitors are selected for comparison. The external benchmark should be a successful competitor, preferably a successful dance school company with schools in the same areas as the Urban Dance schools, or a company that attracts its students from the same 'pool' of potential applicants.

The aim of competitive benchmarking is to establish whether the competitor performs better in the key performance areas, and if it does, to consider ways of removing the 'gap', and bringing performance up to or above the level of the competitor. If the company is able to do this, it should become more competitive, and more successful.

However, the success of competitive benchmarking depends of obtaining useful information about the performance of the main competitors. Rival dance schools are unlikely to volunteer the information, and it would therefore be necessary to obtain information for comparison from whatever reliable sources there might be.

Activity benchmarking, also called 'best practice' benchmarking or process benchmarking, is based on the view that it is not necessary to compare practices with similar types of organisation. Useful information about best practice can be obtained by comparing particular activities within the entity with similar activities in different types of entity. For example, Urban Dance might establish performance measurements for student recruitment activities with similar activities of a music school, or an art school or a private boarding school. Activities relating to normal academic education might be compared with similar teaching in a normal but successful academic school.

Activity benchmarking can help an entity to identify weaknesses in particular areas of its activities. The entity therefore needs to be aware of weaknesses that exist, in order to look for another entity that would be willing to provide the benchmark for that particular activity. The co-operation of the other entity is also required, but this is realistically more achievable than with competitive benchmarking.

(b) The following initial steps should be taken by management of Urban Dance:

(i) Senior management need to identify the fact that there are probably weaknesses in operations that can be identified and rectified by means of benchmarking.

(ii) A decision has to be made about what type of benchmarking would be most appropriate in the circumstances. If internal benchmarking is selected, management would be assuming that best practice was already being achieved in some if its schools. If competitive benchmarking is preferred, management need to recognise that one or more competitors are performing better, and that the differences in performance need to be identified. The choice of activity benchmarking would be appropriate only if management know which activities they wish to improve.

(iii) Having decided which type of benchmarking method to use, the company needs to plan the exercise. With internal benchmarking, the management of the individual schools will probably have to be consulted, and involved in the process. With activity benchmarking, an external organisation to act as the benchmark needs to be identified, and its co-operation obtained.

(iv) The key areas of performance for benchmarking, and the measures of performance that will be used, should also be planned, at least in outline.

(c) Benchmarking has the potential to create problems if it is mismanaged.

Performance measures must be comparable, otherwise the results may lead to costly distractions and mistakes. For example, measuring performance standards in a an area such as dance will be subjective. Different instructors may mark to different standards and generate results that are not comparable.

Benchmarking may also be difficult when the inputs are different. For example, one school might draw heavily from a catchment area where the local state schools place a great deal of emphasis on dance. Students referred from those schools might appear to be progressing more rapidly than those at another school where the local conditions are very different.

Benchmarking also requires the ability to rank different outcomes so that targets are realistic. For example, a competitive benchmark comparing performance in dance and academic subjects might reveal that some schools perform better in the former and others in the latter. That might suggest that schools which focus on dance tend not to devote sufficient time and resources to academic subjects and vice versa. Urban Dance should avoid trying to equal the best performance in both areas unless it can find some means of dealing with the inherent conflict between the two.

219 VIRTUAL

If a company adopts a strategy of becoming 'virtual', its aim is to manage all the operations involved in creating products or services and delivering them to customers, without becoming involved directly in any of those activities. The small number of employees/managers within the virtual company simply focus on their core strengths, which might be to manage the supply chain. A virtual company has no obvious centre, and might consist of individuals linked by computer networks and telephones.

However, in order to deliver products to the customer, there must be operational activities. Resources have to be converted into finished products. If a virtual company does not perform these activities itself, the work must be outsourced to an external organisation. In theory, all activities could be outsourced, and the virtual company would then need to manage its agreements and arrangements with its external suppliers and service providers.

The traditional function of purchasing is concerned with buying items from external suppliers, and getting the best deal available, such as the lowest purchase price. With supply chain management, the approach is different. An entity looks not just at its immediate relationship with its suppliers, but at the entire supply chain from raw materials to finished product, and looks for ways of improving it and adding more value. This will often involve developing long-term relationships with key suppliers, and co-operating to improve elements of the supply chain, and new product developments.

In a virtual company, the entire supply chain is operated by external organisations. Managing this supply chain therefore involves persuading other organisations to deliver supplies efficiently, so that the desired end-product reaches the end-customer on time.

Global sourcing has been made more possible by the Internet and by improvements in the transportation of goods. The Internet allows an entity to identify suppliers in different countries more easily, and to obtain information about them. E-mail and other communication methods allow an entity to communicate with suppliers in any other country. Improved transportation systems mean that goods produced in one part of the world can be shipped to other countries at reasonable cost and within reasonable time frames.

In theory, a virtual company could manage a global network of suppliers and logistics firms, to produce consumer products and deliver them to markets anywhere in the world. However, the virtual company needs to remain an essential element within the overall value chain. It is crucial that the virtual company should remain in control of one or more vital elements of the chain: for example, it might retain control over sales and distribution channels and control over the brand name. With consumer durable products, it is probably also essential to retain a direct interest in product design activities.

A successful virtual company therefore needs to be efficient in managing the sequences of processes that go into making and delivering products or services. Key skills are therefore the management of outsourcing, the management of the supply chain or value chain, developing a successful global supply network, and remaining innovative and competitive.

MARKETING

220 MARKETING FUNCTION: CONCEPTS

(a) Any discussion on marketing mix will include consideration of the 'Four Ps'. These are product, price, promotion and place (or distribution). Their main characteristics are as follows.

Product – is anything that is offered to the market for use or consumption. Factors to be taken into account will include quality, any branding, variety, special features, style, packaging and fashion. Generally, people want to acquire the benefits of a product so they will also be looking for the characteristics of guarantees, after-sales service and general reliability.

Price – is important because it is the only element that produces revenue. Normally this will be characterised by reference to being fixed to both market conditions and also costs of production. Other characteristics will embrace discount policy for quantity or early payment, as a 'weapon' in the introduction of a new product or complementing another line, and also trade-in allowances.

Promotion – is the way in which the product is drawn to the attention of the market place. It covers advertising in all its forms (e.g. press, commercial TV, outdoor hoardings, etc), personal selling, sales promotions and publicity through media coverage.

Place – the purpose of this is to get the product to the consumer, hence the alternative names of placement and distribution. Its characteristics are the channels of distribution and the physical distribution activities. It is also concerned with the location of sales outlets and the infrastructure of warehousing and transport facilities.

(b) The scenario given is one where the skilful application of the four Ps has meant new life for an attraction with declining popularity. Working in the favour of the manager is the fact that with increased prosperity and leisure time for many people, there are opportunities to retrieve the situation and to exploit the attraction very profitably. Two obvious examples in the UK are Alton Towers and Madame Tussauds.

It is essential to recognise that one element on its own cannot be manipulated to give success. It is important that each element be considered as part of the overall approach and that the effect be co-ordinated to ensure improvement. However, for ease of presentation, it may be appropriate to consider each item individually.

Product – the manager must consider just what he is selling and what is so special about his product that encourages tourists to travel to visit the attraction, sometimes at very great expense, e.g. a walk in the main street of Stratford-upon-Avon on any summer's day will confirm the worldwide interest in this particular product. Here, of course, the products are all associated with William Shakespeare and this is very skilfully exploited by the theatre, the Shakespeare Trust properties and all the other attractions that constitute 'the product'.

With this example, the basic concept underpinning what the tourist expects is self-evident. For a museum or theme park, the manager must carefully research the product. Does the visitor want an educational visit, an 'experience', a 'white-knuckle' ride or passive entertainment? Possibly the visitor might want all of these. There are many examples where museums have changed their image, so that instead of passively viewing relics, people can actively experience some of the items on display.

Once the manager has determined his underpinning approach, he can consider what other complementary facilities should be provided. Obvious ones are good rest areas, souvenir stalls, convenient catering provisions and possibly even hire of cameras (as in Tussauds). If the quality is good, there is every likelihood that the additional revenue earned would greatly enhance the profitability of the attraction.

Price – coupled with any changes or developments in the image for the theme park or the museum must be reconsideration of the pricing policy. Typical problems that need to be addressed are as follows.

(i)   How does the price level proposed compare with competing attractions? Will it be seen as value for money?

(ii)   Should there be one overall admission price covering all activities, or would a separate admission charge with extra tickets for rides and other attractions be more appropriate?

(iii)   Will the price level proposed and the estimated attendance ensure that a profit is made?

(iv)   What family schemes, concessions for children and senior citizens, or coach parties, should be arranged?

(v)   A popular development is the provision of package deals for admission and overnight accommodation, e.g. Legoland, Seaside Sun centres, etc. Would this be possible?

(vi)   Should there be different peak charges at weekend and bank holidays?

(vii)   Would the price level be acceptable both to home visitors as well as overseas tourists?

(viii) What price should be charged for franchises such as food and souvenir kiosks?

Promotion – here the concern must initially be with the development of the 'product' and the image it is to portray. Is it a family day out or an educational experience, or should the 'fun' aspect be stressed? Once decided, then the most appropriate means of promotion must be determined. Several outlets might be used. For example, press and commercial television advertising would be satisfactory to attract home visitors but are unlikely to be seen by overseas tourists. Hence, knowledge of what most people do on their first night of a holiday would be appropriate. After unpacking, many people congregate in the reception area of the hotel or campsite picking up leaflets for the local attractions - and this approach was found to be one of the most effective in promoting the new image of Tussauds. Where a small discount token is printed in the leaflet, than it is found that many people cannot resist this bargain.

Place – as the theme park or museum is in a fixed location, particularly in the short to medium term, then consideration of channels of distribution is inappropriate. There are other elements, which may be explored, such as exploitation of the location, and the provision of car parking and conveniences for public transport. Market segmentation is considered under this heading and here there can be opportunities to attract different consumers at different times. One example is the use of a holiday camp for different activities at varying times of the year: for example, holidays during the period April to September and conferences outside these dates. If the marketing manager reconsiders the approach under these headings and is bold in his approach, then popularity of the attraction will be high again. However, having once carried out this exercise, he must not 'rest on his laurels' as people are continually looking for new experiences and he must work all the time to maintain the position.

221   GREEN COMPANY

(a)   A company needs a reasonably reliable estimate of the total size of a market, both within the regional markets or market segments that it currently operates, and possibly in other regions and segments too. This will enable the company to assess its market share, and its competitive position within its markets. Knowing market share will also help the company to decide on an appropriate marketing mix.

For example, if the total market is large and the company estimates that it only has a small market share, it might consider focusing on one segment of the market, and developing a marketing mix that will appeal to customers in the targeted segment. On the other hand, if the total market is fairly small but the company has a large market share, the marketing strategy might aim at trying to protect the market share against competition.

If the total size of the market is known (and total sales within each market segment are also known), it is a simple task to calculate market share. The main difficulty is estimating the size of the total market.

The total size of a market might be estimated in a number of ways:

(i)   In some industries, there might be a suppliers' association (a voluntary association of manufacturers). Where there is such an association, members might have agreed to an arrangement whereby each provides confidential information about their annual sales revenue to the association, which then calculates the total annual sales of its members. If the members operating this scheme represent a substantial proportion of total sales to the market, a reasonable estimate of total market sales can then be given by the association to the participating members. It is not clear here whether or not Green Company has such a manufacturers' association for its particular industry.

(ii)   The company's sales team or marketing team can try to establish from their main distributors what percentage of the total sales of the distributors are for products of the Green Company, and what proportion of their sales are sales of competitors' products. This will enable the company to assess its share of the market in the sales distribution channels that it uses. Having estimated its market share, a total size of the market can be calculated. Since the number of distributors for the company's products is probably fairly small, a reliable sample could be asked to provide information. However, distributors are under no obligation to provide such information.

(iii)   Some information might be obtained by the sales force simply by discussing sales and marketing issues with distributors, or providing information about distributors who do not sell the products of Green Company. However, this information would be difficult to convert into a numerical estimate of market size.

(iv)   If the company's main competitors file annual accounts, some information about total market sales might be obtained from this source, by looking at the sales revenue data. However, it is unlikely that rival companies will provide sales information in their annual report and accounts in a form that is usable by their competitors.

(v)   It might be possible to establish estimates of market size and market share from a market research exercise in which consumers are asked about their buying habits. However, for gardening equipment, it is by no means certain that reliable data could be obtained in this way, since consumers do not buy gardening equipment regularly, and are probably not as 'brand aware' as with frequently-purchased consumer goods.

(b) A company selling gardening equipment will sell mainly through distributors, such as garden centres. There are several ways that the company might use to forecast sales demand for the new products.

(i)   The company could try to establish which of its distributors are likely to sell the new products, and what they expect their purchase quantities to be. This would be a form of survey of buyers' opinions. Opinions could be obtained by members of the sales force in discussion with their contacts in distributor organisations.

(ii)   The sales force might be asked to give their view of the likely demand for the new products, based on their experience of the market and customers. The views of the different sales representatives can then be compared, and a 'composite' view of expected sales can be estimated.

(iii) It might be possible to obtain the opinions of potential customers, by carrying out a market test in a limited number of distribution outlets. Test marketing will help the company to judge what sales might be if and when the products are introduced to the entire market.

(iv)   If the new products are similar to products that have been launched in the past, it might be possible to predict sales on the assumption that the growth in sales will be similar to the pattern of sales for new products in the past. However, this is probably an unreliable method of sales forecasting for new products, since there is no way of being sure whether the products will be well-received in the market.

(v)   It might also be possible to obtain an 'expert opinion' about sales by asking for the views of experienced managers within the company.

(vi)   The company should assess social trends. Long-term changes in demand might be predicted by looking at the types of houses that are being built. If there is a trend towards smaller gardens then that might have implications for the types of gardening equipment that might sell well. If there are fewer gardening programmes on television or sales of magazines are declining, then that could signal a decline in consumer interest.

(vii) The company should investigate historical relationships between sales and factors that might have had an influence on sales levels. For example, if sales were depressed when mortgage interest rates were high, then that suggests customer demand is affected by disposable income. Forecasts of economic trends might then be used to identify potential changes in demand.

222   RESTFUL HOTELS

(a)   There are several ways in which pricing can be used as an element in marketing.

- Restful Hotels might be able to promote itself as a low cost hotel for the quality of service provided, but without putting the four star ratings at risk. The company could then market its hotels as the cheapest in their area for the quality of services provided. To succeed with this pricing strategy, Restful Hotels would need to control costs.

- There are difficulties in generating revenue at new hotels. It might be appropriate to use promotion (for example, web site advertising) to boost the business at these hotels. However, if price is used as a marketing tool, it might be appropriate to charge low room rates until demand is more established, or offering special room prices for a short period of time. For example, it might be possible to have sales promotions offering cut-price rooms at any Restful Hotel in the world to customers who book before a specified date.

- The company should also consider charging different prices in different locations, such as higher prices in city centre hotels than at holiday resorts, because the type of customer is likely to differ between the different types of location.

- It might also be possible to have differential pricing, with room prices varying according to the day of the week or the season of the year.

- Another form of price differentiation to win more customers might be to offer special price deals for pensioners or even students.

- To improve the 'value for money' marketing message, it might be more appropriate to offer more services free of charge (within the room charge), rather than to lower prices. Examples of free add-on services might be a courtesy bus from airport to hotel at holiday resorts.

(b)   The hotel market is segmented in different ways. One method of segmentation is to classify hotels according to quality (number of 'stars') and price. However, a policy of moving from a portfolio of four-star hotels, say to a portfolio of five-star hotels or a mixed portfolio of four-star and three-star hotels, will take time to implement.

If market segmentation is to succeed within a fairly short space of time in boosting total sales revenue, marketing strategy should probably focus on creating a stronger appeal to a sector of the market that does not currently take accommodation at Restful Hotels.

Sectors of the market for hotel rooms might be analysed, for example, as business users, conference participants, and holiday makers. If the hotel group does not currently attract, say, conference business, it might consider a marketing initiative to promote this type of business. If room occupancy is low at weekends, it might be appropriate to promote 'bargain' weekend breaks.

There might also be opportunities for focussing on customers for other services of the hotel, other than rooms. For example, the company might consider developing its restaurant service and promoting these to the general public.

(c)   The company is aiming for the premium range of hotel accommodation. Cutting prices might attract some customers who were previously unwilling to pay market rates for a four star hotel, but might put off some of the company's existing customer base as staying at a Restful Hotels hotel will no longer have the same degree of exclusivity. It might also mean that existing customers are forced to share the hotel with a less select group of residents.

Reducing prices might create a loss of revenue and there is no guarantee that it will generate additional volume. The change in prices might have to be managed so that the reductions are offered in a discreet manner. For example, the 'rack rate' offered at the reception desk for any customer who contacts the hotel directly might remain unchanged, but the discount offered to travel agents could be increased so that the agents can enjoy a bigger commission from each sale. That might give them an incentive to send more customers to Restful Hotels.

The other big danger with cutting prices is that Restful Hotels might then trigger a price war with competing hotel chains. If competitors start to lose business they might cut their own prices, leaving Restful Hotels no more competitive than before but enjoying less profit from each and every sale.

223   CM BREAKFAST FOODS (NOV 06 EXAM)

Requirement (a)

Marketing issues. The involvement of the founder creates the risk that the company takes a production-oriented approach rather than a marketing orientation. If the focus is on selling existing products or the development of new products that are essentially the same as existing products, then the company might fail to spot changes in consumer taste and buying patterns until it is too late. Sales levels have already peaked and this trend is unlikely to reverse itself unless the company takes some active measures.

The company's products have a reputation for being unhealthy at a time when the health implications of diet are coming under increasing scrutiny.

Selling what are essentially the same products as supermarket 'own brands' is a dangerous strategy because of the risk that consumers might recognise the similarity (or be alerted to it by an article in a magazine) and buy the cheaper brands in preference to the branded.

Ethical issues. The company has enjoyed some success because of a family link to a major customer. That customer's board might be unhappy if it were to discover that it was buying heavily from a supplier who had been selected in this way. It might be better for CM to ensure that full disclosure of the relative's involvement is made and that the terms and conditions of the supply of goods have been on a normal arm's length basis.

The company actively sells to children via the packaging, use of gifts and advertising. This is a dubious ethical proposition at present. The fact that the products contain a heavy concentration of salt and sugar increases the risks because of concerns about childhood obesity.

Requirement (b)

The first step is for CM to conduct a strategic analysis of its strengths and weaknesses, its core competences and its resources. This should be drafted in the context of the company's external environment, emphasising issues such as brand recognition, the established distribution chain, etc. This analysis should be thorough and could involve commissioning detailed market research into the attitudes of various consumer groups. CM should not necessarily be thinking in terms of continuing with all of its existing product range at this stage, nor should it discount the possibility of using its expertise to diversify into complementary lines of business. The threat posed by the North American competitor must be analysed. If competing directly is likely to be uneconomic, then CM might have to face up to withdrawing from some of its traditional markets and make best use of its strengths in other areas.

Once the market has been analysed, CM should consider making a set of strategic choices as to which markets to compete in and how. This could leave the company faced with some difficult choices because of the involvement of the founder and the historical attachments to certain markets. The company may decide to carry on much as before, but only after carefully considering the economic merits of doing so. The market can be segmented geographically, by branded versus own goods, by product line and so on. CM must decide where to focus its efforts in the future and then decide on an appropriate marketing mix (product, price, promotion and place) for each. One issue that must be decided quickly is the company's response to the health concerns associated with the product (should it reduce the sugar and salt content?).

Finally, CM must decide how to implement its strategy. Detailed plans and budgets will have to be developed. Decisions should be taken about targets for sales, market share and brand recognition in different markets. These should be translated into advertising and production schedules. A set of benchmarks and a reporting system will have to be developed in order to monitor progress against the plan.

224 TROY BOATS

(a)   The elements or stages of brand positioning might be described as follows.

- Brand definition. The product supplier needs to create an awareness in the mind of consumers what the brand represents, and what type of product will be sold under the brand name. Initially, this will probably mean associating the brand with a fairly narrow range of products. Over time, however, an established brand might be extended to cover a wider range of different products.

- Brand differentiation. When consumers know what a brand represents, the next stage in developing the brand is to differentiate it from the brands of rival products. The aim should be to create a clear and meaningful idea in the minds of consumers how the company's branded products differ from those of rivals. If there is no differentiation, consumers will presumably base their purchasing decision on other factors such as price and convenience. Typically, brands might be differentiated on the basis of product features and price.

- Deepening a brand. With very successful brands, the brand eventually becomes associated in the mind of consumers with their own personal goals and values. This is known as deepening the brand. This process creates strong brand loyalties, and buyers of the brand will continue to do so. For example, a branded range of food items that are differentiated on the basis of 'organic' foods might become associated in the mind of a segment of the market with 'healthy eating and healthy living'. Brand extension becomes easier once a brand has been deepened.

- Defending the brand. Branded products are sold in highly competitive markets. Once a brand has been established and has become successful, it needs to be defended against rival products and new marketing initiatives by competitors.

(b)   To establish an Argo 0 brand, the company needs to decide first of all what range of boats should be sold under this brand name. The aim of brand definition should be to associate the brand name with a particular type of product. There might be a risk that if the company uses the brand name for all the boats that it makes, from small sailing boats up to large motor cruisers, customers will not define the Argo 0 brand clearly in their minds. An alternative approach to brand definition is to start by applying the brand name to a particular range of boats.

If the process of achieving brand identification is successful, the company can go on to create brand differentiation. Since there are no other branded products in the market at the moment, the company must decide how the Argo 0 boats should be presented to customers as being different from the boats made by any other manufacturer. The positioning of the brand in its market might be on the basis of price or quality, or particular design features.

If the company is successful in creating a successful differentiated brand, the next step is to try to deepen the brand. This might be possible by associating the Argo 0 brand with a particular lifestyle that customers would like for themselves, such as 'freedom to get away' or 'life of luxury and leisure'. If the process of brand deepening is successful, the company might be able to extend the brand name to other types of boat.

A successful brand needs defending, often by means of advertising and sales promotion. The company should develop a suitable marketing mix to promote its branded products, for example through regular magazine advertising, and displaying its boats at boat shows, exhibitions and trade fairs. Continual product improvement would also be desirable.

(c)   Creating a brand name requires some means of bringing the brand name and the qualities that the brand espouses to the attention of potential buyers and also to those who might be in a position to influence buying decisions (e.g. journalists). That could be a very costly process. For example, advertising in boating magazines is one option, but it could be a very costly matter and the adverts will have to continue for some time before brand awareness might be developed. The company could also establish a presence at major exhibitions and trade conferences, but that is also an expensive option and one that could generate very few immediate sales, requiring an ongoing commitment.

Potential customers might be wary of committing themselves to a purchase of this type from a relatively unknown supplier when there are better established brands in the market. This is not merely a highly expensive considered purchase, but one that might involve literally staking one's life on the product's reliability. Existing buyers might be happy to trade with Troy Boats because it is a well-established local supplier, but it might be very difficult to branch out into wider markets without this sense of local awareness.

225 4QX (NOV 07 EXAM)

(a) Organisational performance will be dependent on the successful management of the opportunities, challenges and risks presented by changes in the external environment. No organisation exists in a vacuum, therefore it will be affected and will have an effect on its environment. By identifying and understanding the changes within the environment, 4QX will be able to adjust its operations to ensure long-term company profitability and survival.

There are a number of ways of classifying the different aspects of the environment. This analysis divides the business environment into four related but separate systems – political and legal, economic, social and technical (PEST).

The political and legal environment

Regulations governing business are widespread; they include those on health and safety, information disclosure, the dismissal of employees, vehicle emissions, use of pesticides and many more. Changes in the law can affect organisations in many ways. For example, a tightening of health and safety legislation may increase costs and premises failing to meet the higher standards could be closed down. Political factors can also have a direct impact on the way a business operates. Decisions made by government affect our everyday lives and can come in the form of policy or legislation.

In the case of the centre, a number of influences will be relevant. These include:

- the tax incentives to keep the population healthy – the centre may be able to take advantage of these but they may also encourage more competition

- any schemes set up to enable healthcare providers to pay the centre for exercise schemes for patients which could be a potential source of income

- changes in the legislation relating to children swimming unaccompanied – the existing legislation already has an impact on the services offered by the centre.

- the activities of the local council – if the decision were taken to upgrade the public facilities, this would have an impact on the demand for the use of the centre.

The economic environment

All businesses are affected by economical factors nationally and globally, such as interest rates. In addition, the economic climate dictates how consumers may behave within society. Whether an economy is in a boom, recession or recovery will affect consumer confidence and behaviour. When the economy is booming consumer confidence and spending is high. This will have a significant impact on the centre as membership of such facilities is often seen as a luxury and is likely to be one of the first items of expenditure which families cut back on when finances are under pressure. Particular issues for the centre are:

- a healthy local economy which means that confidence and spending are high. Families and other local residents are more likely to sign up as members of the centre. This will also affect the price which they are prepared to pay for memberships and visits to the centre

- changes in the environment will affect the business at the centre – it will therefore be necessary for the management of the centre to pay close attention to the economic environment

- a booming economy may also attract new competitors.

The social environment

Forces within society such as family, friends and media can affect our attitude, interest and opinions. These forces shape who we are as people and the way we behave and what we ultimately purchase. Population changes also have a direct impact on all organisations – changes in the structure of a population will affect the supply and demand of goods and services within an economy. In addition, as society changes and as behaviours change, organisations must be able to offer products and services that aim to complement and benefit people's lifestyle and behaviour.

In the case of the centre:

- Attitudes are changing towards diet and health. As a result there is likely to be an increase in the number of people joining fitness clubs. There is also concern in many countries about the lack of exercise that young people are obtaining. This will have a significant impact on the demand for the centre's facilities.

- The attitude of the local population will also affect the kind of services which they are looking for and their expectations of service quality. The centre may be able to offer classes as well as memberships for example.

- The lifestyle of potential customers will also affect the means by which the centre markets itself. For example, if people are used to networking, then a significant amount of business may come by word of mouth, and the centre could perhaps offer incentives to members to introduce their friends.

The technological environment

Organisations need to be constantly aware of what is going on in the technological environment.

For the centre, technological change could influence the following:

- the type of equipment which the centre can install and the expectations of customers – if increasingly sophisticated equipment is available the centre may find that it has to invest in upgraded equipment to keep customers happy

- the cost of equipment

- new systems which could improve the efficiency of managing the centre

- different ways of marketing the centre and communicating with customers, such as the internet and email.

(b) Market segmentation is the division of a total market into distinct groups or sections. Buyers within each group should share common characteristics that will make them similar in their needs and preferences for products or services, or similar in the way in which they might react to a particular marketing initiative or marketing mix. A challenge for the marketing management is to segment the market in a useful way. To be useful, a group of buyers or potential customers must respond differently from buyers in other market segments to the way a product is priced, or to the quality or features of the product, or to the way it is promoted, advertised or distributed.

If the centre is to segment the market, it needs to divide customers into subgroups which are:

- measurable – that is, the different characteristics can be measured

- accessible – customers in the segment can be easily reached

- substantial enough so that the cost of segmentation does not exceed the benefits.

Markets can be segmented on the basis of a variety of different characteristics, such as:

- demographics (age, socio-economic characteristics, and so on)

- lifestyle

- product usage and purchasing habits

- differing customer needs.

Products can then be designed, priced, promoted and made available in such a way that they will appeal to a targeted segment of the market.

The centre will need to carry out market research before identifying potential market segments. It will need to assess:

- the size of potential segments

- the competition

- the needs of different groups of customers

- the costs of marketing to the individual segments

- the impact on existing business of attracting particular customer groups.

It is likely that this exercise would result in the centre segmenting the market according to lifestyle and demographic characteristics, which are likely to be related. Particular segmentation variables which they would want to consider would be:

- the age of customers and in particular the age of the children in any families targeted; for example, it may not be advantageous to market to parents of very young children if they are likely to want to swim in the late afternoon, as conference delegates swimming after a day's meetings may not be happy to share the pool with a large number of toddlers

- the type of household – which may be families or those without children

- the disposable income of potential customers – the centre will be looking to recruit members and customers with relatively high disposable income who are more likely to pay a high membership fee

- social class – potential customers are likely to come from higher socio-economic groups

- occupation – the centre may decide to target customers with a professional background as this is likely to be linked to the level of income.

(c) The income potential of the centre is the maximum level that can be reached under ideal conditions. This differs from the forecast of sales and income which is a prediction of the actual income that is expected in a future time period for a given level of marketing support. A top-down approach, which can be taken by the company to estimate the income potential, is:

- analysing trends in the industry and economic forecasts, incorporating the impact of the environmental factors described in (a) above

- using this analysis to determine the overall market potential, that is the total potential demand for fitness club memberships or fitness facilities

- determining the local area market potential

- determining the centre's sales potential by considering its past performance, resources and future predicted market share, taking into account any decisions made about targeting particular groups.

An alternative approach would be to take a 'bottom-up' approach, as follows:

- generating estimates of future demand from customers or the company's salespeople

- combining the estimates to get a total forecast

- adjusting the forecast based on managerial insights into the industry, competition and general economic trends.

There are a number of techniques that can be used to forecast the market potential. These may be quantitative or qualitative. The choice of forecasting method depends on costs, type of product, characteristics of market, time span of the forecast, purpose of the forecast, stability of historical data, availability of required information and forecasters' expertise and experience. The most important criterion in the choice of a forecasting method is accuracy.

Quantitative forecasting methods include:

- Fitting a trend line assuming that sales influences fall into four categories:

- trends (long-term changes)

- cyclical changes

- seasonal changes – this may be particularly relevant for the centre as it will include influences such New Year's resolutions leading to increased demand for memberships

- irregular changes.

- Moving average: computes the average volume achieved in several periods and then uses it as a prediction for sales in the next period. With a strong trend in the series, the moving average lags behind. With more periods, the moving average forecast changes slowly.

- 'Simple' regression: trying to estimate the relationship between a single dependent variable (Y or sales) and a single independent variable (X) via a straight-line equation:
  $Y = a + b(X) + e$.

- Multiple regression: estimating the relationship between a single dependent variable
  (Y or sales) and several independent variables.

Non-quantitative techniques for forecasting sales could include:

- Sales force composite: a bottom-up method consisting of collecting estimates of sales for the future period from all salespeople. However this is not likely to be very useful to the centre as this is a new market which the centre has little or no experience of at the moment.

- Looking at the experience of other similar schemes in the same market.

- Jury of Executive Opinion – this opinions of a group of executives are pooled with data compiled by each executive or by marketing research. Individual forecasts may be combined by a specialist or by negotiation as a group. This method is valued as most important to marketing managers.

- Market testing by making the proposed product available to a selected number of customers and measuring their responses to the service and the price.

- Market research by asking local residents what facilities they would use and what price they would be prepared to pay.

Whatever method is used, estimating a forecast is costly in terms of time and money. It must be remembered that it is only an estimate and changes in fundamental conditions can cause the forecast to vary from actual results. There is no best technique for forecasting. Two forecasts undertaken with different approaches are better than one.

226 H COMPANY

(a)   (i)   A 'selling' company probably aims a generic product at a wide market segment and so as almost a 'commodity' i.e. cannot differentiate the product. This means that a high-volume/low price strategy may be evolved and so the emphasis of the business is less on the innovation and creativity to create margin but on selling techniques to ensure its products are chosen over those of a competitor – such as clever merchandising, offers, competitors, goods distribution, etc.

A marketing company however uses the 'marketing concept' which aims to establish customer needs first and then design a strategy to meet them. This may well include 'commodity' products and competition on price, but this should be a deliberate trade-off with other products which can be differentiated in Porter's sense and so create margin which can be used not to reduce prices by internal efficiency but by market research to influence patterns of demand e.g.

women's perfumes at Christmas are sold to male customers buying them as presents so the ads must be attractive not to women, paradoxically, but to men.

(ii) H can adopt this by a change in culture (role to task) and philosophy – 'customer first'. This needs to be the subject of a wide change – management programme, perhaps using TQM as a vehicle. In this way the various parts of it's value chain can be linked, backwards, from the customer through sales and marketing through to purchasing. Clearly marketing must lead the way (in terms of research, etc) but other functions must be part of **Task Force** teams to reduce their resistance to change.

(b) The marketing mix is often referred to as the 4Ps – Produce, Price, Promotion and Place, but nowadays authors have extended the number of factors – some up to seven items.

Product – though it depends ultimately on customers, H must be able to retail products at a reasonable price or, however chic, it may not sell in volume and so overhead costs would increase as a % – if for example its customers want 'designer labels'.

As it is a retailer, it is less constrained than a manufacturer with production facilities and design departments. It can alter its products to appeal to different segments and merchandise them accordingly – with differing point of sale advertising (e.g. larger and smaller sizes for ladies).

Price – It may decide not to put the price on items in the shop windows in order to tempt buyers in who like the basic product. However, this is a dangerous strategy as customers often do not have time to enquire about prices. H has high-street competition and so must match the prices of similar items, while also conforming to traditional sales times, offers, etc.

Promotion – If H has a marketing concept it must differentiate its above-the-line and if possible below-the-line advertising to meet the expectations and values of each of its segments. So, it may re-brand itself generally as The Youth Shop but target older people, the middle-aged, the young executives and children all separately.

Place – The high street is increasingly not the place to be – malls, franchises in-store, catalogues and increasingly the internet are becoming the prime channels of distribution. H must spend money on these.

(c) Inclusion in this feature is likely to prove far more valuable than any formal advertising in the press. This is because the company's clothes will be presented and photographed in a manner that makes them appear to enhance and flatter the wearer. The underlying message of the feature would be that anyone wearing the items recommended to the subject of the makeover will be choosing wisely.

The nature of this type of feature tends to stress that the wrong clothes impair the wearer's appearance and that this can be remedied by switching to a better choice of wardrobe. This association would be beneficial to the company's image.

The newspaper will wish to make the feature interesting in order to capture readers' interest. It will, therefore, be likely to deal with problems that tend to interest significant numbers of potential customers (e.g. how to dress when overweight).

Makeover programmes are popular on television. That will generate additional interest in the newspaper article and might tend to generate further sales for particular lines offered by H Company.

If H Company does not take up this offer then it is likely to be offered to the company's competitors. That could put H Company even further behind.

227   LO-SPORT LTD

(a)   The 'classic' life cycle for a product has four phases:

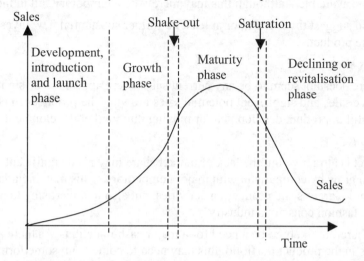

- An **introduction phase**, when the product or service is first developed and introduced to the market. Sales demand is low whilst potential customers learn about the item. There is a learning process for both customers and the producer, and the producer might have to vary the features of the product or service, in order to meet customer requirements more successfully.

- A **growth phase**, when the product or service becomes established, and there is a large growth in sales demand. The number of competitors in the market also increases, but customers are still willing to pay reasonably high prices. The product becomes profitable. Variety in the product or service increases, and customers are much more conscious of quality issues.

- A **maturity phase**, which might be the longest stage in the product life cycle. Demand stabilises, and producers compete on price.

- A **decline phase**, during which sales demand falls. Prices are reduced to sustain demand and to slow the decline in sales volume. Eventually the product becomes unprofitable, and eventually producers stop making it.

A large number of products have gone through this type of life cycle. For example, at the time of writing, it would appear that floppy disks for computers and video recorders are in the decline phase of their life cycle.

(b)   **Rackets**

The manufacture of rackets for tennis, squash and badminton are all within a well-established industry which appears to be in the *maturity phase* of the life cycle model. This is characterised by market saturation and stiff competition. Market growth is thus low.

Implications

Consideration could be given to the continued viability of this product. However, thought also needs to be given to the continuing cash flow generation compared to any disposal price that could be attained.

There could also be wider considerations such as interdependencies between products. For example, the shoe product side of the business may be partly dependent in cash, marketing or operational terms on the continued existence of racket manufacturing.

In the absence of significant other factors, further investment in this product should be questioned.

Existing sports shoes

This industry appears to be in the decline phase of the life cycle model based on the information available – although this may merely be a temporary fall in industry sales.

This would suggest divestment, or at least no further substantial new investment to support the product.

The katex shoe

While there does not seem to be any current sales, there appears to be significant prospective sales and significant potential sales growth. The product can be classified as either still in product development or moving into market development.

Implications

The market is attractive but the lack of market share may need significant investment in order to grow by comparison with major competitors. This may include physical investment in larger scale production activities, but also in advertising to promote the brand in a fashion conscious industry.

There is therefore likely to be a need for a major cash injection. As there are no cash generators in the product portfolio, this may need to come from some form of joint development strategy. Alternatively, or additionally, new debt or equity capital could be raised.

(c) Penetration pricing would involve setting the price low in order to build market share for the new shoe. Ideally, this could lead to the shoe establishing a niche in the marketplace and building up a base of satisfied customers who might become repeat customers once their first pair of shoes reached the end of their lives.

Price skimming might have some benefits if the new shoe really does offer real benefits. The premium price might create the impression of high quality, thereby stimulating sales. The high price might create some interest amongst potential trend-setters (having a celebrity spotted wearing a pair of Katex shoes could be worth more than any advertising campaign).

The biggest drawback to price skimming is the risk that consumers might be sceptical of any claims made on behalf of the new shoe. If the materials are unproven then the public might be unwilling to risk paying too much for it.

Price skimming might also attract competition. If competitors see that Lo Sport Ltd can make significant volumes of sales at this price point, then they might develop their own use of new materials with similar properties. The fact that these would come to market later might create the impression that they offered improvements over the original.

228 SX SNACKS (NOV 05 EXAM)

(a)

Key answer tip:

Make sure you discuss the implications of the issues you have raised.

The main issues to include in the marketing action plan and their implications are as follows:

Product

The new preparation and packaging technology will save on direct labour but also gives SX an opportunity to consider restyling its products. The main emphasis is on high quality fresh products and the designs should reflect this.

The big danger of using packaging technology is that the sandwiches look the same as can be bought from any supermarket and lose their 'home-made' appeal.

Similarly, it is vital that the preparation equipment enhances or maintains quality rather than letting it suffer. For example, will coffee beans be freshly ground?

One implication of this is the need to train staff in the new equipment to ensure that quality standards are maintained.

Place

The plan at present is still to use SX staff to deliver the food and drinks. At some point they may consider outsourcing this activity but, until then, the key issue is to improve the reliability of the deliveries. This is vital, as a lack of reliability will compromise SX's brand name.

The suggestion put forward is to have more drivers, thus reducing workloads. With existing staff being redeployed, this will involve further training in food handling and the outbound logistics procedures (paperwork, scheduling, etc).

As the firm grows there will be a need to recruit further drivers who will also need training and inducting into the SX culture, with a particular emphasis on providing high quality products to customers.

Promotion

Presumably SX will continue to use local radio advertising but the main issue for promotion is the role of drivers. Drivers will be expected to market the products to both existing and potential customers so will need extensive training in sales techniques. SX's reputation will be seriously compromised if staff are heavy-handed in their enthusiasm to win more business.

SX should also consider the use of online and telephone ordering so customers can request further supplies if they run out. This would have resource implications in terms of building a website, assigning someone to deal with telephone orders and may require changes to the production system.

(b)

Key answer tip:

A relatively straightforward requirement – just use the standard contents of a job description and apply them to the scenario.

A job description for the revised post of driver should include the following aspects:

Job title

- Driver (*Note:* You could suggest a different title to reflect the new roles, for example, 'customer service operative').

The purpose of the job

- To improve customer satisfaction through quick, reliable delivery of products.
- To boost sales of products.
- To improve information about competitors.

The position of the job in the organisation

- The driver will report directly to the marketing manager.

Salary

- Presumably comparable with existing wages but slightly higher than normal driver wages.
- Bonus of up to 10% of annual salary, depending on hitting delivery and sales growth targets.

Principal duties to be performed

- Delivering products to customers, mainly petrol stations.

- Getting feedback from customers.

- Encouraging customers to take new product lines.

- Getting information on competitors' products.

- Marketing products to other potential customers such as railway stations and newspaper shops.

The job environment

- Drivers will receive extensive training in the marketing aspects of the role and will be supported by the customer services team.

- Most of the time the driver will work on their own visiting clients' premises.

MANAGING HUMAN CAPITAL

229   TAXIS AND TYRES (PILOT PAPER)

Key answer tips:

To answer this question, you must understand what is a human resource plan. A typical human resources plan looks forward three to five years, and should consider:

- the objectives of the organisation in the planning period

- the demand for employees, and the skills of those employees

- the current numbers and skills of employees

- methods of closing the gap between current staffing and required staffing levels and skills.

(a)   **Outline human resources plan**

Objectives of the organisation

The objectives of the organisation over the next few years are:

- to provide a taxi service at about the same level of sales volume as at present

- to meet the growing demand for tyres

- to provide a wheel alignment service to support the tyre replacement business.

Required staffing, current staffing and the 'gap':

	Immediate required staff levels	Current staff levels	The gap
Management (owner-manager)	1	1	0
Taxi drivers	10	8	2
Tyre fitters	2	1	1
Receptionist/taxi controller	2	1	1

Methods of closing the gap

- There is an urgent requirement to recruit two taxi drivers.

- Recruited staff will probably need training, for example in safety procedures, dealing with customers and learning the local 'street maps'.

- There is a need to recruit an additional tyre fitter. If the recruited individual is not an experienced tyre fitter, training must be provided.

- The existing tyre fitter and new tyre fitter should both be given training in wheel alignment.

- A new receptionist/taxi controller should be recruited. In the longer term, it might be worth considering developing one of the taxi controllers as a junior manager.

- A policy should also be devised for the regular recruitment and training of taxi drivers, since there appears to be a regular annual turnover of about two drivers each year.

The main elements of a human resources plan are:

- setting the objectives of the organisation or department, in order to establish the required numbers and skills of staff over the planning period

- carrying out an 'audit' of existing staff, to establish the current numbers and skills

- identifying the gap between staff requirements and current staff numbers and skills

- devising methods of 'closing the gap' to ensure that the required staff numbers and skills are obtained.

(b) To obtain maximum contribution from the workforce, attention must be paid to the following HR activities, in addition to recruitment and selection, and training and development.

- **Pay and conditions**. The pay and terms and conditions of working need to be established. They need to be sufficiently attractive to attract individuals of a suitable calibre. Staff pay might also include a bonus element, in order to motivate employees to achieve a high level of performance. For example, tyre fitters might be rewarded with a bonus for the number of tyres they have fitted or wheels they have aligned. Taxi drivers might get their 'bonus' from tips from customers, which might encourage them to provide a more customer-friendly service.

- **Health and safety.** It is essential to address health and safety issues at work. In the case of this entity, health and safety concerns apply not only to employees of the entity but also to customers.

- **Performance assessment**. Staff should be encouraged continually to improve their performance. A system of performance appraisal can help to achieve this. Each employee should be encouraged to discuss his strengths and weaknesses with his manager or supervisor, and to consider ways of improving on past performance.

230 T CITY POLICE

(a) The purpose of performance appraisal is to assess the performance of an individual in his or her job, in a process involving the employee (appraisee) and his or her manager or supervisor. There are several ways in which performance appraisal might be used.

- The appraisal should be used to assess current performance of the appraisee.

- The appraisal can also be used to discuss the progress the individual has made since the previous appraisal.

- There can be a motivational element to appraisal interviews, if the individual believes that the organisation is concerned about how he or she is performing, and management is willing to give time to this task.

- An appraisal should also be used to discuss training and personal development plans for the individual. It should therefore be seen as a tool to assist with career development.

- Finally, appraisal can also be used as a basis for deciding the remuneration for the individual for the next 12 months.

- For the T City police force, performance appraisal can be a valuable method of considering the training and personal development requirements of its employees. The individuals should be able to discuss the problems they have experienced in their work, due to lack of familiarity with new techniques and methods. They should also be able to discuss how they feel they can improve their performance by acquiring experience in other areas of policing. Feedback from appraisal interviews can be used both to plan the further training and development programme for each individual, but also to consider the training needs and development needs of the work force generally.

- The information provided in the question also states that the performance appraisal system will be used as a basis for performance-related pay. If the scheme is carefully planned and implemented, employees will be rewarded for achieving certain standards of performance in their work. This ought to motivate staff to achieve the performance levels necessary for obtaining the additional pay reward. As a result, the general standards of performance should improve.

(b)   The potential problems of the performance-related pay system can be explained in terms of an expectancy model of motivation theory. Expectancy theory states that the motivation of an employee to put more effort into his work depends on three factors:

- the employee's perception of his own needs and wants

- the perception that putting in additional effort will succeed in achieving its objectives and result in rewards

- the perception that the rewards from achieving the objectives will satisfy the needs of the individual.

The comments from the staff association spokesman suggest there are two major difficulties.

- Although it is not yet established what levels of performance are required to earn rewards, the poor socio-economic conditions in the T City district will make it difficult for sustainable and significant improvements to occur. The additional effort put in by employees might therefore fail to have enough impact to earn a reward.

- Even if it is supposed that the employees would like more pay and that their efforts can succeed in meeting performance targets, the size of the rewards might be insufficient to satisfy employee needs enough. This is because there is limited government funding, which presumably means that there is not much money to put into a performance-related pay scheme.

The shortage of funds might also make it difficult to implement and administer the scheme successfully, since the scheme will undoubtedly cost money to operate (for example, it will use up the time of the officers carrying out the appraisals, and might therefore result in a requirement for more senior officers).

Although the spokesman did not mention the point, a further problem might arise because of the hierarchical nature of a police force, and the tendency for its management to be autocratic. A successful performance appraisal scheme, whether or not it is related to pay, requires openness between the appraisee and the officer conducting the appraisal interview. Appraisees might feel that they are unable to discuss their performance and problems openly and that the system is too dictatorial and unfair.

Given the shortage of funds for police work, appraisees might also want to argue that the reason they are unable to achieve performance targets is the lack of sufficient resources to do their work properly.

Another issue relating to fairness of the scheme will be the difficulties in identifying key performance targets, and rewarding on the basis of those targets alone. The question mentions that the audit identified crime prevention and convictions as key performance measures (presumably in all types of crime), whereas the general public appear more concerned with response times to emergency calls. Police work involves a wide variety of tasks, and handling many different types of crime and social behaviour. A fair performance appraisal scheme would need to recognise all the different types of police work, and the different measures by which all the different tasks should be appraised.

Another issue identified by the general public is racial harassment. If this is perceived to be a serious problem, for which performance improvement is necessary, it is arguable whether improvements in poor behaviour (a reduction in reports of racial harassment) should be a performance target on which to base rewards – given that the behaviour should not exist anyway.

Clearly there are potential problems with both the performance appraisal scheme and a PRP scheme. The scheme requires very careful planning before implementation if it s to have any chance of success.

231   RECRUITMENT

(a)   The standard procedure in the recruitment process is to first obtain an agreed vacancy: in some firms nowadays the first question after receiving a resignation is not 'where do we get a replacement from' but 'do we need to replace?' If there is a need, then the process should begin by reassessing the job and person description to see if it is current and, if not, altering the duties and/or the qualifications or skills in the person specification. This may be best done by the incumbent who has just resigned, with his or her supervisor.

From here, many firms create **internal job advertisements** first, which go up on notice-boards ahead of any external advertisement. Indeed in some cases, either from experience or from a formal development plan, there is no perceived need to advertise externally: internal candidates may even be identified straight away (such as the incumbent's deputy or assistant) and interviewed. In many cases there may be no competitive interview just an appointment.

Where time is of the essence, media such as agencies and 'head-hunters' may be used, perhaps to fill the position on a temporary basis. Simultaneously, depending on the level of the job and the expert of the perceived labour market, local newspapers and magazines, TV and radio and the Government Employment Agencies can be used to advertise. National jobs markets require advertisements in trade publications, quality daily papers and Sunday newspapers.

Attracting a good field of candidates is often seen as essential and a 'long list' of people who match the criteria can then be whittled down to a 'short-list' either by a paper-sift looking for the best-qualified, or by preliminary interviews. Where there is a national recruitment for a major expansion (e.g. in retail, hotel and catering, market research or sales) interviews can be held locally using hotels or conference centres.

Second or final interviews usually involve senior staff at a Head Office location and may be extended towards an assessment centre format where different skills of the applicant are tested and often an aptitude or personality test given.

(b)   At the stage of selection, the major problem is to find a way of ensuring the selected applicant will do a good job in the real world the firm operates in: this is called 'validity'. To make selection valid it should be as objective as possible, though this is reflected by how far the people the candidate has to work with actually **like** him or her. Thus 'fitting in' is subjective but should be considered an essential part of the process – introduction to colleagues and subordinates may pave the way for a more open relationship later.

Objectivity can be increased by involving several different interviewers (i.e. not one line manager), using the same job and person specification and a structured interview where more-or-less the same questions are asked. Interviewer bias should be circumvented by Panel Interviews and standardisation of questions. However, the use of an assessment centre approach brings in other skills, a group problem-solving exercise, a presentation, an in-tray exercise, a personality test. These are now marketed by major occupational psychologists and are becoming popular.

However, they are artificial. If a sales person has had several jobs with excellent results and does poorly on the selection process, does this mean that the process itself has not been pre-tested? This is the most common failing, the assumption that what you are testing really measures what it sets out to.

(c)   A clear understanding of the job that is to be filled will make it much easier to identify the type of candidate who is required. That, in turn, will enable the organisation to advertise in such as way as to encourage suitable applicants and discourage those who are likely to be unsuitable. For example, if a job requires specific qualifications and some prior experience in the industry this should be stated in the advert. It might also suggest that adverts should be placed in trade publications which will be read by those who are suitably qualified, rather than newspapers which will be read by a wider readership.

A clear job analysis will provide those responsible for selecting a shortlist and conducting interviews with a list of criteria that are necessary and those that are desirable. Candidates who do not possess each of the necessary attributes should not be interviewed. This will provide a more objective basis for rejecting unsuitable

candidates and will also provide the company with a measure of protection in case of claims of bias or discrimination. A candidate who does not have a vital attribute, such as a relevant degree if that is deemed necessary, cannot complain if he or she is not interviewed for the post.

The process of conducting the job design might also alert the company to any problems with the post itself. If the criteria are too demanding, then it might be better to set lower entry requirements and then provide the successful candidate with either training or supervision until s/he has reached the required level of competence.

232   CQ4 (MAY 06 EXAM)

Requirement (a)

Herzberg's theory of motivation is based on the idea that motivation is based on two needs:

- Hygiene factors are those to do with the context of the job rather than the job itself e.g. features such as the working environment (salary, the nature and extent of supervision, job security, etc). These factors are known as 'dissatisfiers' because a lack of attention to these areas can lead to dissatisfaction, but meeting these here will not necessarily lead to employee satisfaction.

- Motivational factors are concerned with the job itself. Generally satisfaction flows from the actual job – the recognition, any sense of achievement from doing it well and so on. Motivational factors meet employees' need for growth and self-achievement.

Focusing on motivating factors is usually more productive because employees will work harder and generally perform better if they are motivated.

The chief executive's proposals can be analysed as follows:

Motivating factors:

- Each manager has a personal 'performance target contract' and is to be left to achieve the required outcome.

- Managers are to be given greater recognition for their role in meeting the company's strategic targets.

- Individual achievement stands a chance of being noticed and rewarded with greater responsibility in the future.

Hygiene factors:

- Bonuses will be paid to reflect the anticipated boost in profits.

- The burden of monthly reports and monitoring has been lifted.

Requirement (b)

There may be constraints on the amount that the company can afford to spend on rewarding good performance. Even if the new system does turn out to give a worthwhile incentive, it may be more than the company can afford.

Some employees may feel disenfranchised and demotivated when they see their managers offered the opportunity to earn a performance-related salary enhancement that is not available to everyone.

Managers might be tempted to focus on the factors of their jobs that maximise their pay, even though that might not be in the very best interest of the company. It can be difficult to design such packages so that managers always have an incentive to do what is best for the company.

Linking pay to outcomes could make managers risk-averse. They might be inclined to adopt a 'safe' course that will guarantee a reasonable bonus rather than to take a better approach that could be more risky.

There has to be an objective mechanism for measuring performance for the purpose of settling the performance-related pay.

The balance between different elements of the remuneration package must be addressed. The relationship between salary and bonus elements is an important one.

The proposed system must be seen to be fair to all sides.

233   MANAGEMENT DEVELOPMENT

(a)   **'Management development'** has been defined as 'the progress a person makes in learning how to manage effectively' (Weitrich). However, as a system, management development is aimed at improving management effectiveness in all areas by a planned process of evaluation, training, experience and performance improvement.

(Many reports in the past five years have shown that management in the UK lags behind our major competitors. It is calculated that Germany spends five times as much as the UK per head of management population.)

(b)   The following steps could occur in a **typical management development programme**:

(i)   The organisation's strategic plan will identify corporate objectives for the next three or five years. This plan should be analysed in terms of manpower needs. A key part of this manpower plan will be the definition of management positions over the coming years. For example, consider a company planning to establish a manufacturing unit in Eastern Europe; the necessary management positions can be defined and a specification of skills and experience levels stipulated. The strategic plan together with the proposed organisation structure provides the basis for this schedule of management positions over the short and medium term and an outline for the longer term.

(ii) Having defined the future needs, the next step could be to evaluate the existing management team. An analysis by skills, experience, age, promotability, past appraisals, career pattern etc, will provide categorisations which can be put alongside the future management schedule. It will be necessary to adjust the present management list for likely turnover for future years. Some turnover, such as retirements can be forecast accurately. Elsewhere, past statistics can be used to anticipate likely numbers leaving in main categories.

(iii) Any specialist skills necessary should be highlighted for separate consideration. Where such skills/experience are rare, the organisation may seek to head hunt selected individuals rather than issue a general advertisement.

(iv) By matching the adjusted basis of present management people against the expected management needs of the future, a gap will emerge. The organisation is now in a position to state the number of managers at particular levels of skill and experience that will need to be developed to fill these gaps. Some general principles will be established as guidelines e.g., younger understudying older, minimum three people identified as development for any management position.

(v) To close the gap, individual managers will need to be developed through training, selective experience, project work etc, whilst other positions will need to be filled through recruitment.

The training section will devise specific individual training programmes where necessary. These may overlap, or form part of, general training courses aimed at developing management effectiveness overall. Also selected periods of experience will be prescribed to develop and test potential of individuals. For example, any individual manager being considered for a senior position in an international company must have spent a successful period as a manager abroad. Appraisal of individual performance will form a key part of the development exercise and an accelerated appraisal scheme may be introduced for the management stream, whereby appraisals are undertaken frequently, not just annually. Such appraisals may be incorporated in a Management by Objectives approach where applicable within an organisation.

(vi) Recruitment of managers will be affected by the development programme. Shortage of time to fill a position, or disappointing appraisals, could lead an organisation to recruit to fill the gap. Some companies (e.g. Tesco, Marks and Spencer) have a policy of strong internal management development; such companies are infrequent recruiters of established managers.

(vii) The success of a management development scheme can be measured by the simple test of 'did the organisation get the right person in the right job at the right time'. This is the fundamental test of success. However, the organisation will need to know that this has been achieved at a reasonable cost. It is therefore important to develop a set of objectives for Management Development section that link achievement with budget stages and that performance should be audited by a senior manager.

Note: That the question requires 'the steps that an organisation should take'. Therefore detailed discussions of individual management responses has only marginal relevance.

(c) Succession planning should be an ongoing process so that staff requirements, particularly at the managerial levels, are anticipated and met.

An assessment of current staff resources should be maintained, analysed by departments, the types of jobs at each level and the number and quality of staff in those jobs.

A forecast of the staff requirements, by grades and skills, should then be assessed and agreed to highlight any shortages in terms of skills or numbers.

If there is a mismatch between job specification and existing employees, then staff development should be focused on resolving the problem.

Significant shortages might require recruitment programmes. Vacancies should be filled in sufficient time to have staff in place with the necessary skills and qualifications before a shortage actually arises. For example, airlines need to be conscious of the implications of losing pilots who are qualified to fly particular types of aircraft. This will often require the recruitment and training of replacements while existing pilots are still in post (and even before they have considered retiring or moving on).

Ideally, succession planning will aim to generate a throughput of staff so that promoted posts are filled from within. This will give staff the opportunity for career progression, which will be motivating. It may also make it possible for organisations to recruit largely in response to vacancies at the lower levels, where candidates will be more plentiful and potentially less expensive to recruit and train.

234   REWARD SYSTEMS

On the assumption that people are at the lower levels of Maslow's hierarchy of needs (basic/physiological) and need money to buy food, the employment relationship is usually characterised by an economic exchange. This means pay for work done. Although it must be emphasised that vast numbers of people work as volunteers, by definition they must be in higher levels of **Maslow's hierarchy**. Clearly in a modern society they or their family must have income – part of an economic exchange somewhere in the background.

To attract people to do work, therefore, employers must provide an attractive reward package. This is a complex amalgam of affordability, perceived internal statuses and the needs of a variety of applicants. Unskilled applicants living with their parents near to the place of work have fewer needs that those with children living some distance away. The cost of working for some is greater than those afforded by state benefits – the 'poverty trap'.

Local labour markets vary with age as well as skills, as older workers often will have paid off debts in raising a family such as mortgages and their dependants may well also have left home. Nevertheless, psychological factors make it unlikely that older applicants will accept lower wages – nor can internal structures and relativities cope with volunteers or age-related pay in most organisations.

What occurs therefore is a hierarchy of jobs, rated in a job-evaluation scheme or by collective bargaining, or by a management 'remuneration committee'. These jobs are often grouped into a number of levels requiring similar levels of skills – for the sake of simplicity if nothing else.

Pay is then attached based on market rates (especially local union rates for skilled workers or minimum wage legislation). Internal relativities are then set – in some firms, supervisors are automatically paid 10% more than those they supervise. For clerical and managerial jobs, skills develop in the job and are paid in a **progression of increments, rate-for-age scales** or **merit (performance-related) pay**. This usually involves a formal annual Appraisal of Performance.

Non-managerial jobs are very often hourly paid whereas managers receive an annual salary. In these cases, additional hours worked are voluntarily given and compensation at a higher rate is usually offered. This may be the hourly rate (time) plus 50% – time and a half – with double time – on days of rest, public holidays etc.

Further, some jobs attract bonuses or commission usually based on increased profitable sales, or production output. It is difficult to calculate the normal rates of performance above which bonuses are paid: **F.W.Taylor's scientific management** gave birth to a plethora of 'time and motion study' experts who measured effort and job difficulty to come to standard times. Sales managers are not fortunate and have to look into the future to estimate budgets and structure commission payments in excess of these. In Japan, profit-related-pay can account for up to one-third of earnings but in the UK it tends to be somewhat trivial, except in partnerships and professional firms (like solicitors).

Added to pay is a wide range of **non-incentive benefits from pensions**; through sick pay to expense allowances, even company cars, subsidised canteens and so on. The job of the 'compensation and benefits' manager becomes more complex daily.

235 DISMISSAL, RETIREMENT, REDUNDANCY

Planned leaving normally refers in the HR plan to retirements at the state retirement age. An age profile of current employees is easily built up and scheduled retirements each year can be filled in quite automatically so that future demand can be anticipated and recruitment planned for. Typical examples might be in manufacturing, where many employees joined 'en masse' when a factory opened, and were in their 20s. Thus, 40 to 45 years on they will be retiring 'en masse' over a period of five or so years. Mass recruitment may be needed at that time.

Unplanned leaving is of course more complex and disruptive, often called 'turnover' or 'labour turnover' and is **voluntary** i.e. employees leaving by resignation for better jobs elsewhere. Monitoring turnover can give indications of poor management or working conditions, stress, or low wages compared with the market-place. A reasonable level – 5% to 10% is healthy however as it enables the introduction of 'new blood' and the possibility of promotions. **Involuntary leaving** is not usually measured – this involves dismissal for various reasons under the contract of employment.

Capability often is given as a reason and may include long-term or frequent sickness absence. Early retirement on grounds of ill-health is an option for those in the pension plan and with sufficient service, while others must rely on state-provided benefits. Frequent absences however are difficult to handle as it is not easy to appear fair and reasonable: employees are usually counselled, then given targets to achieve well before dismissal, and this type of treatment spills over into an issue of 'conduct'. Poor job performance is similarly quite hard to prove definitively - there is always an element of judgement and comparison with other jobs/personnel. Issues of bad faith by employer's inept recruitment of people who prove unable to do the job can sometimes by circumvented by transfer to other work in a different department. Otherwise, dismissal is the only option.

Conduct, likewise, is a difficult area unless the firm has strict, written rules, which are made public to all employees (such as during induction training). Fighting, drunkenness, theft, refusal to follow a reasonable instruction, absenteeism and the like are more easy to handle than insubordination and rudeness to colleagues. The issue is whether dismissal is really necessary.

Redundancy is an acceptable reason and quite clear – but so long as criteria for selection are open and fair. Redundancy exists where the business ceases to be, where the job the employee is performing becomes outmoded or disappears, or when work is transferred to another location. This last category can be quite confusing especially in major cities where employees live near to main roads or railway lines which they habitually use to get to work. If the Head Office moves across town it might become extremely difficult for those employees to reach the new location in good time and so they may claim to have been made redundant. Employers also must consult staff, minimise the effect of the scale of the redundancy and its timing, giving advance notice, calling for volunteers, reducing overtime and part-time/temporary or contract work and so on. Following the redundancy the employer then has the problem of maintaining the morale of those left: not an easy proposition.

236   B3 PERSONNEL AGENCY (NOV 06 EXAM)

Requirement (a)

Opportunity 1. These new technologies might improve the quality of service by permitting B3 to contact potential recruits more quickly than by other means. It might not be possible to telephone applicants during normal working hours because they will not wish their present employers to be aware that they are in touch with a personnel agency. Many people have access to email at home and most carry mobile phones (some of which can access email as well as text messages), so electronic communication is likely to be faster and more efficient.

Email is probably better for communicating detailed information. Text messages are restricted in length. Texts could, however, be better for passing on relatively urgent information such as a change of time for an interview.

Some senior candidates for executive posts might find this form of communication too informal and would be slightly offended at the prospect of having career information passed on by means of email.

This would be a relatively inexpensive option. The computing requirements to send emails and text messages via the internet are modest and staff will not require any specific training because virtually all will be able to use this technology anyway.

Opportunity 2. Filing CVs electronically should make filing easier. Electronic documents should not go missing or get lost provided they are filed correctly when they are first received. B3 could create a database with basic details (name, type of post applied for, dates) and each database record could be linked to the associated CV.

Each recruitment consultant should have access to all current CVs without the problems that would be created if several people were working on the same group of files at once.

Electronic CVs could also be emailed to clients along with a short-list.

Requirement (b)

The first step should be to quickly review the members of the short-list to confirm that all candidates are suitable. This should have been done by B3, but there could be issues that might not be known by the personnel agency. For example, the shortlist could contain candidates who are known personally to the selection panel and could be deemed unsuitable for personality or other reasons. Candidates from some competitors might be regarded with slight suspicion because they might be using the interview process to gather information on behalf of their employers.

The short-listed candidates should be invited for an interview as quickly as possible. This is partly a matter of courtesy and of showing the candidates that their applications are being treated seriously and partly a matter of reducing the risk of them taking up posts with other employers.

The screening process offered by B3 should make it possible to proceed to the final interview. Candidates should have been briefed on the nature of the post, terms and conditions, etc before being short-listed.

The interview itself should be conducted by a small panel. Having more than one interviewer reduces the risk of personal bias. Sharing the responsibility for interviewing and selecting the best candidate should give more confidence. The interview should be planned in advance with a standard set of questions for each candidate, although there should be some opportunity to follow up points made. There should be a designated convener to chair the panel so that each interviewer has an opportunity to participate, but in a controlled and orderly manner.

237   HUMAN RESOURCE PLAN

(a)   Human resource planning (HR planning) was previously described as manpower planning, and has been defined as 'a strategy for the acquisition, utilisation, improvement and retention of an enterprise's human resources'. Manpower planning still provides a good starting point for the development of a human resource plan, but in recent years it has been recognised that there is more to people planning than quantitative estimates of the demand and supply of personnel.

Four main phases are involved in manpower planning:

(i)   an analysis of existing staffing resources – its strengths and weaknesses, age spreads, experience and training levels, etc

(ii)   an estimation of likely changes in resources – flows into, within, and out of, the organisation, and the ability of relevant labour markets to supply existing or future demands

(iii)   an estimation of the organisation's future manpower needs in terms of numbers, type, quality and skill composition

(iv)   the identification of gaps between supply and demand and the development of policies and plans to close these.

The HR planning process goes beyond this simple quantitative exercise by taking into account the broader environmental factors, for example patterns of employment and developments in automation and uses qualitative techniques, such as scenario planning, for estimating future manpower requirements. The process is also linked to the development of the organisation as a whole, and should be related to corporate objectives and to an organisation structure capable of achieving those objectives. It is also concerned with developing people so that they have the skills to meet the future needs of the business and with improving the performance of all employees in the organisation by the use of appropriate motivation techniques.

(b)   Briefing paper: Development of a human resource plan for the finance department

The key considerations for developing the human resource plan for the department will focus on three main areas:

(i)   making the required reductions, in line with the downsizing strategy

(ii)   addressing the changes that are affecting the department

(iii)   identifying the future role, in playing a fuller part in the management of the business.

Reducing staff numbers from 24 to 17 over the next two years and to 12 by the target date (in five years' time) will be by using natural wastage and early retirement wherever possible. Hopefully, this will avoid (or at least reduce) the need for compulsory redundancies, and will avoid or reduce the adverse effects on staff morale and motivation.

There is a good chance of achieving the reductions over the time period set, provided that the necessary steps are taken. Three of the older members are within five years of retiring; two more will move into this category within the five years set by senior management. If those employees nearest retirement could be encouraged to leave by offering them a generous retirement package and an enhancement of their pension, it would be the least painful option.

One or two of the younger qualified members of staff are already looking for posts elsewhere, so they may be encouraged to leave earlier when the news that the organisation is looking to slim down the department has been communicated to the department. One of the trainees has applied for maternity leave. She will have the right to return to work, provided that she comes back within the period set out in legislation, so we have no room for manoeuvre there. Some of the trainees will qualify within the time period under consideration, and the reduction in costs will not allow me to increase salaries substantially, so I think that they will look elsewhere for work.

The age/experience of the existing people, spread over financial accounting, management accounting and the treasury function, is a mix of older, experienced specialist staff, a young to middle-aged group of qualified accountants (many of whom also possess MBA degrees), and a group of trainees with limited experience who have yet to qualify. I would like to keep a similar spread and one of the problems will be retaining the most able of my staff. This will mean planning a package of financial inducements and a clear career structure.

Reducing staff will be possible, but coping with the current workload with the reduced resources will be more difficult. There are several solutions to help me to deal with this problem:

- The department's existing operations will be thoroughly reviewed to make sure that it matches the corporate objectives, and its structure is capable of achieving those objectives. It may be that, following the general downsizing, there may be a reduced need for some of its services.

- There are many changes in technology and the department can make more use of IT and the latest developments in computer software. This could allow an increase in productivity and result in better quality output from the department. It will mean developing some of the staff, so that they have the skills to meet the future needs of the business. Although staff training is expensive, it will provide some motivation and reassurance to staff that the organisation is still prepared to invest in them and is ready to equip them with the latest IT skills.

- The department has been under increasing pressure to outsource transactions, and some of its other routine work, to one of the new service centres. Although I am not keen to do this, it may be the only way of coping with the existing volume of work.

For the **future plans**, the department will have to monitor its expenditure to keep in line with the budget. Early retirement and additional staff training will add considerably to costs, but perhaps outsourcing some of the routine work will allow us to offset some of these costs.

It is inevitable that some of the department members will have to become more flexible and be ready to take on a wider range of responsibilities. The younger staff will welcome this, as their education and training has already prepared them for wider management responsibilities, and those with MBA degrees are in a good position to accept more responsibilities. However, additional training and development to handle future demands will need to be planned for some members of the department.

238 APPRAISAL

(a) The objectives of a formal appraisal process are:

(i) To **highlight areas of good/above average performance** in order to assist in reward systems and/or career development opportunities.

(ii) To **highlight areas of poor performance** which can be rectified by a Training Needs Analysis.

(iii) To **de-brief on targets set and achieved** thus creating a mutual understanding and opportunity for creative criticism. Some firms operate 180° Appraisal where the subordinate also appraises the supervisor.

(iv) **As a control mechanism** e.g. as part of Management by Objectives ensuring the ongoing improvement in critical areas.

(b)   Appraisal systems are fraught by their very nature of formality.

Having a certain time for feedback may ensure it is done, formally correct, logged and actioned but may result in managers 'saving-up' issues for the predetermined time rather than addressing them as they occur.

Many managers see the process as one enabling them to set additional 'projects' for staff rather than an attempt to measure them against what they are supposed to do. This is easier than trying to create objective measures, for example in a finance department where adherence to standards is far more important than individual creativity and where many employees are doing very similar, repetitive tasks.

Frequently, managers see the appraisal as an opportunity for criticism and to bring out all the faults of the employee in circumstances where this would otherwise not be possible. Employees whose everyday work is exemplary and who have no cause to be worried can face a very personal judgement about their personal characteristics within a formal, confidential, one-to-one appraisal.

They suffer from the 'halo and horns' effect in that human judgement is poor, often based on impressions, so it is easier for a manager to look for faults or success in an otherwise patchy performance and bias his/her judgement one way or the other – particularly when the appraisee is generally seen as having 'potential' and it is politically expedient to emphasise success (e.g. in graduates).

Finally, most managers are not trained in, nor are they comfortable with, the process. They may tend to do it passively, aim for a 'middle level' to avoid conflicts, and spend little time in preparation or execution of what can be an extremely resource-hungry activity.

Some of these problems can be alleviated by:

- education and training of managers and subordinates

- central direction of target-setting, scale and indices of performance

- 360° appraisal involving peers and a judgement of the managers

- increasing the frequency.

All this can be greatly assisted by slick software, eliminating the 'paper chase'.

(c)   The appraisal interview is the vehicle for giving feedback to the employee where strengths and weaknesses can be identified and the possibilities of improvement discussed. It also provides employees with an opportunity to describe their perspective of such concerns. This two-way communication is so important that the interview is a crucial part of the appraisal process. If managed properly it can ensure that the feedback is positive and that the overall effect is motivating.

The interviewer must be willing to listen to the subordinate and be prepared to change an evaluation in the light of valid evidence presented in support of any claims made. The emphasis should be on the future rather than the past, with both sides stressing opportunities rather than apportioning blame. It is often helpful to focus on specific job behaviour rather than on more general issues of personality or attitude.

If conducted properly, the interview can create a sense of self-appraisal in the employee and that should encourage improvement and development in those areas where they are necessary.

One of the biggest problems to be overcome is that the subject of the interview will have a natural desire to push for the best possible evaluation and that might make it difficult to be frank about weaknesses or areas where improvement is required.

239   R COMPANY

(a)   An induction programme is a programme for introducing a new employee into an organisation. Ideally, it should be planned and structured, rather than a variety of ad hoc arrangements. An induction programme should enable a new employee to:

- learn what they need to know about the organisation, how it operates, what its rules are, and its way of doing things and culture

- understand the work that they will be doing, and their responsibilities

- meet the individuals in the organisation that they need to or ought to know.

- An induction programme should have a clear time frame. Typically, an induction programme might last three months, six months or as much as one year. At the end of the induction programme, the individual should be able to think of himself or herself as a fully-integrated member of the company's work force.

The key activities in a planned induction programme should be as follows.

Before the new employee's first day	The human resources department should write to the individual, with details of: • the job title and job description • conditions of employment, such as hours of work, holiday entitlement, sickness arrangements and so on • rate of pay, including any entitlement to overtime, bonuses There should also be a covering letter welcoming the new employee, and giving details of where to go on the first morning, who to meet and at what time.
On Day 1	The new employee should be met by a person in the HR department, who will welcome him/her, discuss 'personnel' matters such as the company's rule book and its pension scheme. The induction scheme should be explained, and then the new employee should be taken to meet his/her office manager. The office manager will either act as a mentor for the new employee throughout the induction period, or (more likely) will assign someone else to carry out the tasks of mentoring. The role of a mentor is to explain the work environment to the new employee and deal with any questions or problems he or she might have. The mentor will introduce the new employee to the work environment, for matters such as introducing work colleagues, touring the office building and facilities (canteen facilities, drinks machines and so on). The mentor will also introduce the new employee to the work that he or she will be doing, and the computer software that will be used.

Early in the programme	The HR department should contact the individual again, to provide 'regulatory' information, such as information about fire drill, health and safety, discipline procedures and grievance procedures.
At planned intervals	In a planned induction programme, the new employee might go through a rotation of duties, assisting with different elements of finance work in order to familiarise himself/herself with the organisation's systems, and to meet a variety of colleagues. The training needs of the individual might need to be reviewed. If there is a large enough number of new recruits each year, it might be possible to arrange an in-house course, where the employees are given a fuller introduction to the organisation and its operations, as well as a chance to meet each other.
At regular intervals	The new employee should have short, formal meetings with the mentor (in addition to any unofficial discussions they might have) to discuss how the employee is settling into the company and whether there are any problems. If problems arise, it may be possible to take action to deal with them and address concerns.

(b)   The problems that the finance department is experiencing are:

- the loss of several new employees within the first year

- under-performance by several of the staff.

It is by no means certain that the lack of a planned induction programme is to blame, nor that the introduction of such a programme will remove or even reduce the problem.

The process of recruitment might be inadequate. New employees might find that they are not entering the type of job that they had been led to expect. The HR department might also be failing to recruit people of the right calibre.

Alternatively, the problems could be due to poor management and/or low employee morale.

An induction programme might possibly help to reduce both problems.

Reducing staff turnover

An induction programme can help a new employee to become integrated more quickly into the organisation, by meeting work colleagues and learning how the organisation operates. If an individual feels 'at home' rather than an outsider, he or she will be less likely to resign.

Through introducing new employees to each other, it might be possible to create a 'self-help group' of individuals who are able to discuss their induction experiences and problems. Shared problems are generally more easily dealt with and resolved.

If an individual knows that there is a programme for induction, and can see a purpose to what he or she is doing, he or she might be prepared to be more patient in waiting for training, and to put up with mundane accountancy work in the short term.

Regular meetings with the mentor, if properly conducted, should provide an opportunity for the individual to discuss problems and concerns. To the extent that the mentor can help, the new employee will feel more valued and appreciated, and so might be less inclined to resign.

Improving performance

Lower-than-expected performance could be caused by a number of factors. These include:

- not understanding fully the tasks of the job and its responsibilities
- failing to appreciate the systems of the organisation and how they operate
- a lack of regular performance review after joining the organisation.

An induction programme could help to overcome these problems. The job responsibilities of the employee should be set out clearly in the job description, and the mentor should be able to give advice and guidance. An induction programme should also introduce the individual to the systems and the culture of the organisation, so that the individual appreciates more clearly how things operate and how his/her job fits into the 'general scheme of things'. By helping the individual to understand what is expected, he or she might perform better.

In addition, if the individual has regular meetings with the mentor, the mentor can give 'unofficial' guidance about the individual's performance, and discuss the difficulties the individual is experiencing.

240 CX BEERS (MAY 05 EXAM)

Examiner's comments

There was a real range of performance on this question from well-prepared candidates who successfully applied known theory to the scenario in a purposeful manner to those who merely reproduced their understanding of general HR issues.

Common errors

- A tendency to adopt an 'all I know about.....' approach.

(a) The main issues and stages involved in developing a human resource (HR) plan for the CX buy-out idea are as follows:

Issues

The HR plan must incorporate all three of the suggested initiatives:

- the museum
- bottled beers
- flexibility.

The HR plan must preserve the good reputation of the firm.

The company must be profitable in the longer term. Ultimately this is likely to be the main constraint on how many workers can be employed.

Stages

Four main phases are involved in HR planning:

1   Auditing the current labour force in the company, its strengths and weaknesses, age spreads, experience and training levels.

2   Forecasting the future labour demand in terms of number, type and quality of people the company should employ to meet planned requirements.

3   Forecasting the expected labour supply, looking at both existing workers, expected staff turnover and future training plans, and at the external labour market.

4   Developing a plan to ensure that supply equals demand in the future. If supply exceeds demand, then this could involve redundancies, relocating staff and/or reducing recruitment. If demand exceeds supply then the plan will involve recruitment, staff relocation, training programmes and so on.

These stages can be applied to CX beers as follows:

Stage 1: Auditing the current labour force

- Given that the factory has just shut, strictly speaking there is no current labour force to audit. However, unless they have already found alternative employment, most of the previous workers will want a job with the new firm if possible.

- The firm will want to identify and recruit the employees with higher levels of experience and skills. This will reduce the need for training and ensure a quicker start up for the new strategy. Previous HR records can be used here along with interviews.

Stage 2: Forecasting future demand

Since labour is a derived demand, the overall number of employees needed depends on the demand for each of the initiatives. The managers will thus have to estimate the number of likely visitors to the museum, the annual demand for bottled beer from supermarkets and future demand for current beers for the third initiative. Each of these demands will have to incorporate seasonal aspects and will be for both the immediate short-term and the longer-term future.

The precise nature of future demand for labour will depend on the three elements of the strategy:

- The museum option would require the minimum workforce to operate the older plant together with the most experienced workers to give authority to presentations, to be able to answer queries from tourists and maybe act as guides. This would also suggest that older ex-workers are likely to be preferred.

- The bottled beer for supermarkets plan may require new technology and methods. The type of machinery used will have a major impact on how many employees are needed and what skills they will need. The managers will have to decide whether to try to recruit workers with experience of the new techniques or ex-workers who will then need extensive training. If the latter plan is followed then it is important that workers who have shown an aptitude to learning new processes are specified in the recruitment plan.

- Employing a flexible but experienced workforce will involve specifying the type of flexibility required (see section (b) below) and the level of experience needed. There may be conflicts here as older workers may be more experienced but may want more stability due to having families. Younger workers may be more willing to accept seasonal work but have less experience.

Stage 3: Forecasting future supply

The immediate supply will be fairly easy to forecast, as most ex-employees will be available to work, given the area's high unemployment. Existing HR records will also detail their skills, experience, ages, etc. Whether they have the skills required depends on which of the three elements of the plan is being considered.

Future supply is harder to predict, as it will be affected by whether or not ex-workers manage to find alternative employment.

Stage 4: Developing a plan

The immediate plan would involve a mixture of recruitment and training. It is likely that any workers re-employed would be highly motivated, having been given a second chance.

The main training aspects will be for:

- conducting tours for the museum
- learning new skills for the bottled beers.

(b) **Numerical flexibility**

One of the main problems facing CX was the seasonal nature of its trade, with the winter being the busiest. With the new initiatives of the museum and bottled beers demand will be less seasonal but there will still be a seasonal element that the buyout team will have to deal with.

This will require the firm to have numerical flexibility – the firm can adjust the level of labour inputs to meet fluctuations in output.

The buyout team can achieve numerical flexibility by the following:

- temporary contracts

- part-time workers

- use of sub-contractors

- overtime

- outsourcing non-core activities.

Charles Handy suggested the idea of a 'shamrock' organisation, which would work well for CX. Such an organisation would have three inter-related 'leaves':

- a small managerial/technical core leaf

- an outsourced business-to-business relations leaf

- the contract and temporary contingency workforce leaf.

Functional flexibility

The new organisation would also benefit form functional flexibility – the ability to adjust and deploy the skills of its workforce to match the tasks required by changing workloads.

For CX this could mean museum staff being able to assist in production and vice-versa, or having brewers who can also carry our routine maintenance, for example.

This flexibility will be achieved by the following:

- training staff in a wider range of skills

- recruiting staff with a wider range of skills

- introducing a programme of job rotation.

241 COMPANY A AND B

(a) **Staff concerns**

The staff of Company B will have a number of concerns, depending on their age, position in their career and personality.

Benefits

Most staff will be concerned that the overall benefits package they receive in Company A is not inferior to their existing terms. As well as the obvious issue of pay, this will incorporate:

- pensions

- holidays

- study leave.

Legislation may ensure that the new employment conditions of Company B staff are no worse than they enjoyed in Company B before it was taken over, depending on the country concerned.

Status

Senior managers in Company B will be concerned with whether or not they will enjoy a similar status in the new organisation.

Promotion

Junior managers in Company B will be concerned about opportunities for progression in Company A.

Cultural differences

Most employees moving to the Company A headquarters will be concerned about the different policies, practices and procedures of Company A. This could include:

- the quantity and quality of the work
- the technology and systems they will be using
- whether or not they will be able to work with the new team in Company A.

Routine matters

Staff will be concerned about routine issues such as the best way to travel to the new work place and whether there will be parking space.

Induction programme

All of these issues can be addressed via an effective induction programme. A well-structured induction programme should achieve the following:

- a greater sense of belonging in the new firm
- a greater sense of Company A's commitment to them – they will feel more valued
- a greater commitment to organisational goals
- reduced staff turnover
- a quicker understanding of new technology and systems.

Staff will be more aware of company rules and procedures and will be less likely to break safety rules, for example.

Together these should result in better quality work, fewer disciplinary problems, better morale and cost savings.

(b) **Induction programme**

An induction programme to assist finance staff from Company B to become quickly effective in Company A could take the following form:

Timing	Focus	Responsibility
Prior to move	• Send background information about Company A (history, mission, products, etc)	HR department
	• Send copies of terms and conditions of employment, covering pay, holidays, pensions, study leave, sickness policy, etc	
	• Send details of rules and procedures, for example, unauthorised use of company computers, Internet policy, procedures for smokers, etc	

- Send practical details, including hours of work, map of location, parking arrangements, start time, dress code, what to bring and who to report to on the first day

Timing	Focus	Responsibility
First day	• Introduce new staff to colleagues	Line manager
	• Explain department culture, covering lunch arrangements, tea breaks and personal phone calls	
	• Communicate locations of canteen, telephones, drinks machines, etc	
	• Clarify job description and role	
First week	• Clarify performance appraisal systems and targets	Line manager
	• Training session covering health and safety regulations, fire training, discipline and grievance procedures and trades unions/staff associations	HR department
First month	• Opportunity for feedback	Line manager
	• Training session to understand the company's aims, objectives, strategies and plans	Senior management
First six months	• Full appraisal of performance to date and future plans	Line manager

(c) There should be a clear system for voicing grievances so that perceived problems can be dealt with as quickly as possible. This situation is one in which misunderstandings and rumours might circulate very quickly and a great deal of resentment might arise on both sides.

All possible care should be taken to reassure staff who raise a grievance that they should not fear any form of reprisal or retribution. Cases should be handled confidentially and those raising grievances should be treated courteously throughout.

All staff, from whichever company, should know to whom to address any grievances. Ideally, this should be their immediate line manager for matters associated with day-to-day working arrangements or a designated member of the personnel department for matters that are more related to terms and conditions of employment. It may be that an informal discussion with the designated manager will resolve the issue. If not, then the member of staff should know exactly who to raise the matter with in order to make a formal complaint.

Formal grievances should be dealt with as quickly as possible, consistent with gathering all relevant information and giving the matter appropriate consideration. The person raising the grievance should be informed of the results of this in writing and as quickly as possible.

The results of the grievance process should remain confidential. If there is an outcome that arises from an individual's complaint (e.g. the decision to give Company B staff travelling costs to cover the additional journey to work), then this should be communicated without referring to the fact that there had originally been a complaint.

242   ZNZ (MAY 07 EXAM)

Key answer tip:

This answer provides more detail for each stage than would be required in an exam. However you do need to provide enough information to demonstrate that you understand what is involved in all stages in the process.

(a)   A systematic approach to the training and development of professionally qualified staff is likely to be the responsibility of the human resources department, although it should be carried out with the involvement of managers and staff from across the organisation. The approach can be described in terms of the following stages:

1   identify training and development needs

2   plan training

3   implement plans

4   follow up.

Identify training and development needs

- The training needs will be indicated by a job training analysis. A job analysis will reveal the 'training gap' which is the difference between the knowledge and skill required for the effective performance of a specific job and the knowledge and skill already possessed by the employee.

- The knowledge and skill gap needs to be defined for the future needs of the organisation and expressed for each of the future time periods. This will involve an assessment of the organisation's strategic objectives, current performance and any indication of poor organisational health such as absenteeism and staff turnover.

- Individual training needs can be established by feedback on individual assessments. A major objective of appraisal schemes is to make both superior and subordinate aware of the need to train and/or re-train employees.

- Some training and development needs may be general, such as the need for interpersonal skills. Others may be specific to the job such as technical skills and knowledge.

- In a case such as ZnZ where there are a number of staff studying for professional qualifications, the needs assessment must also take account of specific requirements of the professional bodies. This will vary for different groups of employees.

Plan training

- A plan needs to be developed which takes account of the different groups of employees who need training as well as the skills requirements of particular groups.

- The planning process needs to consider the most appropriate way of providing the training required. The plan may include a mix of a number of different methods:

  - in-house or external courses

  - on-the-job training

  - classroom courses or individual learning.

- The planning will also need to take account of the cost of providing the training and this may also influence the choice of training methods used. The cost assessment should include the cost of time away from normal work.

Implement plans

- Careful briefing of employees and their managers should take place, in order that they know what is happening, when and why.

- Some managers may be involved in delivering the training as well as allowing staff time to attend training courses.

Follow up

- This is perhaps the most difficult stage of the process. The aim is to evaluate the effectiveness of the investment, in terms of resources, and find out whether it has achieved the stated objectives. The following questions need to be asked:

  - Was the training **effective**? Did the employees acquire the knowledge and skills that the activity was intended to provide? Can the employees do the job, which requires the knowledge and skills that they have acquired?

  - Was it **worthwhile** in terms of return on expenditure incurred in giving the training? Is there some other way that the organisation can secure a suitably skilled employee that is less expensive, e.g. effecting different training arrangements, buying-in the skills.

- Follow up should include reviewing the system on a regular basis to ensure that it is still satisfying the organisation's training and development needs.

- Managers need to ensure that staff are given opportunities to use the new skills gained – this is an important part of the development process.

(b) **Advantages of the proposed scheme**

- The scheme should provide evidence of ZnZ's commitment to people development and reinforce the culture of supporting and developing its employees.

- The scheme will provide support to staff who are particularly key to the success of the organisation:

  - middle managers who have promotion potential and who the organisation will not want to lose

  - trainees who are gaining technical skills which are needed by the organisation.

- Enhance communication within the organisation, particularly where staff from different parts of the organisation participate in the scheme together.

- Provide development opportunities and enhanced job satisfaction to experienced staff who are involved as coaches.

- Improve recruitment and retention as the scheme is likely to be seen as an important benefit by current and future staff. This will have an impact on ZnZ's effectiveness and costs.

- Improve the effectiveness of the existing training provision.

- Have the potential to improve the satisfaction and motivation of all staff involved in the scheme, resulting in improved performance.

- Including all trainees and middle managers with promotion potential rather than just minorities and disadvantaged groups should reinforce ZnZ's reputation for providing equal opportunities.

(c) **Disadvantages of the scheme**

- Whilst the scheme is wider than originally proposed there are still some staff who are not covered by it and may resent this and attack the scheme for being unfair. This may cause the staff who are not eligible to become demotivated. The human resources department may need to consider other ways of supporting those staff or widening the scheme further. The staff not covered include:

- junior and senior managers

- non-professional staff

- newly qualified professional staff.

- There may be opposition to the scheme from staff who see it as 'flavour of the month' and are suspicious of the motives of managers behind the scheme.

- There may be conflict between coaches and line managers of staff on the scheme if managers consider that coaches are taking on some of their responsibilities.

- There will be significant costs involved in setting up the scheme:

  - Training of coaches.

  - Cost of time lost from coaches and participants. The cost of time lost from coaches is likely to be high as they will be senior members of staff.

  - Setting up a scheme such as this will be time-consuming and use resources both in HR and other departments in the company, as it will require careful communication about the scheme and its objectives in addition to the cost of designing the scheme and setting up training provision.

- The effectiveness of the scheme will need to be measured – finding suitable indicators and obtaining feedback is likely to be difficult as it will be largely based on opinion.

243   JANE SMITH

(a)   The concept of symptoms and problems is a useful way of viewing the 'people' situation at the Casterbridge office. In other words what may be perceived as problems – such as high staff turnover, sickness, deteriorating quality and increased mistakes – are quite likely to be symptoms of an underlying problem which, if removed, would then lead to an improvement in staff performance. The symptoms can be viewed as indicators. In fact organisations can track these indicators as part of their non-financial performance measurement so as to identify to management areas of concern. Experience suggests that a deterioration in the human resource indicators such as sickness and staff turnover are generally linked to a deterioration in staff morale which is itself a condition of the level of employee motivation. Given no other differences between Casterbridge and the other practice offices, then the incidences of high staff turnover, high sickness and poor work quality are classic outcomes associated with low staff morale.

It follows therefore that an understanding of what motivates and de-motivates employees is crucial to identifying the cause of the lack of motivation at the Casterbridge office. Motivation conditions behaviour, that is, motivation drives people to take certain actions. For example, if you are cold then you may put on warmer clothes - the objective thus being to feel warm which if you are feeling cold drives you to seek ways to change this state. Such objectives can be described as needs, and theory *(Maslow)* suggests that people have levels of, or a hierarchy of, needs ranging from basic physiological needs (such as keeping warm) through higher level needs such as social needs (friendship), ego needs (self-esteem) to self-actualisation. The work environment at the office must thus be satisfactory (clean, warm, spacious, etc) but staff need to feel self esteem, which can be achieved through management encouragement and the recognition of good quality work – an occasional 'well done' or 'thank you for that'.

Once basic needs are fulfilled then people will seek to satisfy the needs at the next highest level. Motivation theory (and common sense) also suggest that people themselves are different and that at the higher level differences arise (McClelland) in the way that different individuals are driven by achievement, power and affiliation objectives. For example some people are ruthless and others not, some people need close friendships at work and others less so. Managers themselves differ in their management style toward employees which is in part a reflection on how they themselves view peoples' relationship to work. Some managers, (McGregor) described as Theory X managers, are driven by the view that people basically do not like work and therefore need to be pushed to perform, be constantly watched and closely controlled. However, Theory Y managers hold the view that people do not inherently dislike work but, given self-direction, recognition and self-esteem, will respond through improved work performance. The Theory X view appears to fit the attitude of the senior partner and would account for the probable lack of encouragement and recognition.

Other theories (Hertzberg) suggest that the satisfaction of some needs will help to remedy de-motivation but will not in themselves motivate behaviour while the satisfaction of other needs will actually motivate towards the type of behaviour we are seeking. Examples of the first category which are sometimes described as hygiene factors include salary and physical working conditions, while examples of the second category described as motivators includes recognition and opportunity for advancement. In other words the partners in Jane's firm cannot assume that paying a good salary will automatically result in motivated staff.

Taken together the theories allow us to make some observations about the likely motivational problem at the Casterbridge office:

- the senior partner appears to have a Theory X view of the problem – 'a case of far too slack management control and supervision'

- paying staff 'above market rates' and providing good working conditions will remove staff dissatisfaction but these are simply hygiene factors and will not in themselves provide motivation

- the unavoidable but frequent changes in the staff partner responsible for the Casterbridge office will have resulted in instability, uncertainty and probably little recognition of individual staff achievement.

(b)   If understanding motivation theories helps to identify problems then it also gives us a guide as to how to remedy the poor staff morale which is giving rise to low levels of motivation with the subsequent performance problems. In a sense Jane starts with an advantage in that the hygiene factors in the Casterbridge office are in place in that working conditions and pay are to standard and inherently there is no reason why the type of work activity carried out in a practice office cannot be made stimulating.

Jane's strategy should focus on confirming the probable cause of the poor performance through discussing with individual staff their thoughts about their job, the office itself, their aspirations and ways for improvement. Jane should spend more time listening than talking and should use a combination of open and closed questions to identify problem areas.

Theory suggests that, if Jane follows up her talks by removing any obvious remaining dissatisfiers and then adopts a management style which involves two-way communication about work issues, encouragement and praise for tasks well done, and delegates responsibility where possible, then her staff will respond through improved behaviour, underpinned by improved motivation, commitment and team spirit.

The firm should bear in mind that each of its offices is a work group of professional people. They are likely to be ambitious and keen to develop themselves and to progress. The firm has to take care to avoid giving signals that suggest the staff might be better off elsewhere. For example, the frequent replacement of the partners in charge of Casterbridge might have been perceived as indicative of a problem. Either partners see the office as a 'hardship posting' and wish to leave or the firm does not care about the disruption and uncertainty caused by constantly changing the management of that office. Either way, professional staff are less likely to be motivated. If changes are necessary then it might help to ensure that staff are told why.

Recruitment may also play a part. If staff are recruited locally then care should be taken to ensure that those selected are team players. If the culture in the Casterbridge office has been lacking in that area in the past, then local decision makers might not attach a great deal of value to that attribute in assessing potential staff.

It might help to provide greater opportunity for staff from Casterbridge to interact with colleagues from other offices in order to generate a greater sense of loyalty to the firm as a whole. Joint training programmes, or the use of staff from a variety of offices in any firm-wide committees or working parties might help.

244 NS INSURANCE COMPANY (NOV 05 EXAM)

(a)   **The role of the HR division**

Key answer tip:

With this requirement it is difficult to understand what the examiner is looking for as the term 'role' could be interpreted in many different ways.

Michael Armstrong sees the role of HRM as:

'A strategic and coherent approach to the management of an organisation's most valued assets: the people working there who individually and collectively contribute to the achievement of its objectives for sustainable competitive advantage.'

The role of HRM, as defined by Armstrong, can thus be viewed as follows:

Suggesting a strategic approach to the personnel function

The previous 'personnel' function probably had a more operational role than strategic. The new HRM division should have a more pivotal role within the firm's strategic planning. This will involve:

- using the value chain to see how human resources can contribute to the firm's competitive advantage

- increasing the weight given to human resource aspects within the firm's SWOT analysis

- viewing staff as contributing to the firm's core competences

- changing attitudes so staff are viewed as assets to be developed rather than costs to be controlled

- encouraging all line managers to see HRM as their responsibility.

Serving the interests of management

Management wants staff to make and implement decisions and to become more customer focused. The HR division will be instrumental in the training aspects of this (see part (b) below).

Dealing with gaining employees' commitment to the values and goals laid down by the strategic management

Management is keen to encourage staff to become more creative and innovative. This will require a change of culture within the firm and, again, the HR division will be central to facilitating that change.

Development of the human resources would help the organisation add value to *their products or services*

Traditional 'personnel' departments tend to focus on training, i.e. filling an identified skills gap, rather than on long-term development. The HR division should see development as a priority looking to enhance the competences of individuals and, in so doing, enhancing the competences of the firm.

(b) The following aspects of HR strategy will change significantly:

Recruitment and selection

To help change the culture of the firm the HR division should seek to recruit people who have experience of the new culture. Ronald Corwin argues that an organisation can be changed more easily if it is invaded by creative and unconventional outsiders with fresh ideas.

Training

The training strategy will be key to encouraging the changes wanted by management. This could include:

- training in the new culture – especially the values involved as part of continuous improvement

- training in customer service – for example, telephone answering techniques, selling, etc

- training in decision-making techniques.

Development

The firm must initiate development programmes to incorporate:

- career planning

- long-term education in general skills as well as specific job-related ones.

Target setting and performance appraisal

Senior management wants a new system of performance measures. The HR team can interview managers and staff to help agree new performance targets and how they should be linked into remuneration.

Remuneration

To encourage innovation the firm may wish to offer some form of bonus system for good ideas – for example, offering staff a bonus equal to 5% of any cost savings or profit gains that result from staff suggestions.

Job descriptions

The changes in expectations of staff should be reflected in revised job descriptions.

245 NYO.COM

(a) Any disciplinary procedure must take account of local legislation. In the case of NYO there are a number of steps that should be followed:

- The company should write the procedures down to avoid misunderstandings and provide all members of staff with a copy.

- It should be very clear which sections apply to which staff (for example, some parts may only be relevant to senior executives).

- The procedures should state very clearly the forms of disciplinary action which can occur, for example verbal warnings and written warnings.

- The procedures should also state which levels of management are able to use certain kinds of action (for example, only senior executives being able to issue written warnings).

- Detail the steps that will be taken to investigate complaints that might lead to action being taken.

- Detail the procedures of how the employee will be notified of any complaint and of any action being taken against them.

- Detail the appeal procedures for workers who feel that the action taken is unmerited.

(b) At its most fundamental level, the existence of a written disciplinary procedure is designed to protect both the employer and the employee.

Benefits to employer

The employer should be protected from facing future actions (for example, for unfair dismissal). If the company has clearly set out what it views as unacceptable behaviour and the actions that will be taken if this behaviour is undertaken, then it becomes very hard for the employee to claim they have been mistreated.

If an employee does undertake some action that is deemed unacceptable, the sliding scale of various different punishments should mean that the employee is less likely to repeat the action.

Looking at the big picture, the point of a disciplinary scheme is to deter employees from breaking the rules, in other words, to make sure that the scheme never has to be used.

Benefits to the employee

The employee of an organisation benefits from having a formal disciplinary procedure since it reduces the risk that they will be arbitrarily accused and punished for their actions.

This is becoming more important as more individuals are left to their own devices at work rather than being given detailed rules and procedures (as organisations move from a mechanistic to an organic approach). This is likely to be particularly important in a company like NYO, which is growing and changing rapidly.

(c) Employers are under a statutory duty to demonstrate that any dismissal is fair, otherwise the dismissed employee would have a vairiety of rights and responses.

An employee might be dismissed on the grounds of a lack of capability or qualifications. This arises when the employee is effectively incapable of doing the job properly, for example because ill health has had an impact on his or her performance. In this case the employee must be given the opportunity to improve the position or, in the case of ill health, be considered for alternative employment.

An employee can be dismissed for misconduct if he or she is guilty of refusing to obey lawful and reasonable instructions, absenteeism, and insubordination over a period of time. Criminal actions relating directly to the job might also constitute grounds for dismissal.

An employee could be dismissed if he or she was unable to pursue normal duties without breaking the law. For example, if one of the company's sales staff was banned from driving and was unable to visit clients then that would probably consitute grounds for dismissal.

Any other good work-related reasons for dismissal might be treated as valid grounds, for example, if the business needed to change and the employee refused unreasonably to adapt to the change.

MAY 2008
EXAM QUESTIONS

SECTION A – 40 MARKS

[The indicative time for answering this section is 72 minutes.]

Answer ALL 15 sub-questions.

QUESTION ONE

1.1 The evaluation of candidates for a job using a comprehensive and interrelated series of selection techniques is known as:

    A   psychometric testing

    B   developing a balanced scorecard

    C   job evaluation

    D   an assessment centre

                                                   (2 marks)

1.2 The systematic comparison of key factors between sections or departments within the same organisation is called:

    A   internal benchmarking

    B   performance appraisal

    C   environmental auditing

    D   quality assessment

                                                   (2 marks)

1.3 In the expectancy theory of motivation a person's preference for a particular outcome is referred to as:

    A   a valence

    B   a hygiene factor

    C   a motivator

    D   preference discrimination

                                                   (2 marks)

1.4 **The concept of 'reliability' of staff selection techniques means:**

    A   effective testing of a candidate's desire for the job and natural abilities

    B   overcoming poor performance in the interview due to nervousness

    C   that if the test is repeated a consistent test score would be achieved

    D   choosing the best candidate every time   **(2 marks)**

1.5 **M-marketing refers to marketing practices using:**

    A   mobile telephone technology

    B   manipulation and image projection

    C   market forecasting of current and future product demand

    D   marketing decision support systems   **(2 marks)**

1.6 **In purchasing, the 'Reck and Long' positioning tool is by nature:**

    A   strategic

    B   independent

    C   supportive

    D   passive   **(2 marks)**

1.7 **The use of 'skim pricing' as a marketing technique will result in:**

    A   non-recovery of promotional costs

    B   enticing new customers to buy a product or service

    C   high prices normally at an early stage of the product lifecycle

    D   low prices so denying competitors opportunities to gain market share   **(2 marks)**

1.8 **The technique PDCA represents:**

    A   a programme development control activity used in information management

    B   a framework for bringing about quality improvement to a process or system

    C   a software inventory system used in warehouse management

    D   people, developments, controls and appraisal in strategic human resourcing   **(2 marks)**

1.9 **Undifferentiated market positioning involves the targeting of:**

    A   a single market segment with a single marketing mix

    B   a single market segment ignoring the concept of the marketing mix

    C   an entire market with a different marketing mix for each segment

    D   an entire market with a single marketing mix   **(2 marks)**

1.10   The internet is an example of:

A   parallel processing

B   distributed processing

C   a local area network

D   a wide area network

(2 marks)

(Total for sub-questions 1.1 to 1.10 = 20 marks)

Required:

Each of the sub-questions numbered **1.11** to **1.15** below requires a brief written response. Each sub-question is worth 4 marks.

Your response should be in note form and should not exceed 50 words per sub-question.

1.11   **Identify the qualities normally associated with the workforce of a 'learning organisation'.**

(4 marks)

1.12   **List the types of internal failure cost that might arise for a manufacturing organisation considering quality issues.**

(4 marks)

1.13   **Identify the potential challenges arising from the introduction of a database management system (DBMS) within an organisation.**

(4 marks)

1.14   **Identify the means of recruitment that exist for an organisation other than using journal or newspaper advertising.**

(4 marks)

1.15   **Describe the likely features of an organisation that has fully embraced the marketing concept.**

(4 marks)

(Total for sub-questions 1.11 to 1.15 = 20 marks)

(Total for Section A = 40 marks)

SECTION B – 30 MARKS

[The indicative time for answering this section is 54 minutes.]

Answer ALL 6 sub-questions. Each sub-question is worth 5 marks.

QUESTION TWO

K1S is a fast growing chain of hair and beauty salons (shops) located throughout the prosperous north of the country. The company is due to expand from thirty to thirty five salons within the next year. K1S's policy is to buy existing salons in fashionable city centre shopping malls which, it believes, are 'underperforming' by offering too limited a range of treatments and charging too low a price. (All K1S's salons charge 'top' prices but provide excellent customer care. In addition to hairdressing services, K1S offers beauty treatments.) K1S also plans to sell own-brand products at premium prices from its premises. K1S's managing director (MD) sees training as critical to 'keeping our service sophisticated and professional, with a distinctive K1S style'. K1S now operates its own hairdressing training academy from purpose built premises.

The MD has, however, identified a number of areas which need to be addressed if K1S is to continue to prosper:

- The opportunities for the use of information technology (IT) need to be taken, particularly in the implementation and running of the information system network and in support of management operations.

- Information systems (IS) need to be developed primarily based on the needs of the company as a whole but also mindful of the need to support salon management operations locally.

- The threat posed by competitors who are copying K1S's approach.

The MD has appointed a management consultancy team to conduct a complete organisational review. Its report identifies a number of issues, some of which are highlighted below.

- Information systems are generally weak and the benefits of modern software applications lacking. The accuracy and completeness of information received from salons needs to improve, and there needs to be better coordination of activities. Several different systems are used and some are very inefficient. (For example, over 40% of salon receptionist/ administrators' time is spent manually analysing and searching for information.) Through its acquisition policy, K1S has 'inherited' a series of salons operating independent systems of varying sophistication and effectiveness. Some still use manual systems, others use stand-alone computers, but none take full advantage of software capabilities and most only use basic software functions. It seems that the more complex a system the salon has, the more the staff resistance to its full use seems to be. Internet possibilities are being missed and there is no wide area network (WAN). Common computerised stock records will also be required when hair styling products and treatments are sold.

- Brand development and management is crucial to competing successfully. A more recognisable K1S brand should be supported by consistent shop style, uniforms, paperwork, etc. and a user-friendly website needs to be developed.

- There is a need to strengthen management locally. Salons are currently managed by senior stylists who have much industry knowledge but little management training. These senior stylists are assisted by a receptionist/administrator. Each salon keeps its own set of accounts and makes its own staffing arrangements including recruitment, selection, rotas, holiday cover and remuneration, etc. Managers should be appointed with responsibility for a few salons each (so leaving stylists to concentrate full time on hairdressing) and a centralised HR and Finance function should be established to support salons. Staff flexibility between salons would also lead to more efficient operations.

You are part of the management consultancy team responsible for the report and have been asked to prepare a series of notes on key themes for discussion with the MD.

Instructions

You should use no more than one page per sub-question. Use a separate page of your answer book for each sub-question (meaning that your notes are contained on no more than six pages in total). Your notes can take any form and might include diagrams, tables, sentences or bullet points, etc.

Required:

(a)   Explain how information systems (IS) should be developed to serve K1S's management operations both centrally and within salons. **(5 marks)**

(b)   Explain how K1S's operations can be improved through the use of information technology (IT) generally and a wide area network (WAN) specifically. **(5 marks)**

(c)   Discuss the significance of 'people' to K1S within the context of the 'marketing mix'.
(5 marks)

(d)   Explain the concepts of 'physical evidence' and 'process' and their importance in developing brand awareness for K1S. **(5 marks)**

(e)   Explain the role a central human resource management function could play in supporting salons. **(5 marks)**

(f)   Discuss the factors that need to be considered when developing staff training associated with the installation of a new computer system for K1S. **(5 marks)**

(Total for Question Two = 30 marks)

(Total for Section B = 30 marks)

SECTION C – 30 MARKS

[Indicative time for answering this question is 54 minutes.]

Answer ONE question only.

QUESTION THREE

QW9 is a large insurance company. The industry conditions are very competitive and QW9 is under constant pressure to achieve higher standards of customer service and improve profitability for shareholders.

You have recently taken up a post in QW9's central project and technical support team working directly for the Director of Strategy, who is also relatively new to the organisation. In an initial briefing with you, the Director explains that he has met with most senior managers and discussed their feelings on the strengths and weaknesses of the company. He has concluded that there are a number of areas that need to be addressed, including two from the area of human resource management, namely, performance related rewards and performance management.

- Performance related rewards. QW9 experiences difficulty in recruiting staff even though it pays comparable salaries to its rivals. Senior managers do not feel that there are problems with either staff morale or the external image of the company. The Director of Strategy explains that although QW9 offers a number of benefits to its employees beyond basic pay, this is not made explicit enough either internally or externally. The Director has so far identified a good pension scheme, flexitime, personal insurance cover at reduced rates, a subsidised canteen and a social club. You have also heard it said that the balance between a professional and personal life is a distinguishing feature of being a QW9 employee. It is the Director's view that all benefits should be examined and a 'total reward package' approach should be progressed. This would draw together all the financial and non-financial benefits (including working practices, development opportunities and the challenge of working for QW9 itself) into an integrated package which would be available to all employees.

- Performance management. A formal performance appraisal system supported by standardised procedures and paperwork has operated for a number of years. The scheme has clear organisational objectives centred on staff development and improved performance rather than as a basis for paying individual annual bonuses. It is, however, not well regarded by either managers or staff and its objectives are not being met. Senior managers complain about the time that is taken up with the process. Exit interviews are conducted whenever someone leaves QW9, and a review of a sample of recorded comments indicates staff feelings on the scheme very clearly: 'appraisal is just a paper exercise', 'a joke', 'a waste of time and effort'.

Required:

(a) Discuss the advantages and disadvantages of QW9 developing a 'total reward package' approach. **(10 marks)**

(b) Explain how QW9 should conduct research that would help inform the design of a total reward package. (Assume that research is conducted by QW9 staff.) **(10 marks)**

(c) Explain the possible reasons why the objectives of the formal appraisal system are not being met. **(10 marks)**

(Total for question three = 30 marks)

QUESTION FOUR

DOH is a long established family run firm which supplies parts for local motor car manufacturers. For the past thirty years DOH has exercised quality control over its manufacturing processes by employing one quality control (QC) inspector for every 40 workers. (QC inspectors sample completed batches and remove defective parts before they are despatched.)

Recently, DOH was reluctantly forced to subcontract a batch of work to another firm so that it could meet new delivery deadlines. Fears by DOH's managing director that this subcontracted work might be of an inferior standard proved to be unfounded. In fact, no defects whatsoever were discovered in the subcontracted batch. At the same time, DOH's main customer is unhappy with some of the batches it has received and is insisting that in future quality failures due to defective parts produced by DOH will incur strict penalty charges, including the cost of labour involved in removing the part from the vehicle under construction. The managing director is worried that unless DOH improves its quality standards, it might in future lose contracts with key customers.

At the next staff liaison committee, the managing director raises the issue of quality processes and a frank discussion follows. Apparently the workforce believes that 'mistakes happen' and 'we are all human after all'. Scrap and reworking costs are thought to be 'inevitable in our business'. It is also a generally held view that

- senior managers are 'out of touch' with the problems of maintaining quality standards whilst meeting production targets;

- the value of middle managers is not apparent;

- QC inspectors are not liked but are respected because they are hard working and exercise their individual professional judgement diligently when deciding which parts to reject as unsuitable for despatch.

Worried by these developments, the managing director discusses DOH's quality problems with an advisor at the government funded regional trade and industry office. The advisor negotiates access for him to see first hand how other manufacturers are improving quality in similar industries so that lessons might be learned. The managing director is very impressed by

- teamwork within the workforce;

- an absence of middle managers and QC inspectors;

- the way in which individual workers demand better quality and get senior manager support to achieve it.

The managing director organises a weekend hotel meeting for all senior managers, where he presents his analysis of the problems of quality within DOH. He makes it clear that he is looking beyond temporary 'quick fixes' to overcome the challenges DOH faces. After much discussion he formulates a plan for bringing about change through a programme he calls 'putting quality first'. The programme aims to drive up quality standards through training, improved teamwork and a review of roles within DOH, particularly quality control inspectors and middle managers. If successful, he believes the programme will bring lasting improvements and longer term, increased customer satisfaction and reduced costs. Senior managers support the programme but have warned that it needs to be both 'sold' to the workforce and carefully implemented.

Required:

(a) Analyse the problems of quality that DOH is facing. **(10 marks)**

(b) Discuss the way in which the problems of quality are being addressed by DOH. **(10 marks)**

(c) Explain the extent to which DOH's 'putting quality first' programme is based upon the principles of organisational development. **(10 marks)**

(Total for Question Four = 30 marks)

Section 8

ANSWERS TO MAY 2008 EXAM QUESTIONS

SECTION A

QUESTION ONE

MULTIPLE CHOICE QUESTIONS

Key answer tip: Use some of the 20 minutes reading time to begin working through the MCQ's. You can mark the answers on the question paper. Once the 3 hour writing time begins, 36 minutes should be more than adequate to write out the answers to the 10 MCQ's.

Tutorial note: This was a reasonably straight forward and typical set of questions. The syllabus areas of operations management, marketing and managing human capital featured heavily.
Two minor syllabus areas, namely M-marketing and the PDCA cycle, were tested. Otherwise, the questions covered core areas and a well prepared candidate should have scored well here.

1.1 D

Assessment centres refer to the use of trained assessors to observe and evaluate individuals using a comprehensive and interrelated series of selection techniques.

1.2 A

Benchmarking is the systematic comparison of a service, practice or process. Internal benchmarking is one type of benchmarking and relates to the comparison of sections or departments within the same organisation.

1.3 A

Valence is a person's preference for a particular outcome, e.g. a promotion.

1.4 C

Reliability refers to the need of a selection process to give consistent results.

1.5 A

M-marketing refers to the use of mobile phones to market products or services.

1.6 A

The extent to which supply chain management is a strategic issue can be considered through Reck and Long's strategic positioning tool.

1.7   C

Skim pricing involves the setting of a high price for a new product in order to benefit from those wishing to be early adopters of the product.

1.8   C

The PDCA (Plan-Do-Check-Act) cycle is a framework for bringing about quality improvements to a process or system. This cycle encourages continuous improvement.

1.9   D

Undifferentiated marketing is the delivery of a single product to the market with little concern for segment analysis.

1.10   D

A wide area network (WAN) can link computers in different geographical locations or organisations. The internet is an example of a WAN.

SHORT QUESTIONS

Key answer tip: The use of bullet points or short notes is perhaps the most effective approach, allowing good coverage of points in the 36 minutes allocated.

Tutorial note: There were no surprises in this section. All syllabus areas, except for change management, were examined. Again, a well prepared candidate should have scored well here as only core areas were examined.

1.11

Senge believes there are five core workforce competencies involved in building a learning organisation:

1. Building a shared vision

2. Mastery of learning by individuals

3. Challenging existing practices

4. Team building and learning

5. Systems thinking with a focus on long-term solutions

1.12

Internal failure costs are costs arising within the organisation due to a failure to achieve the quality standards specified. These may include:

- Re-inspection costs

- The cost of re-working parts

- The cost of scrapped parts

- Losses due to lower selling process for sub-quality goods

1.13

Potential challenges arising from the introduction of a DBMS include:
- Ensuring the system is resilient to failure and that there is a contingency plan

- Development costs may be high

- Staff may be resistant to the change. Training will be required

- Problems of data security and integrity

1.14

Recruitment methods, in addition to newspaper or journal advertising, include:
- In-house methods such as the use of an intranet or notice boards

- Recruitment fairs and headhunting

- Recruitment agents

- Career services such as job centres

- Web based and radio adverts

1.15

Features include:
- Establishing customer needs, using market research

- Developing products/ services with features to fulfil these needs

- Promotion should not be hard sell but should focus on the ability of the product's features to satisfy these needs

- The concept should be embraced by the whole firm

SECTION B

QUESTION TWO

Question overview: The question was based on a common workplace scenario involving a chain of hair and beauty salons. Three syllabus areas, namely information systems (IS), marketing and managing human capital featured heavily.

As with previous sittings, question 2 was not as well answered as question 1. Common errors included:

- Lack of development of written points

- Poor application of knowledge to the scenario

- Too much repetition of question content, rather than demonstration of understanding

This may appear to be a lot to achieve given candidates only have 8 minutes for each requirement. However, a good candidate will have completed a number of section B questions during revision and should feel comfortable with these areas. Use of headings, sub-headings and bullet points should help to break up the answer and make it easier to mark.

A separate page should be completed for each requirement. This gives plenty of scope for candidates to start on the requirements that they feel most comfortable with and to gain the easy marks first. However, answer all requirements and stick to 8 minutes for each one.

(a) Key answer tip: The requirement asked how information systems could be developed within the company. Easy marks were available for explaining the key stages in the systems development life cycle (this is a core knowledge area). Good candidates developed their points using full sentences and linked their discussion back to the scenario.

Tutorial note: A large number of candidates answered the question in terms of IT, rather then IS. Candidates should refer back to the requirement several times to ensure that their answer reflects it.

(a)

The current information systems (IS) in K1S are weak and inefficient. A project team, led by a competent project manager, should be appointed to implement a new IS in order to ensure that K1S continue to compete successfully in the market.

A number of formal stages should be followed:

Feasibility

This involves a review of the existing system and the identification of a range of possible solutions. Factors such as cost (economic feasibility), resistance and retraining needs (social feasibility), organisational fit (operational feasibility) and availability of an appropriate solution (technical feasibility) must be considered.

Potential solutions may range from a transaction processing system to carry out routine day-to-day processing, e.g. stock and payroll, to a management information system used to provide salon management with the information required to monitor and control the salons. The package could include a website.

Analysis

Staff buy-in is essential. Fact finding methods, such as staff questionnaires, should be used to establish the current system problems and the needs of the new system.

The results can be translated into technical diagrams, such as a data flow diagram.

Design and Development

The results of the analysis will be used as the basis for developing an IT solution. A development choice must be made between the development of bespoke software or the use of off-the-shelf solutions. K1S is a fairly typical business and so a ready-made package should be able to fulfil most of their needs.

Implementation

This involves a number of activities, such as testing and training, to bring the system into full use. Care must be taken in ensuring the accuracy of data when transferring it from the old system. The new and old systems may be run side-by-side for a period (parallel running) to ensure the system fulfils K1S's requirements.

Review and Maintenance

The success of the project should be reviewed and any maintenance carried out.

(b) **Key answer tip:** The requirement asked how IT generally, and a WAN specifically, could improve operations. Easy marks were available for discussing how IT could address some of the problems mentioned in the scenario and through the basic discussion of the improvements that a WAN would bring, e.g. email access and website development.

(b)

OPERATIONAL BENEFITS OF IT

1. Improved efficiency

The use of an online booking and diary system could dramatically reduce the time spent by receptionists and administrators manually analysing and searching for information.

2. Simplification

IT could simplify procedures for producing accounts and for managing staff.

3. Standardisation

The use of an integrated IT system should assist in co-ordination and control of the business.

OPERATIONAL BENEFITS OF A WIDE AREA NETWORK (WAN)

1. Improved efficiency

A WAN will allow computers and other devices to be linked across a number of geographical locations. This will increase the speed of communication between individual salons and managers.

2. Information and resource sharing

This should become much easier between salons, e.g. through the use of email.

3. Website as a source of competitive advantage

A new, well branded, website, could be used for advertising and booking.

(c) **Key answer tip:** The requirement asked for a discussion of the significance of people to K1S within the context of the marketing mix. This should have been a relatively straight forward requirement. A well prepared candidate will have had good knowledge of the marketing mix and there were easy links to be made regarding the significance of people for K1S.

Tutorial note: A large proportion of candidates failed to recognise people as both customers and staff. A brief discussion of both was required to obtain a good mark.

(c)

The Marketing Mix

The marketing mix will be used to positively influence KIS's target market. People are just one of the elements of this mix. People relates to both staff and the need to understand customer needs.

Customers as People

K1S must continue to understand and prioritise the needs of its customers. This will ensure continued business success.

K1S has established its target market as those customers who are willing to pay top prices for excellent customer care.

Staff as People

The quality of the personal relationships between the staff and the clients and the level of customer care will be vital to K1S and can act as a source of competitive advantage.

New staff joining K1S will need thorough training and constant monitoring.

Staff leaving the business may take customers with them and so investing in staff retention is vital.

Staffing costs will be a big percentage of K1S's cost base and so proper strategies for recruiting, training and safeguarding relationships should be put in place.

(d) **Key answer tip:** The question required an explanation of the concepts of physical evidence and process, with a particular focus on how these could be used to develop brand image. Candidates should have included a definition of the terms and some practical examples of how they could be used to develop the brand.

A well prepared candidate should have had few problems explaining the terms. A good candidate was able to expand their answer to include the required discussion of brand image.

(d)

Physical evidence, process and people are the additional P's contained within the marketing mix for a service organisation suck as K1S.

Physical Evidence

K1S must be able to physically demonstrate the quality of its service. This can help to develop K1S's brand awareness, e.g. by using a consistent approach to:

- The design of its salons – including the shop front, layout and furnishings.

- The salon location – this should help reinforce the quality image.

- Use of appropriate magazines, music and beverages to appeal to the target market.

Process

This can be considered as the whole customer experience. Processes can be used to differentiate the brand, e.g.

- Immediate and professional greeting on arrival combined with short waiting times.

- Personalised customer consultation to ensure the needs of the individual are established and fulfilled.

- After sales care such as personalised product recommendations and appointment reminders.

(e) **Key answer tip:** Most candidates should have performed well in this requirement. Easy marks were available for explaining the role of the HRM function. This should not have caused too many problems. In fact, many students would have struggled to keep the answer brief enough. Time management is important for success in section B and so coverage of a few of their key roles would have been fine.

Good students will have linked their points back to K1S and specifically how a HRM function could assist the salon.

(e)

A central human resources management (HRM) function could work with the salons to help ease their workload and to develop a strategic approach to HRM whilst still embracing local knowledge and expertise.

The HRM function carries out a wide variety of activities including:

1. Organisational Design and Development

Input into the appropriate company structure and the development of company culture.

2. Staffing

- The **planning** of staff needs as K1S expands.

- Assisting salons with advice on appropriate **recruitment** methods and **selection** techniques.

- **Training** is of key importance to K1S. HRM could assist in identifying training needs and developing appropriate training programmes.

- HRM could implement a standardised **appraisal** process and assist the salons with its implementation.

- HRM could assist salons in setting appropriate **remuneration** levels, developing incentive schemes and maintaining staff morale.

3. Employee Services

HRM could help to ease the local burden of having to keep personnel records and deal with health and safety legislation.

(f) **Key answer tip:** This requirement asked candidates what factors needed to be considered when developing staff training for the new system. Little or no technical content was required and this allowed candidates the freedom to apply some a common sense.

Tutorial note: Candidates may have chosen to bring in their technical knowledge of some of the change theorists, e.g. Lewin and Kotter & Schlesinger.

(f)

The following factors will need to be considered when developing staff training for the new computer system:

Resistance to Change

The use of more complex systems has previously resulted in some resistance amongst staff. Lewin concluded that for any change to be successful these restraining forces must be removed.

Kotter and Schlesinger identified a number of techniques for overcoming change. E.g. education and communication, through techniques such as staff briefings and the training itself, should assist in getting buy-in from staff.

IT Competence

Some salons still use manual systems and so will require thorough training, starting with basic computer literacy. Other salons use computers with basic software but will still require in-depth training on the new system.

Cost

The cost of the training must be established and budgeted for. It will not be essential for all staff to complete training. It can be limited to the main users such as the salon receptionists, managers and head office staff. It is worth noting that initial and one-off training can be capitalised.

Training Tools

There are a number of training tools available such as formal courses, on-the-job training, individual web-based training or home study. A number of factors should be considered when establishing the most appropriate tool, e.g. the cost, training contents and preference of the trainee.

SECTION C

Section overview: Section C was particularly poorly answered.

Common errors were:

- Lack of content. Outline notes are not sufficient for the more substantial requirements in this section.

- Poor planning resulting in an unstructured answered and a failure to address all the issues in the scenario

- Some candidates took the approach of writing down everything they knew, highlighting an inability to link their knowledge to the scenario.

- Poor time management in the rest of the exam resulting in a rushed answer.

Candidates should not feel overwhelmed by the scenario question.

Top tips include:

- Allocating the time to and working through each requirement in turn. This helps to break the question into manageable chunks.

- Remember, there will always be easy marks available for book knowledge and common sense ideas.

- Depth of answer is important. Use full paragraphs and explain each point made. The use of headings is advised to break up the answer and make it look professional.

QUESTION THREE

Question overview: The question focused the 'managing human capital' part of the syllabus. It required the application of knowledge and understanding to the scenario of a large insurance company.

(a) A discussion of the advantages of a total reward package approach was required.

Key answer tip: Candidates may have panicked when they realised there were 10 marks available. However, by keeping calm, candidates should have been able to get 6-8 marks here.

- Brainstorm 6-10 points in a plan. By forgetting about the structure and depth of the answer for a minute it will be surprising how easy it is to come up with enough ideas.

- Use these points as headings in the answer.

- Explain each point fully, linking back to QW9.

Tutorial note: It may be difficult to get enough depth into the answer. Overcome this by explaining the points using one or two of the motivational theorists.

(a)

A total reward package (TRP) would draw together all of the financial and non-financial benefits available to employees.

ADVANTAGES

1. Attract and retain staff

QW9 offers a number of attractive benefits to its employees but these are not made clear to current or prospective staff. The use of a TRP would address this lack of knowledge and should help in solving any problems that the company has in attracting and retaining staff.

2. Improved quality of staff

Some of the benefits, e.g. a good work-life balance are a distinguishing feature of being a QW9 employee. By making this clear, the company would improve its ability to attract and retain the best staff.

3. Improved motivation amongst staff

Employees are motivated by a number of factors, not only a competitive basic salary. It appears that there are a number of potentially motivating factors in place within QW9. Maslow identified a hierarchy of five different needs. As each need is satisfied so the individual moves up the hierarchy, with successive levels of needs dominating behaviour.

The needs from bottom to top are:

- Physiological needs such as competitive basic pay in QW9

- Safety needs such as a good pension scheme in QW9

- Social needs such as the social club in QW9

- Ego needs such as opportunities for a merit pay increase.

- Self-fulfilment needs such as a challenging job and achievement in work.

It is not clear if the last two needs are in place in QW9. However, many of the needs do seem to be in place and by pointing this out to staff in a TRP, employee morale and hence productivity should increase.

4. Recognises employees as individuals

Different employees will be motivated by different factors e.g. some by the flexitime and good work-life balance (perhaps allowing work to complement a family life) and others by the social club allowing them to meet friends at work. The TRP should allow flexibility in that employees can choose a selection of benefits that will suit their own individual needs. QW9 will be able to use this to attract a broad range of suitable employees and, once again, staff retention and motivation should improve as a result of this flexibility.

DISADVANTAGES

1. Cost

The TRP will itself be costly to implement. The benefits must outweigh the cost. However, it may be difficult to measure the benefit of the implemented package since recruitment and retention can be influenced by a number of factors and staff motivation can be hard to measure.

2. May not recognise all employee needs

As discussed above, all employees have different needs. A prospective or current employee may review the TRP and may conclude that their needs are not met. As a result, good staff members may be lost or potential high quality recruits may go elsewhere.

3. Actions of other companies

There is a risk that other companies will also implement a TRP and may even compete using a much better package of benefits. As a result, the advantages discussed above, such as retention of staff, may not be achieved. QW9 must ensure that it can compete in terms of the benefits offered and also has a number of unique benefits to offer.

4. Other impacts on recruitment

Other factors may have resulted in the problems that QW9 are experiencing regarding recruitment e.g. an inappropriate choice of recruitment techniques. If this is the case, a TRP will have to be complemented by other changes within the business.

(b) This question asked candidates how to conduct market research into the design of the TRP.

Key answer tip: Again, it would be a good idea to start by planning the answer and brainstorming ideas. Don't stop until there are a sufficient number of points.

Tutorial note: Some book knowledge could be applied here, e.g. the use of primary and secondary research. This would also help to give structure to the answer. Alternatively, candidates could have applied common sense. By keeping calm, and relating the points made back to QW9, a reasonable mark could have been obtained.

(b)

There are two main methods of market research available to QW9, namely field (primary) research and desk (secondary) research.

FIELD (PRIMARY) RESEARCH

This is research by direct contact with an identified contact group. Sources include:

1. Employees working for competitors

Discussions with members of staff who work for the competitor companies (if possible) or with current QW9 staff who have previously worked for the competitor companies. These staff should have knowledge of the TRP in place.

2. QW9's HR department

The HR department should have a detailed knowledge of the benefits currently in place. This may include other benefits in addition to those that the Director of Strategy is already aware of. The HR department are a key information source and their input from the start should help to achieve buy-in into the process.

3. QW9 employees

A representative sample of QW9 employees/ potential employees should be chosen. Methods such as questionnaires, interviews and group discussions can be used to ascertain their views on the current benefits system and opinions regarding any changes they would like to be made to this system. Employees are a valuable knowledge source and obtaining their buy-in should increase the probability that the new package will be successful.

4. The finance department

The finance department should be able to provide the detailed costing information on the current benefits in place and any prospective benefits.

DESK (SECONDARY) RESEARCH

This is concerned with the collection of information from readily available secondary sources. Collection of desk research should help to reduce the amount of field research required. Sources include:

1. Academic research

Research may have been carried out on the effective design of a TRP.

2. Publications

Trade or industry publications may be available which outline the TRP available in competitor companies and review the industry norms regarding benefits.

3. Internet searches

The internet can be used to investigate TRP's offered by other insurance companies or by other companies with well regarded TRP's.

4. Recruitment information

Recruitment information could be obtained from other insurance companies. This may highlight the benefits that are offered to staff members.

CONCLUSION

The expertise of the marketing department should be embraced when carrying out the research. Once the research is complete it should be possible to design and implement an effective and economically viable TRP.

(c) This requirement asked the candidate to explain the reasons why the objectives of the appraisal system were not being met.

Key answer tip: Most candidates were able to come up with a number of reasons, either by applying common sense or using book knowledge, e.g. Lockett's theory. The gain a good mark, candidates had to discuss several key reasons and link their discussion back to the scenario.

(c)

There are a number of possible reasons why the objectives of the formal appraisal system are not being met. Lockett pointed out that appraisal fails due to six key reasons:

1. Confrontation

There may be conflict between both parties involved in the appraisal.

2. Judgement

The appraiser may take a one-sided view of the process and QW9 staff may feel that they are being judged unfairly.

3. Chat

The appraisal may lack purpose or outcomes being set. This may well be the case in QW9 because employees have commented that the appraisal is "a joke", "a waste of time and effort".

4. Bureaucracy

Senior managers complain about the time taken up with the process and staff feel that the "appraisal is just a paper exercise". Staff fears, ignorance, lack of involvement and suspicions of unfairness can create open hostility. The scheme should not be seen as a form filling exercise but should be fair, with an appeals procedure for those who think they have been treated unfairly.

5. Unfinished business

The appraisal should be part of a continuing process towards performance management. It may be that the facts are not being recorded and that there is little follow up to the actions required as a result of the appraisal, e.g. the arrangement of training for the appraisee.

6. Annual event

An appraisal is often an annual event. Annual targets may be irrelevant after a few months and therefore meaningless.

In addition to Lockett's six reasons, there are a number of other reasons why the current system may be failing to achieve its objectives:

Lack of support by senior managers

We are told that the scheme is not well regarded by managers and that they complain about the time taken up by the process. Support and buy-in from management is essential for an effective system.

Lack of training

The appraiser should be given full training before they carry out any appraisals.

Mixed objectives

Appraisals are often used to achieve a number of outcomes such as performance management, promotion and salary reviews. It may be difficult to use the same process to achieve all of these.

Poor design

Poor design or implementation of the scheme is a possibility.

QUESTION FOUR

Question overview: This question involved a manufacturing company that is seeking to change in order to improve the quality of its products. The syllabus areas of 'operations management' and 'change management' were tested.

(a) This requirement asked candidates to analyse the problems of quality that DOH is facing. Little book knowledge was required.

Key answer tip: Many candidates focused on the problem of poor quality in isolation, rather than discussing the individual problems surrounding quality. Candidates needed to explain the problems and not just copy them from the question.

A good mark could have been obtained by using 6-7 key headings, with well explained points and referenced back to the scenario.

(a)

DOH is facing a number of problems:

Old fashioned quality control (QC) system
The current system takes a traditional approach to QC. The system focuses on checking the quality of the parts produced as opposed to producing for quality. At present, defects are accepted and expected. This is an inefficient system and will result in a number of costs such as:

- Appraisal costs – the costs of quality inspection and tests.

- Internal failure costs – the costs of detection and rectification of quality failure.

- External failure costs – the costs incurred after a faulty part has been passed onto the customer.

Potential loss of customers

If the problem of substandard quality continues, customers may be lost or they may impose penalties. Key customers are becoming more demanding and will not continue to tolerate mistakes.

Threat from competitors

Other industry competitors have taken substantial and successful steps in improving quality. There is a risk that DOH will fall behind its competitors and lose market share.

Defects still occur

The current system results in defects, despite the hard work of the inspectors. This may be because the inspectors carry out their work too early in the process and as a result some faults may be missed. In addition, we are told that inspectors are allowed to exercise individual judgement. The absence of formal standards may not be effective.

Workforce resistance

The workforce is complacent, believing that "mistakes happen". There is no buy-in to the quality process. It appears that most of the responsibility for quality has been passed to the quality inspectors.

Managers are out of touch

Senior managers are out of touch with quality standards. Unless this is addressed, it will be very difficult to solve the problems surrounding quality.

Role of middle managers and quality inspectors

Other manufacturers have improved quality whilst also removing the needs for middle managers and quality inspectors. This may be an unnecessary and costly resource and an alternative approach to quality control may be more effective.

(b) This question asked candidates to discuss the ways that DOH is addressing the problems of quality.

Key answer tip: Some candidates failed to get enough depth to their answer. A few of the key changes could have been used as headings. Each change should have been discussed fully, e.g. considering the impact of the change, any potential problems and recommendations.

(b)

The problems of quality are being addressed is a number of ways:

1. PRIORITISATION OF QUALITY

Initiative

Senior managers recently devoted an entire weekend to formulating the quality programme. This demonstrates that the issue has been prioritised and that improved quality is seen as a key part of the business strategy.

Potential problem

The MD, together with the senior managers, was responsible for implementing the programme. Without the input from lower level managers and employees, key implementation issues may not be identified and it may be difficult to spread the quality ethos throughout the organisation.

Recommendation

Input from all levels should be obtained. This should reduce the number of potential problems, help to obtain buy-in and help to change the culture of the organisation to one where all employees embrace quality.

2. TAKING ADVICE FROM THIRD PARTIES

Initiative

DOH has sought advice from a government advisor and has visited other manufacturers who have taken steps to improve quality. The lessons learnt have been used to develop a quality improvement programme called "putting quality first".

Potential problem

In addition to the lack of employee involvement discussed above, simply copying competitors may not work. The techniques used may result in a host of new problems, current problems may not be addressed and competitive advantage will not be obtained by simply mirroring competitors.

Recommendation

A proven quality improvement programme should be implemented. One such programme is total quality management (TQM). Fundamental features include:

- Prevention of errors before they occur, e.g. through the use of top quality supplies and highly trained staff.

- Participation by all employees.

- Recognition of the need for continual change and improvement.

- Recognition of the vital role of customers and suppliers.

3. SELLING THE PROGRAMME TO THE WORKFORCE

Initiative

Senior managers have recognised that the changes will only be successful if they are sold to the workforce.

Potential problem

This is a fundamental change. Employees may have concerns about changes to their roles, potential redundancies or new skills and therefore training required. The success of the change may be dependent on more than a process of simply selling the change to the workforce.

Recommendation

For change to be successful, any restraining forces must be removed by addressing the concerns of the workforce. As mentioned, a TQM approach involves all employees embracing the quality ethos. Rather than simply selling the changes, other methods, as recommended by Kotter and Schlesinger, could be used. E.g.

- Education and communication using small group briefings and training.

- Participation and involvement using small groups or employee representatives.

4. ROLE REVIEW

Initiative

The roles of the quality control inspectors and middle managers are going to be reviewed.

Potential problem

The removal of these roles may result in key tasks not being completed or senior managers becoming overburdened as they take on some of the middle managers' workload.

Recommendation

A detailed review should be carried out before any decision is made. If a decision is taken to remove these roles, senior manager must be given sufficient resources to implement the change programme effectively and to ensure that they are not overburdened.

(c) This requirement asked candidates to discuss the extent to which DOH's quality programme is based upon the principle of organisational development.

Tutorial note: A large number of candidates did not understand organisational development and as a consequence this requirement was poorly answered.

(c)

Organisational development (OD) is an educational strategy intended to change the beliefs, values and structure of an organisation so that it can better to adapt to the change. It is seen as a continuous, all embracing process. The quality programme in DOH is an example of OD and embraces many of the principles of OD.

AIMS OF OD

- Designed to solve problems that reduce operational efficiency – this is a key aim of the quality programme.

- Create an open, problem solving organisation – this was partly achieved through the weekend attended by the senior managers. However, full achievement of the aim will only be achieved by involving all staff.

- Build trust amongst individuals and groups in the organisation and increase autonomy– simply selling the change to employees will not be enough to achieve this aim. Full buy-in must be obtained (as above).

- Swapping the authority of role or status with that of knowledge – this aim has, to some extent, been achieved. The role of the quality inspectors and middle managers will be reviewed and a programme of putting quality first will be implemented.

OD PROCESS

1. Discussion of the aims of the programme – the aim of improving quality was established by the MD. The MD could choose to involve a third party, such as a management consultant.

2. Analysis and diagnosis – used to identify and clarify the problems. This was carried out by the MD through discussion with the trade advisor and knowledge gained from

visiting other manufacturers. Detailed analysis took place during the senior managers' hotel meeting.

3.   Agreement of aims between managers and employees – discussion has occurred between the MD and senior managers but there has been no discussion with other employees.

4.   Planning the sequence of activities required to bring about improvements - the QC programme must be structured and detailed.

5.   Evaluation of progress and implementation of new plans – this should be carried out once the programme has been implemented.

CONCLUSION

DOH's "putting quality first" programme is on the whole based upon the principles of OD.

Section 9

NOVEMBER 2008 EXAM QUESTIONS

SECTION A – 40 MARKS

[The indicative time for answering this section is 72 minutes.]

ANSWER *ALL* 15 SUB-QUESTIONS.

Instructions for answering Section A:

Each of the sub-questions numbered from **1.1** to **1.10** inclusive, given below, has only ONE correct answer. Each is worth two marks.

QUESTION ONE

1.1 Computer to computer transmission of structured data in standard business documents is referred to as:

    A   technology interface

    B   process compatibility

    C   electronic data interchange

    D   business networking   **(2 marks)**

1.2 Herzberg's contribution to understanding people in the workforce included:

    A   personality testing

    B   explaining factors associated with job satisfaction as 'motivators'

    C   problem-solving processes that encourage team spirit and cooperation

    D   an integrated framework involving appraisal, training and motivation   **(2 marks)**

1.3 The unwritten expectations that the organisation and the individual have of each other is referred to as:

    A   a valence

    B   work/life balance

    C   the psychological contract

    D   expectation management   **(2 marks)**

1.4 An example of a network typology that is hierarchical by design is called :

A   a star network

B   a ring network

C   a tree network

D   an authoritarian network   **(2 marks)**

1.5 A duplication of data held by an organisation is called:

A   data synthesis

B   data redundancy

C   data integrity

D   data archiving   **(2 marks)**

1.6 Aptitude testing is most commonly used in:

A   staff appraisal processes

B   exit interviews

C   staff selection

D   market research and testing   **(2 marks)**

1.7 Direct mailing, branding activities and public relations campaigns are all examples of :

A   market process

B   product placement

C   promotion

D   market research   **(2 marks)**

1.8 Economies of scale and manufacturing experience might help a firm to compete successfully by:

A   pricing its products more cheaply than its competitors

B   introducing value adding features to its products

C   better understanding buyer behaviour

D   offering a broader product range   **(2 marks)**

1.9 Selling at a low price with the intention of damaging weaker competitors is referred to as:

A   price skimming

B   opportunistic pricing

C   penetration pricing

D   predator pricing   **(2 marks)**

1.10 The product life cycle is depicted on a chart or diagram as a line against the variables of:

A   cash flow and market share

B   number of customers and sales value

C   sales volume and time

D   relative market share and market growth rate   **(2 marks)**

(Total for sub-questions 1.1 to 1.10: 20 marks)

Required:

Each of the sub-questions numbered 1.11 to 1.15 below requires a brief written response.

Each sub-question is worth 4 marks.

Your response should be in note form and must not exceed 50 words per sub-question.

1.11 Describe four likely variables a private health scheme company might investigate as a basis for segmenting the market.

(4 marks)

1.12 Many commercial retail websites contain the opportunity to purchase goods and services online. Describe four features of a 'good' retail website.

(4 marks)

1.13 Explain four advantages of centralised data processing

(4 marks)

1.14 Explain four reasons for job redesign.

(4 marks)

1.15 Identify eight factors that influence employee productivity.

(4 marks)

(Total for sub-questions 1.11 to 1.15 = 20 marks)

(Total for Section A: 40 marks)

SECTION B – 30 MARKS

[The indicative time for answering this section is 54 minutes.]

ANSWER *ALL* 6 SUB-QUESTIONS

QUESTION TWO

OK4u is a national leisure and sports chain selling specialist equipment and clothing for 'every sport'. A relatively young organisation, all OK4u's growth has been internally generated and has been led by its entrepreneurial founder and Chief Executive Officer (CEO) who is known for his creativity and person centred approach. Store managers are given discretion to display items in imaginative ways and use promotions to generate sales locally. All store managers report directly to the CEO who tries to oversee all aspects of the organisation's functioning without the help of a management team.

In its advertising, OK4u makes a feature of the creative way in which it is reducing non- recyclable packaging. It also claims to follow ethical policies. It has a few trusted long term suppliers of sports equipment and clothing. All suppliers are personally known to OK4u's CEO, and some are close friends. Good logistics mean that valuable floor area is not taken up by excessive in-shop storage. Known for good design, broad appeal and no 'stock outs', OK4u has established itself over the past five years as one of the country's favourite high street brands. Unfortunately, all that changed last year.

A year ago, OK4u expanded its product range by introducing fashion clothing into its stores. This was manufactured by a number of new suppliers. Initially sales were disappointing, until OK4u decided to discount prices. Thanks to tightly negotiated contracts, OK4u was able to pass the costs of the campaign on to its many new suppliers. As sales improved, these same suppliers were pressurised by threats of financial penalties into meeting late orders to tight deadlines.

Six months ago, a national newspaper ran a story under the front page headline "The Shame of Sweatshop OK4u". The article claimed that the chain was using workers from third world countries and paying them a fraction of the selling price. Further, it had discovered cases of children as young as eight years old working long hours. This was television news for two days and sales fell by 40% within a week.

The CEO's investigation of the newspaper's claims found that:

- The incidents related to a few of the new fashion range items.
- None of the workers featured in the story were OK4u employees. The fault lay with its new clothing suppliers, some of whom OK4u knew little about.
- In some cases, these new clothing suppliers had sub-contracted work in order to keep costs low and meet delivery deadlines. In doing this, they had exploited vulnerable workers.

OK4u immediately withdrew its new fashion range and issued a public apology. In it, it explained that the fault had been with its suppliers and that it would be more careful in developing new supplier relationships in future.

Although sales have recovered over the past six months, they are nowhere near their previous levels. The brand was also voted one of the most poorly regarded in a recent independent survey. The events have also affected morale and staff turnover has increased.

Last week, OK4u's CEO reviewed the situation and acknowledged a need to combat the negative public perception. He sent a personal letter to all employees in which he explained that OK4u intended restoring confidence with the public that OK4u is still following ethical policies. He explained that "the key to becoming one of the country's favourite high street brands again is to deliver excellent customer satisfaction. This can only be achieved through a superb combination of marketing, HRM and operations".

Required:

(a) Explain OK4u's ethical and management failings associated with its expansion into selling fashion clothing. **(5 marks)**

(b) Describe appropriate measures OK4u might take in order to restore public confidence that it is following ethical policies. **(5 marks)**

(c) Explain how marketing, HRM and operations in OK4u could deliver "excellent customer satisfaction". **(5 marks)**

(d) Evaluate OK4u's strategic relationship with the two sets of suppliers – those supplying sports equipment and clothing and those who supplied fashion clothing. **(5 marks)**

(e) Explain the past year for OK4u using the basic marketing mix variables as a framework. **(5 marks)**

(f) Explain OK4u's past growth and recent crisis in terms of the early stages of Larry Greiner's organisational growth model. **(5 marks)**

(Total: 30 marks)

(Total for Section B: 30 marks)

SECTION C – 30 MARKS

[Indicative time for answering this question is 54 minutes.]

ANSWER *ONE* QUESTION ONLY.

QUESTION THREE

ARi9 is an information systems solution company employing 250 staff. When staff are not at clients' premises they work from a corporate headquarters (HQ) in the country's capital city. The premises, which are owned by the company, are spacious and modern but have extremely limited car parking.

A senior staff meeting takes place every month. The agenda for last month's meeting included a number of significant issues. Unfortunately, the start of this meeting was delayed because of a public transport strike which led to gridlocked roads during rush hour. Those travelling by car found public parking spaces scarce, and parking charges high. When the meeting eventually started, a report by the Director of Human Resourcing identified a number of difficulties:

- ARi9 is losing talented staff when they take career breaks or maternity leave and never return.

- Competition amongst firms in the industry for talented individuals who live within a reasonable commuting distance is intense.

- Recruitment is becoming more difficult as local property prices are very expensive.

- ARi9 employs significantly fewer people with disabilities than the Government's suggested quota.

- Clients are making demands on staff outside normal working hours resulting in staff dissatisfaction and increasing claims for overtime payments.

- Staff productivity is declining, in part due to interruptions to work caused by the office environment (which is 'open plan' and has crowded workstations where conversations can be easily overheard).

At the same meeting, a review by the Finance Director of the company's cost structure showed the high cost of office space, which was contributing to reduced profitability. Someone joked that ARi9 is in the technology not the property business!

In the debate that followed, the option of relocating the HQ to somewhere outside the capital was suggested. The Chief Executive tasked both directors to collaborate and produce some 'radical solutions' for the future.

At this month's meeting their joint report outlined a number of ideas:

- ARi9 should sell its HQ and relocate to much smaller accommodation outside the capital. When they are not at clients' premises, staff would be expected to work mainly from home. On the occasions when they were required to be at the HQ, the new building should contain a flexible area where staff can 'hot desk'. There should also be some meeting rooms that could be booked in advance, if needed.

- In future, staff working from home would be expected to stay in touch with colleagues and clients through email, webcams and teleconferencing (so-called 'teleworking' or 'telecommuting').

- New equipment purchased for staff would be financed from anticipated improved productivity gains.

The report concluded with the claims that the proposals were 'win/win/win'. The company would produce significant HR and financial gains, society would benefit environmentally through reduced travel, and the employees would be given greater autonomy to structure their own working arrangements.

Required:

(a) Evaluate the claims made by the report's authors that the proposals would produce significant gains for the company. **(10 marks)**

(b) Discuss the potential benefits and potential difficulties of the proposals from the employees' perspective. **(10 marks)**

(c) Explain Maslow's motivation theory in the context of the potential impact of the move to teleworking by ARi9. **(10 marks)**

(Total: 30 marks)

QUESTION FOUR

ENO9 has, for many years, operated a mail order catalogue scheme selling top brand name clothing, electrical goods, home furnishings, kitchen utensils and jewellery. Quarterly glossy catalogues (containing between 1,000 and 1,200 pages) are produced and delivered to members of the public, who act as agents. Agents show the catalogue to their friends, place orders on their behalf, collect money owed and post it monthly to ENO9. In return, agents receive a commission on sales and are alerted first to sale items towards the end of each quarter. ENO9 promises delivery of goods (excluding furniture) by a complimentary courier service within three working days of receipt of an order. ENO9 accepts returns on faulty goods free of charge and promises to replace or refund items, provided they are returned complete and unused, within 14 days of receipt by the customer. Taking advantage of advances in technology, the company also operates an online shop facility to place orders, obtain catalogues, browse products and email queries.

ENO9 recognises that it operates in a highly competitive environment and periodically monitors its share of the market and compares its prices with those of its competitors. Recently, ENO9 appointed a Director of Performance Enhancement to bring about greater performance improvement. So far the new Director has identified the need to operate a more systematic method of performance improvement. To this end, she believes that benchmarking is necessary and has information that at least one of ENO9's main competitors benchmarks already. In conjunction with senior managers, she has identified performance measures of price, product quality, delivery, quality of product information, and customer service, for which data needs to be collected. The intention would be to compare performance on a regular basis to that of its competitors and drive improvement accordingly.

The new Director will present a comprehensive report at the next Board meeting. The report will contain her proposals, accompanied by full costings, an analysis of likely benefits and an implementation schedule that she herself will oversee. The report recommends that the effectiveness of benchmarking should be reviewed after six months.

Required:

(a) Analyse the way in which the new Director is attempting to bring about the change she believes is necessary in ENO9. **(10 marks)**

(b) Discuss the potential advantages and disadvantages of benchmarking for ENO9. **(10 marks)**

(c) Explain how objective data for the performance measures identified might be collected **(10 marks)**

(Total: 30 marks)

(Total marks for Section C: 30 marks)

Section 10

ANSWERS TO NOVEMBER 2008 EXAM QUESTIONS

SECTION A

QUESTION ONE

MULTIPLE CHOICE QUESTIONS

Key answer tip: Use some of the 20 minutes reading time to begin working through the MCQ's. You can mark the answers on the question paper. Once the 3 hour writing time begins, 36 minutes should be more than adequate to write out the answers to the 10 MCQ's.

Tutorial note: The syllabus areas of operations management, marketing, information systems and managing human capital were all examined in this section. A well prepared candidate would have been able to correctly answer the majority of questions. As can be expected in this section of the exam, a number of minor syllabus areas were examined. However, a logical application of knowledge would have resulted in most candidates selecting the correct answer.

1.1 C

Electronic data interchange, or EDI, is used predominantly by large business organisations with bespoke computer systems. It works by converting messages, such as purchase orders and invoices, into a standard format that the computer systems of both participants can interpret and respond to.

1.2 B

Herzberg suggested that factors which cause job satisfaction (motivators) were different to those which would cause dissatisfaction if not present (hygiene factors).

1.3 C

A psychological contract describes the unwritten expectations that the organisation and the individual have of each other.

1.4 C

A tree network comprises a hierarchy of computers. The computer at the top of the tree is the most powerful, for example a mainframe. Computers at lower levels are less powerful, for example microcomputers.

1.5 B

Duplication of data items is referred to as data redundancy.

1.6   C

Selection is the process of choosing a suitable candidate for the role. Aptitude testing may be used as part of this process.

1.7   C

Direct marketing, branding activities and public relations campaigns are all examples of promotion.

1.8   A

Manufacturing experience and economies of scale (such as discounts for buying in bulk) reduce the costs associated with production. This helps the firm to compete by pricing its products more cheaply than its competitors.

1.9   C

Penetration pricing is the selling of items at a low price in order to stimulate rapid growth in market share and damage weaker competitors.

1.10   C

The product life cycle shows sales volume against time.

SHORT QUESTIONS

Key answer tip: The use of bullet points or short notes is perhaps the most effective approach, allowing good coverage of points in the 36 minutes allocated. Any part of the answer over the 50 word limit will not be marked.

Tutorial note: This section examined the syllabus areas of marketing, managing human capital and information systems. Candidates should have scored well here. The questions either examined core knowledge areas or required straightforward application of knowledge.

1.11

- **Age:** influences a person's desire to join the scheme and the benefits required.

- **Income:** influences the type of cover that will be targeted at an individual.

- **Family life cycle:** the need or desire for cover will differ at each stage of the cycle.

- **Social class:** influences the desirability/ affordability of cover.

1.12

- **Design:** this should be attractive, appropriate for the web and compliment brand image.

- **Web address:** should be easy to search for and/ or remember.

- **Navigation:** this should be quick and simple.

- **Secure:** customer details must be kept safe and secure.

1.13

- **One set of files:** standardised data is readily accessible by everyone.

- **Staff quality:** less staff required and so higher quality specialists are affordable.

- **Ease of control and security:** one system only

- **Economies of scale**: due to removal of duplication of activities and replacement of small **computers** with one large computer.

1.14

- **Understanding:** improved performance due to better understanding of and empathy with others.

- **Skills:** redesign is essential due to new skills required by the organisation.

- **Needs:** redesign ensures that an individual's job suits them in terms of what motivates them.

- **Development:** redesign is part of the continuous process of developing the individual.

1.15

- **Salary**

- Job **security**

- **Pension** provision

- **Challenge** of work

- **Appraisal** system

- **Promotion** opportunities

- Social interaction/ relations with colleagues

- **Working** conditions

SECTION B

QUESTION TWO

Question overview: The question was based on a common workplace scenario involving a national sports and leisure chain. All syllabus areas, apart from information systems, were examined. This was a fair question and only core syllabus areas were tested.

Common errors in this question were:
- Points made were too general in nature with little reference back to the scenario.
- A lack of development of points or not having enough separate points.

There may appear to be a lot to achieve given candidates only have 8 minutes for each requirement. However, a good candidate will have completed a number of section B questions during revision and should feel comfortable with these areas. Use of headings, sub-headings and bullet points should help to break up the answer and make it easier to mark.

A separate page should be completed for each requirement. This gives plenty of scope for candidates to start on the requirements that they feel most comfortable with and to gain the easy marks first. However, candidates must answer all requirements and stick to 8 minutes for each one.

(a)

Key answer tip: This requirement asked for an explanation of the ethical and management failings of OK4u . Easy marks were available for discussing the problems associated with the new suppliers. Good candidates expanded on this area and used sub-headings or separate paragraphs to explain the key issues. Little book knowledge was required here. Instead candidates were expected to apply the information in the scenario to their answer.

There have been a number of ethical and management failings associated with the expansion into selling fashion clothing:

Ethical image undermined

OK4u's past advertising has claimed that the business follows ethical policies. This ethical image has been shattered as a result of the recent media exposure that the business has been involved in the use of extremely cheap, and in some cases child, labour

New suppliers

OK4u's past success was in part due to the strong relations with trusted suppliers. This helped to drive competitive advantage through improved quality, reduced costs and consistency with OK4u's ethical image. However, due to its desire to move into a new market selling fashion clothing, OK4u decided to use a number of new suppliers. This was not in itself a mistake. However, it appears that OK4u did not take the time to research potential suppliers and develop relations with them. The end result of this rushed decision has been costly damage to the organisation's reputation.

Marketing strategy

Sales of the new fashion clothing range were poor until a decision was taken to reduce prices. This may indicate that the there was not an appropriate marketing strategy in place for this new range. Such strategy is essential in order to ensure that the needs of potential customers are understood and met with regards to the products itself, its price, the place of sale and the promotional techniques used. Investment in this area could have removed the need to slash prices.

Pressure on suppliers to cut costs

The cost of the discount campaign was passed onto the new suppliers, some of whom were forced to sub-contract the work in order to achieve their target cost. This extra pressure may have resulted in the use of low paid workers, including children. Cost reduction is only beneficial if the ethical standards of the business are maintained.

Pressure of suppliers to meet tight deadlines

This additional pressure forced some suppliers to sub-contract the work. The sub-contractors were unknown entities, some of whom exploited vulnerable workers.

If OK4u had not pressurised suppliers on costs and to meet tight deadlines, it appears that many of the problems encountered could have been prevented.

(b)

Key answer tip: This requirement asked candidates to explain how public confidence could be restored. Again, limited book knowledge was required. Candidates would be wise to plan their answer first, in order to ensure that they have enough separate points and to assist in structuring the answer.

The removal of the new fashion range combined with a public apology was not sufficient to prevent a fall in OK4u's sales. A number of steps should now be taken to restore public confidence:

Development of a robust supplier policy

Formal procedures should be put in place for investigating potential suppliers and maintaining open and honest communication with them. An improved understanding of the way in which the suppliers operate should prevent the problems of the past from happening again and as time goes by should help to restore public confidence.

Transparent supplier policy

It will also be important to communicate such procedures to the general public who are the company's potential customers. A transparent set of policies involving supplier selection, screening and monitoring should be made available, for example via OK4u's website. A summarised version of the new policies could be communicated using a newspaper article or advert.

Ethical code

OK4u has made a feature of a number of its ethical policies in the past. Ethical actions, such as the use of recycled packaging, could be a key source of competitive advantage. However, OK4u must establish a comprehensive ethical code of conduct for the business and this should be communicated to all staff. Ethics must become an integral part of the culture of the organisation. Again, this code could be communicated to the public via the website.

Support for those affected

A public apology may be viewed as an empty gesture. OK4u could take steps to correct the damage that their actions resulted in. For example, they could compensate employees and the families of those who were affected by the poor pay.

Ongoing support for the community

It may be difficult to directly compensate those workers who were affected. However, OK4u can be seen to be making a difference to society through the support of community projects. For example, they could get involved in a local recycling project or an overseas project helping communities impacted by poor pay and conditions in the workplace.

(c)

Key answer tip: This requirement asked how marketing, HRM and operations could deliver excellent customer satisfaction. Relatively easy marks were available for a brief explanation of each area in the context of customer satisfaction.

Marketing

Marketing aims to anticipate and meet the needs of the customer and can be key to excellent customer service.

Comprehensive market research could be carried out to establish the needs of customers in terms of the features of the products, their price, the place of sale and the most effective way to promote them. The fulfilment of customer needs should result in excellent customer satisfaction.

Operations

Operations refer to all the activities involved in making the product. Therefore, there is plenty of scope to deliver excellent customer service via operations.

By putting the customer at the core of all operational decisions, satisfaction should improve. For example, strong and long term relations with suppliers could help to reduce costs and improve quality.

HRM

HRM is the process of obtaining, developing and motivating employees and making the best use of their skills.

Investment in HRM should have positive implications for customer satisfaction. Employees across the organisations will have the necessary skills required to anticipate and meet the needs of the customer and they will be more motivated to do so.

(d)

Key answer tip: This requirement asked for an evaluation of the relationship of OK4u with its two sets of suppliers. Good students will have used the information in the scenario to discuss each relationship in turn and to analyse the relationships in terms of pros and cons for the business.

Tutorial note: A general evaluation of the strategic relationship was sufficient. However, candidates who based their answer around a strategic theorist, such as Reck and Long, may have found it easier to score well and to develop their points.

There are vast differences in the relationship between OK4u and its two sets of suppliers:

Sports equipment suppliers

This relationship involves a small number of trusted, long term suppliers, many are known personally to OK4u.

Reck and Long recognised that purchasing and the supply chain are a strategic issue for organisations. The relationship with suppliers should be seen as collaborative, with OK4u and its suppliers working together to find ways to enhance value and to drive competitive advantage.

OK4u appears to be at the final, integrative stage of development with regards to its sports equipment suppliers. Viewing suppliers as key strategic partners has assisted in good logistics. Cost savings are made through reductions in floor space and customer reputation is enhanced due to the lack of stock outs. This helped to drive OK4u's past success as one of the country's favourite high street brands.

Fashion clothing suppliers

This clothing was manufactured by a number of new suppliers. In some cases, these suppliers sub-contracted work and in doing so exploited vulnerable workers.

Reck and Long argue that is inappropriate to view the relationship with suppliers as an opportunistic one, where OK4u would try to obtain the lowest price possible. Every price gain for OK4u is a loss for the supplier and it was this pressure on suppliers that resulted in the significant damage to OK4u's image.

If OK4u is to continue to operate in this market, it must develop a collaborative relationship with its suppliers and the purchasing function for fashion clothing must develop so that suppliers are seen as vital strategic partners.

(e)

Key answer tip: candidates should have scored highly in this requirement which examined the core knowledge area of the marketing mix. Easy marks were available for describing the four P's and good candidates linked their discussion back to the scenario.

Tutorial note: This is a commonly examined area. Detailed knowledge of each area of the marketing mix has been required in a number of past sittings.

The marketing mix is a set of controllable variables that can be used to ensure that the needs of the target market are met:

Product

The features of the product should help to satisfy customer needs and act as a source of differentiation and hence competitive advantage for the organisation.

This appears to have been the case with the specialist sports equipment clothing and equipment which is known for its good design and broad appeal. However, the last year saw the launch of the new fashion clothing range in OK4u's stores. Sales were disappointing initially and this may have indicated that customer needs were not being met. This forced OK4u to discount prices in order to increase sales.

Price

When pricing its products, OK4u needs to consider how much the customer is willing to pay, its competitor's prices and its costs. It appears that OK4u carefully considered these factors in the past since the organisation managed to establish itself as one of the country's leading high street brands.

Poor sales of the new product appear to have resulted in a strategy of penetration pricing, where the price is set artificially low in order to gain market share. However, this resulted in the excessive pressure being put on suppliers and the resultant damage to OK4u's reputation.

Promotion

In past advertising, OK4u made a feature of its reduction in non-recyclable packaging and it claimed to follow ethical policies. This promotional activity has been undermined by the recent media exposure.

It is unclear how OK4u promoted its new fashion range. However, it appears to have been ineffective as indicated by the poor initial sales. Careful choice of promotional tools should be made in the future.

Place

The last year has seen little change in OK4u's 'place' strategies with sales continuing to be made via a national high street chain of stores. This appears to have been an effective strategy in the past and so there is no reason that, once public confidence is restored, it can't continue to be a recipe for success in the future.

(f)

Key answer tip: This requirement asked candidates to use Greiner's growth model to discuss OK4u's growth. Easy marks were available for identifying the relevant phases of the model. Many candidates failed to link their explanation back to the information in the scenario or were inconclusive as to which stages OK4u had passed through.

Greiner concluded that organisational growth takes place in discrete phases. Each phase is characterised by two things:

- Evolution: a distinctive factor that drives growth.

- Revolution: a crisis through which the organisation must pass before moving onto the next phase.

There are five phases in total. OK4u, as a relatively young company, has not passed through all the phases as yet.

Phase 1

Growth through creativity: OK4u started out as a small organisation managed in an informal way by its entrepreneurial founder, the CEO.

Crisis of leadership: As the organisation grew the CEO would have found it increasingly difficult to co-ordinate its activities.

Phase 2

Growth through direction: As the organisation grew the CEO recruited store managers and additional employees.

Crisis of autonomy: The CEO would have found it difficult to keep detailed control of all the organisation's activities, and to retain a sense of the wider picture. Employees would also have resented their lack of autonomy and their performance would have fallen as a result.

Phase 3

Growth through delegation: The CEO responded by giving the store managers the discretion to display items in an imaginative way and to use promotions to generate sales locally.

Crisis of control: This delegation may have resulted in the stores acting sub-optimally and taking decisions to cut the prices of the new fashion range. As a result, OK4u's reputation has been damaged.

There will now be a need to move onto the next phase, growth through co-ordination. Co-ordinated policies and a degree of centralised decision making should help to address the poor decisions that were made with regards to suppliers over the last year.

SECTION C

Section overview: Section C was particularly poorly answered.

Common errors were:

- Lack of content. Outline notes are not sufficient for the more substantial requirements in this section.

- Poor planning resulting in an unstructured answered and a failure to address all the issues in the scenario

- Some candidates took the approach of writing down everything they knew, highlighting an inability to link their knowledge to the scenario.

- Poor time management in the rest of the exam resulting in a rushed answer.

Candidates should not feel overwhelmed by the scenario question.

Top tips include:

- Allocating the time to and working through each requirement in turn. This helps to break the question into manageable chunks.

- Remember, there will always be easy marks available for book knowledge and common sense ideas.

- Depth of answer is important. Use full paragraphs and explain each point made. The use of headings is advised to break up the answer and make it look professional.

QUESTION THREE

(a)

Key answer tip: This requirement asked for an evaluation, from the **Company's** point of view, of the new flexible working arrangements. Candidates must ensure that they produce a balanced answer with both pros and cons and that each of the three areas (HR, financial gains and society) are discussed. These three areas could be used as key headings.

This was not a difficult question but some candidates failed to score well due to lack of depth or structure to the answer.

Tutorial note: Book knowledge could have been used by candidates to answer this requirement. However, it would have been just as appropriate to use knowledge and experience from their own workplace.

The report recommendations appear to indicate a move towards a more flexible way of working in ARi9. These new working arrangements could have a number of positive and negative implications for the company:

1.   **HR Implications**

Benefits of report recommendations:

Recruitment: The organisation may find it easier to recruit the right calibre of employee since high quality staff may be attracted by the flexible working arrangements. These arrangements bring potential cost and time savings for employees and greater autonomy for staff during their working day.

Staff retention: ARi9 are losing talented staff due to increased property prices close to the office. In addition, demanding clients have resulted in long hours being worked by staff but no overtime pay. These factors, together with a crowded and noisy office environment, have made staff retention difficult.

All of these issues could, in part, be addressed by the new flexible working arrangements. Employees would no longer be required to live close to the capital and could therefore relocate to cheaper housing. Time would be saved commuting and this would reduce the need for overtime working. Finally, staff would be able to concentrate once away from the distractions of the office. Each of these factors should help to increase staff satisfaction and hence increase staff retention and reduce absenteeism.

Positive discrimination: The new flexible working arrangements may help, in part, to address the fact that ARi9 employs fewer people with disabilities than the government's recommended quota. The flexible working policies may assist in attracting high quality, skilled disabled staff. The current need to commute to the capital and to work in, what may be, an unsuitable office environment may have discouraged individuals with disabilities from applying for roles within the organisation.

Drawbacks of report recommendations:

Co-ordination problems: the new arrangements may make it difficult to co-ordinate staff. Teleworking and telecommuting will, to some extent, address this issue but it will still be difficult to retain the same level of co-ordination and control if staff are not working in a traditional office environment.

More difficult to attract and retain staff: Not all prospective and current employees will be attracted by the new working arrangements. Some individuals will enjoy the commute to the capital and the kudos that comes with working in an office in the city. Others may prefer the discipline and social interaction that comes with a traditional office environment. As a result, good staff may be lost and it may be difficult to attract the best staff.

2.   **Financial Implications**

Benefits of report recommendations:

Reduction in staffing costs: Recruitment costs in particular may be lower since it may be easier to attract and retain staff.

Increased productivity: Productivity should increase due to better quality staff being attracted to the new system, increased motivation due to staff appreciation of the new flexible arrangements and more time on productive work as staff will spend less time commuting.

Lower head office costs: Significant savings in head office costs should be made due to the move to a smaller, out of town office.

Drawbacks of report recommendations:

Additional costs of moving head office: Additional costs could arise because the new head office may have to be adapted to suit the needs of ARi9 and the move from a prime city centre location to an out of town office may damage the company's image and impact profitability.

Additional costs of home-working: Suitable equipment will have to be provided to all employees who work at home. This will prove to be a significant additional upfront cost. There will also be costs associated with complying with employment and health and safety legislation relating to home working. The working environment of all employees (including disabled employees) must be safe and suitable for work. Furthermore, some employees will be less productive at home due to feeling isolated and this will have associated costs. While difficult to quantify, there may also be additional costs associated with the control and co-ordination of staff.

3.   Social Implications

Benefits of report recommendations:

The move towards home working could have significant environmental benefits. Employees will be travelling to the office less often and the commute to the new out of town office may be shorter for many employees. This will have a positive impact on the environment and on the company's image.

Drawbacks of report recommendations:

The move towards home working could, however, have negative implications for the environment. Each employee working at home will need to heat and light their home and power their computers. This could result in a significant increase in energy use. This combined with the energy used by the new head office may exceed that uses currently in the city centre head office.

Although employees will be travelling to the new office less frequently, they may travel further to the new out of town location. The use of public transport may no longer be a practical option and as a result more employees may use their car to get to and from the office. This would have a significant environmental impact.

Conclusion

Each of the benefits and drawbacks should be reviewed in detail before a final decision is made with regards to the report recommendations.

(b)

Key answer tip: This requirement asks candidates to discuss the benefits and drawbacks of the new working arrangements from the **employee's** point of view. Candidates should be careful not to answer part (b) in part (a).

Tutorial note: Book knowledge could have been used by candidates to answer this requirement. However, it would have been just as appropriate to use knowledge and experience from their own workplace.

Benefits from the employee's perspective

Cost savings: Employees will no longer be required to make frequent trips into the head office and will therefore save money that was previously spent on regular commuting into the capital. The savings made by those who used public transport or their own car could prove to be significant.

Time savings: Work-life balance should be improved due to the reduction in the regular commute to the head office. This should save a significant amount of time.

Other benefits of eliminating daily commute: Many employees will find the regular commute to the capital draining and demoralising. Public transport may be crowded and unreliable and employees driving to the office may face congestion and expensive parking. Removing the need for this regular commute should result in more contented employees.

Increased enjoyment: Employees may feel a greater commitment to the company and increased enjoyment of their work since they may feel that ARi9 is listening and adapting to their needs.

Lifestyle balance: Employees may enjoy the flexibility to work at home and may find it easier to fit their work around family life and other interests.

Drawbacks from the employee's perspective

Increased costs: Employees may find that, although they save on the cost of commuting, they will in fact incur extra expenditure on utility, telephone and broadband bills. ARi9 may agree to reimburse any incremental expenses.

Loss of social interaction: Employees may miss the social interaction and enjoyment of regular trips to the head office.

Loss of social status: Some employees may enjoy working in a traditional office environment in the city and may feel a loss of status when the move is made towards home working.

Lack of support: Some employees may feel unsupported when working from home and may miss the face to face support of other members of staff.

Cost cutting exercise: Some employees may question the motives behind the move and may view the changes as a cost cutting exercise as opposed to a reaction to changing employee's needs.

(c)

Key answer tip: This requirement examines the candidate's ability to apply their knowledge of Maslow's theory to the scenario. Candidates must demonstrate that they understand the five needs but they are also required to link each need back to the scenario and, more specifically, to teleworking. There were relatively easy marks available here for core knowledge.

Technology has made it possible for individuals to work away from the traditional office environment. They can be linked to the computer systems of the organisation through remote terminals and can communicate with colleagues via email, phone and fax. The potential impact of this teleworking arrangement in ARi9 can be linked in a number of ways to Maslow's motivational theory:

Basic/ physiological needs

This is the first need that an individual will seek to satisfy. It relates to the basic needs required to stay alive, such as food and shelter. These needs can be satisfied with money.

ARi9 employees may feel that they are financially better off as a result of working at home, due to the removal of the regular commute. Therefore, this need is more likely to be satisfied.

Safety/ security needs

Once basic needs are fulfilled, employees will seek to satisfy their safety/ security needs. People want protection against unemployment, the consequences of sickness and retirement. These needs can be satisfied by employment legislation, sick pay and company pension schemes.

Teleworking may result in limited change with regards to these needs. However, if ARi9 does benefit financially as a result of the changes, they may be able to pass some of these savings onto the employee, for example by increasing pension contributions. Hence this need would be better satisfied by teleworking.

Social needs

Once the safety/ security needs of the employee have been fulfilled, individuals will seek to satisfy their social needs. The way in which work is organised, allowing individuals to feel part of a group, is fundamental to the satisfaction of this need.

Teleworking may result in employees feeling that this need is no longer satisfied. However, the use of tools such as email and teleconferencing could help to fulfil this need in a different way.

Ego needs

The next need that the employee will seek to satisfy is their ego needs. This relates to wanting the esteem of other people. Job status, promotion and allowing the employee to organise their work will all help in the fulfilment of this need.

The move to teleworking may actually increase the fulfilment of this need if employees feel that they have greater autonomy to organise their own work. However, employees may feel that their status and promotional opportunities are diminished by the move to home working. ARi9 will have to work hard to ensure that this need is satisfied.

Self-fulfilment needs

This is the final need and is simply the need to achieve something worthwhile in life. It is the need that is satisfied by continued success.

ARi9 will have to work hard to ensure that the potential for employees to fulfil this need is not diminished in any way by the move to teleworking. If employees feel that they can continue to thrive within the organisation there will be no negative impact on motivation.

QUESTION FOUR

(a)

Key answer tip: This requirement asks candidates to analyse the new Director's approach to implementing change using benchmarking. 'Analyse' means examine in detail. Therefore the candidate is required to give a detailed explanation of what benchmarking is and how this could be implemented in EN09.

The new Director has recognised that EN09 operates in a highly competitive environment and that a more systematic method of performance improvement that looks outside of the company is required.

What is benchmarking?

Benchmarking is the process of systematic comparison of a process against one of similar activities.

The process involves the establishment of targets through data gathering and comparison. For EN09, the performance measures of price, product quality, delivery, quality of product information and customer service will be used. These appear to be a suitable and broad range of financial and non-financial performance measures. Benchmarking aims to facilitate continuous improvement in these areas.

As a result of the benchmarking exercise, good or best practice can be identified. Detailed analysis will allow EN09 to understand how this is achieved and to take steps to replicate this good practice.

There are a number of different types of benchmarking. EN09 is considering carrying out competitive benchmarking. This will involve the comparison of EN09's activities with those of its competitors.

The benchmarking process

The benchmarking exercise in EN09 should follow a number of formal stages:

1. **Decide what is to be benchmarked**: This has already been established by the new Director. She believes that competitive benchmarking is necessary and that performance measures in this area should be set.

2. **Identify benchmarking partners**: EN09 must then decide which competitors to benchmark against. Companies with good or best practice should be used. It may be useful to investigate the process of benchmarking that is currently being used by one of its competitors.

3. **Agree and collect relevant information**: This can be a difficult process. (Refer to later discussion in requirement c).

4. **Analyse and evaluate information**: The information collected must then be analysed and evaluated in order to make it more meaningful for EN09.

5. **Identify best practice**: Once the information has been analysed, best practice can then be established for each of the areas identified.

6. **Develop an action plan for implementation**: EN09 will seek to adapt its processes so that it can meet or exceed the best practice in the processes reviewed. A pilot

scheme could be carried out prior to full implementation. It will be important to monitor the process throughout.

(b)

Advantages of benchmarking

Improved performance

Benchmarking could be a key tool in enabling EN09 to improve its performance and increase profitability in this highly competitive market. There should be improvements across all of the areas discussed, i.e. product quality and customer service etc.

Achievability

The improvements will be seen as achievable since the new methods have actually been used in another organisation. This should encourage managers and employees to buy-in to the change process.

Improved understanding of environmental pressures

The benchmarking process should enable EN09 to get back in touch with the needs of its customers and to better understand its competitors. The industry is highly competitive and so this greater awareness will be essential for future success.

Eliminates complacency

Benchmarking can help EN09 to overcome complacency and to drive organisational change.

Continuous improvement

Benchmarking can be carried out at regular intervals and can therefore drive continuous improvement in the business.

Disadvantages of benchmarking

Identifying best practice

It may prove difficult to identify the organisations that are best in class.

Cost

The actual benchmarking process will be costly for EN09. It is essential that the benefits of the exercise are greater than the associated costs.

Impact on motivation

If comparisons are unfavourable the information could have a negative impact on employee motivation and this would result in further inefficiencies.

Deciding which activities are to be benchmarked

This is a difficult process. EN09 may not realise that there are better ways of doing things until they have seen their competitors carrying out certain processes.

Managers become too target driven

Benchmarking can result in managers becoming obsessed with hitting targets. This could sometimes be counterproductive. For example, delivery times may be improved at the expense of accuracy.

Collection of data

The actual collection of data can be time consuming and costly. Data may not be readily accessible for all of the areas of performance measurement and competitors may be unwilling to share details.

(c)

> **Key answer tip:** A more difficult requirement which asks for an explanation of how data for each of the performance measures could be collected. Candidates need an in depth application of their book knowledge to do well. It would be appropriate to base discussion around each of the performance measures discussed in the scenario.

Collecting data for the performance measures identified can be difficult. Competitors will have little incentive to give away their secrets or reveal any weaknesses and may even communicate incorrect information.

Price

Financial information about competitors will be easier to obtain than non-financial information.

Competitor's prices should be easily accessible. This information would be readily available to customers via catalogues and company web sites.

Product quality

This could be obtained using:

- **Reverse engineering**: This may prove useful for EN09. It involves buying a **competitor's** product and dismantling it, in order to understand the content and make up.

- **Media comment**: Press articles may be available with comments on the positive and negative aspects of competitor's product quality.

- **Trade associations**: Some information on product quality may be available from **these**.

Delivery

Delivery information may be readily available from competitor's catalogues and on-line. However, EN09 should be aware that there may be a difference between the delivery service that is offered and the service that actually occurs.

EN09 appear to have a robust delivery process. The company delivers products within three working days at no charge, accepts returns of faulty goods at no charge and make refunds of items that are unused and returned within 14 days.

It would be useful for EN09 to compare themselves with those who are considered to be best in practice in delivery. EN09 may find that improvements and/ or cost savings could be made in the area of delivery.

Quality of product information

Competitors will print a significant amount of information about their products in their catalogues, on their website and on the product packaging itself. This may assist in bringing about quality improvements.

Customer service

This could be obtained in the following ways:

- **Direct from competitors**: Competitors may be willing to provide customer feedback directly to EN09. Alternatively, customer testimonials may already be available, for example on the company's website. The problem with this feedback is that it may be biased and only review the positive aspects of customer service.

- **Other online tools**: The growth in the popularity of online forums and blogs may result in a wealth of information with regards to customer satisfaction. Customer comments could be reviewed to gain an understanding of their level of satisfaction. This could also be used for feedback on other areas of performance measurement such as price, product quality, delivery and quality of information.

- **Market research**: This could be carried out to establish the public's perception of EN09 compared to that of its competitors. However, it may be difficult to get a representative sample of data.